PRAISE FOR
THAT WHICH CANNOT BE DENIED

"If you want a romp through history woven like a novel by an enchanting storyteller, you must read *That Which Cannot be Denied*. From the beginning, the stories grip and engage us so that we feel we accompany the unusual character through his adventures to fascinating places around the globe. A brief introduction to his ancestors explains how their life choices impacted their descendants, including Roger's immediate family.

"The author's lens is through his personal experiences, but the book reads more like a riveting novel than a memoir. His clarity of historical events and how they impacted people are captivating and serve as the backdrop for the stories. The son of a Top-Gun fighter pilot, Hughes uses humor to defuse some explosive situations he experienced as a military child and later in life as a young man. You'll find yourself rooting for the protagonist as he guides us through his unusual and compelling observations and encounters. The photographs add even more delight and impact to his entertaining book. Enjoy!"

—Nannette Rundle Carroll, Author of
The Communication Problem Solver

"*That Which Cannot Be Denied* is the compelling memoir of Roger Hughes, a retired lawyer who grew up in the 1950s and '60s as his military-career father shuffled his family across multiple continents. Part homage to his father, an accomplished Marine Corps fighter pilot dedicated to the service of his country, and part nostalgic memories of how his family's nomadic travels and world events defined his developmental years, this skillfully researched book is a sure-fire hit for history buffs, travel enthusiasts, and fans of coming-of-age narratives."

—Jill Hedgecock, Book Review Columnist for the *Diablo Gazette*,
Author of Award-Winning *Rhino in the Room*

"*That Which Cannot be Denied* is a true story of Roger's father, Harry J. Hughes, a Marine pilot who served in WWII and the Korean war. He was an American patriot and hero. Harry earned 'Top Gun' in every training session. Roger lived in the shadow of his older brother, Terry, and craved love, compassion, and support from his father. He witnessed his father's achievements and dangerous experiences as the family lived throughout the world. The classified secrets Harry took to his grave contributed to peace during the Six-Day War in 1967. Roger received the love and support he desperately needed but didn't receive from his father from a couple in the Pacific Northwest while his father was still living. This book is filled with adventure that brings tears, laughter, and surprises that lift your spiritual awareness. A MUST-read."

—Ken Calvert, Director, Business Development, Peet's Coffee & Tea (Retired)

"The real-life saga of the Hughes family, a complex American family with an indomitable spirit, spans over 100 years, five wars, four continents, and many thrilling and hilarious adventures. There are many heroes in the Hughes family. The adventure begins with great-grandsire Elsworth Hughes, who worked and fought his way to prominence in Bakersfield, California, earning the reputation as the 'meanest man in Bakersfield' in the 1920s.

"The story then moves on to Elsworth's son, Harry, a 'Marine tough man' who overcame his lack of a college education to become a Marine Corps officer and 'Top Gun' Marine pilot. Upon retirement, Harry was an indispensable covert operative for the US through the Cold War, years traveling all over the world with the family in tow—though the family did not really know what Harry Hughes was doing.

"Roger, Harry's younger son, is the book's author and narrator. He unspools the story of his family as seen through his own eyes and evolving maturity. He shares the 'aha!' moments that helped him unlock the family secrets, enabling him to understand his family and himself and the events that shaped them all. Roger shares his personal path to wisdom. Hard-won wisdom requires Hughes's indomitable spirit to overcome the challenges on his way to becoming one of the best trial lawyers in California and a man of ever-blossoming personal religious faith. *That Which Cannot Be Denied* is a thrilling ride."

—David Alexander, Partner, Hanson Bridgett LLP, Former General Counsel, Port of Oakland

"Roger Hughes offers a colorful mosaic of memory in *That Which Cannot Be Denied*. Beginning with the poignant death of his grandfather, he presents first the inner history of the family who formed him and then one of the most unique coming-of-age adventures imaginable. In a Forrest Gump manner, Roger, as a result of the mysterious career of his father, appears in a myriad of worldwide places at just the moment that they supply a story of note.

"Beginning humbly in Bakersfield, then on to Surf City, the mountains of Utah, Hawaii, Japan, Egypt, East Germany, Paris, Berlin, Florence, Cook's Inlet, and more, his tale unfolds. Comedy, tragedy, and adventure all serendipitously merge into the kaleidoscope of his memory and the reader's pleasure. I put the book down, asking myself, 'And then?' Such a beginning cries for the closure of knowing the rest of his story."

—Gary Strankman, Administrative Presiding Justice, California Court of Appeal, First Appellate District, Division One (Retired)

"Roger Hughes was my law partner for two decades. Over that time, I came to know him as an adventuresome, fun-loving prankster, inspiring to all who crossed his path, and, above all, a genuine and kind man. He loved the law. He was a fierce and powerful advocate. And he was a master storyteller: in the courtroom, in front of a jury, in the office, around a dinner table, in church.

"He has brought all these qualities to this marvelous memoir about a peripatetic youth, growing up the son of a decorated Marine combat flyer and professional spy. *That Which Cannot Be Denied* is a coming-of-age tale that passes through Bakersfield, California; Salt Lake City, Utah; Hawaii; Japan; Irvine, California; Cairo, Egypt; Europe; and the Alaskan Kenai Peninsula. It's a tale full of adventure that touches on history, ideas, and spirituality. A great read."

—Roland Nikles, Attorney, Writer
http://rolandnikles.blogspot.com

"The author's grandfather, 'the meanest man in Bakersfield,' and his father, a World War II Marine Top-Gun fighter pilot, are right out of Steinbeck's *Grapes of Wrath* and Tom Brokaw's *Greatest Generation*. These powerful characters, the author's muses, form the backdrop of *That Which Cannot Be Denied*, giving context to a compelling coming-of-age story of a young man groping for direction and meaning in life in the 1960s. Accompanied by well-developed humorous anecdotes involving the perils encountered during the travels of the adventuresome author, the reader tours Asia, the Middle East, Europe, and Alaska, wondering how it will end. The serendipitous journey concludes with a powerful discovery."

—Monte Lake, Retired Lawyer, Author

"*That Which Cannot be Denied* centers on a young man's journey from childhood to adulthood, but it's a much bigger story than that. It is so artfully and richly crafted that it transports readers to a different time and lets them feel the experiences that come from heart-racing adventures around the globe."

—Michael White, Senior Vice President, Strategy and
Group Account Director, Young & Rubicam (Retired)

"History doesn't always reflect the details of what real people experience. However, in *That Which Cannot be Denied,* Roger Hughes provides not only the experiences of four generations of his family, but he also delights the reader with his storytelling expertise, making for a captivating reading adventure. Roger skillfully tells their remarkable stories as well as his own, with affection, admiration, and a captivating sense of humor. After reading this poignant memoir, you will feel like you were there, experiencing the ups and downs of his family's everyday lives and their incredible feats of courage as they gave back to their communities and served as examples of what makes America great."

—Loella Haskew, City Council Member, City of Walnut Creek, CA

"Roger Hughes's autobiography, *That Which Cannot Be Denied*, takes you on his worldwide journey of discovery. Sit down and enjoy the ride."

—Shellye Archambeau, Author of *Unapologetically Ambitious*, *Fortune* Top 10 Business Book of 2020

"Roger Hughes entertains us with his incredible family history and thrilling worldwide travels in *That Which Cannot Be Denied*. I have known Roger for decades, and after reading this autobiography, I now understand why he is so special. I can't wait for the next book!"

—Roy Van Pelt, Lathrop Construction Associates, Retired Partner

"Roger's enthralling book, *That Which Cannot be Denied*, engages the reader in his and his ancestors' history. His mix of pithy humor with prosaic accounts of world travel, blended with world events, makes for a compelling read."

—Alan Bailey, Worldwide Travel Advisor, CruisePlanners

That Which Cannot Be Denied

by Roger M. Hughes

© Copyright 2023 Roger M. Hughes

ISBN 979-8-88824-122-6

All rights reserved. No part of this publication may be reproduced, stored in a retrieval system, or transmitted in any form or by any means—electronic, mechanical, photocopy, recording, or any other—except for brief quotations in printed reviews, without the prior written permission of the author.

Published by

3705 Shore Drive
Virginia Beach, VA 23455
800-435-4811
www.koehlerbooks.com

That Which Cannot Be Denied

A Memoir

Roger M. Hughes
Foreword by Earl F. Palmer

To my beloved wife, Natalie. Without you, I could not have finished this book. Thank you for your love, patience, humor, intellect, and, most of all, for sharing "Us-land" with me for all these years. You are my forever love, my heart, and my soul.

TABLE OF CONTENTS

Foreword by Earl F. Palmer 1
Prologue: Three Vignettes 3

Part One 5

Chapter One: Henry and Agnes 7
Chapter Two: The Meanest Man in Bakersfield 13
Chapter Three: Last Call 23
Chapter Four: World War II 27
Chapter Five: South Side of Chicago 30
Chapter Six: Top Gun 33

Part Two 39

Chapter Seven: Big Boys Do Cry 41
Chapter Eight: Who am I? Why I'm Calvin! 48
Chapter Nine: Things Were Getting Gnarly 54
Chapter Ten: Anchors Aweigh! 58
Chapter Eleven: Land of the Rising Sun 64
Chapter Twelve: Shadows on a Wall, 1956 73

Part Three 77

Chapter Thirteen: Leaving Santa Ana 79
Chapter Fourteen: Stranger in a Strange Land 89
Chapter Fifteen: The Best of Times, the Worst of Times 93
Chapter Sixteen: A Collection of Stories 98
Chapter Seventeen: 3300 Manhattan Beach Blvd., California, 1963 ... 116
Chapter Eighteen: Mira Costa High School, 1963–1964 121

Part Four 135

Chapter Nineteen: Arrival Cairo, Egypt, 1964 137

Chapter Twenty: The Portico 145

Chapter Twenty-One: The Test 156

Chapter Twenty-Two: On the Wall 159

Chapter Twenty-Three: On Thin Ice 164

Chapter Twenty-Four: Rhythm of the Streets 182

Chapter Twenty-Five: Full Throttle! 191

Chapter Twenty-Six: Alexandria 199

Chapter Twenty-Seven: The Valley of the Kings 211

Chapter Twenty-Eight: On My Own 214

Chapter Twenty-Nine: The Deep Desert 247

Chapter Thirty: The Six-Day War 1967 256

Part Five 265

Chapter Thirty-One: Return to Bakersfield 267

Chapter Thirty-Two: Fuji-san 272

Chapter Thirty-Three: UOP and Leo 274

Chapter Thirty-Four: The Quickening of My Soul 279

Chapter Thirty-Five: The Fool 291

Acknowledgments *294*

FOREWORD BY EARL F. PALMER

That Which Cannot be Denied is a true story of a young boy, Roger Hughes, and his journey to manhood in the midst of many influences: a grandfather known as "the meanest man in Bakersfield;" and a father, a top-of-his-class flyer with the discipline of Marine Corps training; and a mother with flexible boundaries when it came to raising two boys often in the absence of their father. Her signature statement would admonish their sons with the words, "Clean up; your father is coming home!" Added to the environment was the constant presence of an older brother who was perfect in every way—a perpetual feature and reminder of success.

Because of his father's deployments to places near and far during his school years, Roger grew up with wide-flung experiences in schools and cities worldwide: Bakersfield, California; Mira Costa, California; Honolulu, Hawaii; Salt Lake City, Utah; Tokyo, Japan; and Cairo, Egypt. These episodes reveal intrigue and challenge as Roger describes significant markers in his growing years.

The intermix of people and places with his stories provokes the reader to fear for this eighteen-year-old as we read about him hitchhiking alone from Trieste, Italy through the Yugoslavian Alps in the middle of winter to reach the ship he needed to board for his return to Cairo. As part of this journey, we read about Roger falling asleep alongside the road, alone and cold in the penetrating chill of a major snowstorm. The reader experiences Roger's wonder as he deals with a hangover in the aftermath and disorder of a fraternity rush party and the surprise visit by his father's best friend, who questions, "What would your father say if he knew?" (Apparently, the father never found out.)

Throughout Roger's narrative, there are questions interwoven that he asks about life and the purpose of his own future. Roger searching for his sense of being propels him to get out on his own as a twenty-year-old man. The series of events that follow are filled with character-forming experiences. With strains in his tie with his parents, Roger heads to Alaska. Here he experiences challenging, physical, and exhausting work under precarious circumstances. Roger also experiences the caring discipline of the family who took him in and where the strands of Roger's life were gathered to culminate the story and lead to the resolution of his journey and the title, *That Which Cannot Be Denied*. As Roger ends the story of his formative years at this juncture, I encourage you to read on and discover that it is actually just the beginning. It reveals the turning point for this young man—the "fool" (as he refers to himself)—in his journey to fulfillment.

* * *

Earl F. Palmer is a biblical scholar; founder and active minister and teacher of Earl Palmer Ministries; cofounder of New College Berkeley; author of twenty books; Board of Trustees emeritus for the Princeton Theological Seminary; and has served as a pastor of congregations nationally and internationally over the past six decades.

PROLOGUE

Three Vignettes

Go Tell Grandma Goodbye, July 6, 1950
Bakersfield, California—Terrace Lane

I was sitting on my grandfather's lap in the breezeway of my grandparents' home in Bakersfield, California, when he laid down The Tale of Peter Rabbit and said quietly, "Roger, go tell your grandmother I said goodbye."

"What, Grandpa?" I remember replying.

He repeated quietly, "Go tell Grandma I said goodbye." I got off his lap, went to the kitchen, and did as I was told. My grandmother, who was washing dishes, looked out the window and then hurried outside, but he had already passed. The book lay open on his lap. I was three years old.

The El Alamein Lagoon, September 1964

The emerald green surface of the El Alamein Lagoon along the Egyptian Mediterranean coast lay before us, clear and calm but not for long, not with our DC-3 ripping through the air, propelling us forward, my father at the controls. The bucolic serenity of the El Alamein Lagoon, with its emerald water and sandy bottom surrounded by palms and deep reed banks, was not for us to appreciate, not now. The thrust provided by two Wright R-1820 Cyclone 9 engines demanded total concentration as we skimmed the lagoon's surface. We had work to do.

Cook Inlet, Kenai Alaska, June 1967

The view displaced every rational thought. I beheld first the mist and wondered how many shades of gray there could be. The sea was the dark gray of a black goose; the horizon shone like an old man's beard, luminescent in the last of the sun's glow; gray mullet trenches rippled the wet sand following the receding tide; intermittent idiosyncratic wonders, brackish and slick or briny darkened greens, swirling and stretching like dancers, were mysteries I could not comprehend. I wondered at the light along the horizon smeared laterally, a thin razor delineating the day's light from the darkened sea.

But it was wrong! All was inverted.

Part One

Child labor in the coal industry.
Image via Wikimedia Commons.

A hurrier and two thrusters heaving a corf full of coal as depicted in the 1853 book *The White Slaves of England* by J. Cobden.

CHAPTER ONE

Henry and Agnes

My great grandfather Henry Hughes, the second son of James and Elizabeth Hughes, was born on August 28, 1837, in Coalbrookdale, England. Acknowledged as the world's most productive coal fields, the mines of Coalbrookdale produced great riches for over four hundred years. However, the townsfolk who mined those fields did not share in the wealth they created for the industrialists. The town was self-proclaimed as *The Cradle of the Industrial Revolution*, a fancy sobriquet that belied the brutal existence of the men, women, and children who toiled deep into the Coalbrookdale mines. Such was the insatiate nature of the times that children were commonly utilized to carry explosives deep into the narrowest passages of the mines where only the children could reach.

Henry's parents were adamant that their children would never be listed with the names of the dead as a result of the latest mine catastrophe.

Agnes Seddon was the third daughter of James and Agnes Seddon. Months earlier, Henry and Agnes had agreed to marry with the understanding that Henry's life would never end amid collapsing timbers and broken rocks while families waited for news, knowing that when it came, it would be heartbreaking for some and heartfelt joy for others. Henry and Agnes were equally determined that Henry would not succumb in the dark of a mine to the dreaded *black lung disease*. Known colloquially as *fugitive dust*, this dust was so fine that once inhaled, it never left the lungs, resulting in a tragic death by slow suffocation.

Citizens of Coalbrookdale wanting to escape the tyranny of the mines had only a few options. First, they could seek work in London, the city known as *The Big Smoke*, portrayed by Claude Monet's garish orange sky paintings in his late London series.

The only other alternative to the filth of the coal mines was the one resource that would never be depleted—wheat, Britain's most significant crop grown for human consumption. Since land ownership was passed down from generation to generation, a non-land-owning family interested in farming could only accept subjection to one of the English manors as a so-called tenant farmer, who could cultivate specific fields within the manor to maintain their subsistence.

Henry and Agnes Marry

Henry and his betrothed Agnes Seddon, the third daughter of James and Agnes Seddon, were married at the Cathedral Church in Manchester, located in Lancashire County. The legal formalities were deemed complete when the couple's names and places of birth were entered into the County Marriage Registry by the officiant and then affirmed by their signatures or, more likely, by their mark. At least one witness was required, and then the couple would be confirmed as man and wife.

In normal times, these procedures could easily be managed, but the 1860s were far from normal. Interminable lines formed as, for many reasons, marriage nuptials were a must before an unmarried woman would dare to cross the Atlantic with a man. The line stretching behind them, the betrothed would wait for their moment on *the spot*, as they called it, as the ceremony was conducted literally with the bride and groom standing in one particular place. Once the civil requirements were fulfilled, the public official would cede the spot to the priest who would then step in to conduct the religious services—on the same spot.

Coming to America

Within days of their marriage, Henry and Agnes were on their way to America. Following the Homestead Act of 1862, the United States gave away prime cattle and agricultural land in the heart of the new state of Kansas to citizens or intended citizens. The Homestead Act allocated up to 160 acres to the chosen individuals as long as they had never borne arms against the US government. The Act stated that all claimants were to improve the plot by building a dwelling and cultivating the land. After five years on the land, the original filer was entitled to the property, free and clear.

Henry and Agnes joined the flood of immigrants who, in 1862, made the momentous decision to immigrate to America, more specifically to Kansas. Certainly, they wanted to escape the crushing poverty of Coalbrookdale and the ruthless class systems imposed by virtually every country in the world, but mostly, they came in response to the promise of free land—and lots of it. It is uncertain how much these newcomers valued the free land versus the freedom to live and worship as they pleased based on their hard work, ingenuity, and tenacity. The scant notations in my grandmother Myrtle's Bible provide hints about Henry and Agnes's station in life. They were by no means paupers, nor were they well-to-do. They were hardworking and frugal. Otherwise, they would never have chanced such a move.

Undoubtedly, theirs was not a romantic honeymoon, as they likely traveled steerage class which involved long lines and other unpleasantries under sail. Ocean voyages took six to fourteen weeks, depending on the weather and currents, as well as the captain and crew's skill, courage, and boldness. Regardless of the duration, the crossings were a fixed price. Consequently, no value was placed on the safety or comfort of the passengers. This assured a very rough passage. Such was the experience of Henry and Agnes. After the harrowing ocean voyage, they faced a daunting 1500-mile journey overland until finally, they reached their destination.

Their travel was not measured by time or distance but rather by their conjoined spirits with the tide of immigrants from all over Europe who shared the same desire: to roll up their sleeves and get to work.

Bloody Kansas

In the midst of the Civil War, in 1862, Henry and Agnes acquired 160 acres of prime wheat and cattle land in Kansas, but nothing came easy. Section 19 of the Homestead Act years before had allowed settlers to determine, by popular vote, whether Kansas would enter the Union a free or slave state. The consequences were steeped in blood, but Kansas ultimately rejected slavery and became the thirty-fourth state on January 21, 1861. Still, the hard feelings of the previous decades lingered. It's hard to know if Henry and Agnes understood the caldron they were entering, but if they didn't, they quickly learned.

Typical sod house built by homesteaders.
Image via Wikimedia Commons.

What then?

I know very little about what happened to Henry and Agnes or how they fared as landowners in Kansas. We do know that their son Elsworth was born in 1877 and that Agnes died of scarlet fever in 1882 when Elsworth was only five years old. I don't know how long Henry stayed in Kansas after Agnes died, but records show Henry died in Tulare, California, in 1913.

Henry did not remarry, and to the best of my knowledge, he continued to live and work on the Kansas property alone for many years. At some point, when Henry could no longer manage the property, at Elsworth's urging, Henry moved into Elsworth and his wife Myrtle's home in Tulare, California.

After Henry's death, Elsworth and then Myrtle continued to lease the land in Kansas to the family that occupied and worked it for more than fifty years.

A few years after Myrtle died, in the early 1970s, I went on a road trip with Dad to help him drive his cars to Oklahoma City. He had just received a promotion as Chief Aviation Safety Inspector at the Federal Aviation Administration Headquarters. Every FAA pilot was required to submit to rigorous flight checks to renew their credentials each year. Dad was responsible for ensuring the proficiency in flight of every FAA pilot, and he relished the challenge.

On the way, we stopped at the family's homestead in Kansas, which neither Dad nor I had ever seen. Dad had contacted the tenant family who worked the property and asked them to meet us and show us around. After touring the property, Dad asked me to go back to the car so he could speak privately with the patriarch of the tenant family. I waited in the car as I watched him walk and talk with his tenant.

Upon my father's death, I learned that he had given ownership of the Kansas property to the tenant. It took me a long time to understand and reconcile why Dad gave away the 160 acres of prime land in Kansas that had been in our family for three generations. Of course, it was not my job to question what my father chose to do with his birthright. Over the years, I've come to understand my father's deeply held belief that he had not earned the land, but the tenants had. It was imperative for him to know that he had made his way in life without taking anything from anyone.

Momentous Decisions—The Three Pledges

At a young age, Henry made three life-altering decisions. First, no matter his circumstances, he would never make his living underground as his father had. Second, he would own the land he toiled and never become indentured. Third, he would never take on debt of any kind.

These pledges were passed from Henry to Elsworth and then to my father, not by word of mouth but by example. These commitments certainly kept my grandfather and father from becoming wealthy, but they were never beholden to anyone, and there was always food on the table. I am quite certain these early admonitions kept the family afloat throughout Prohibition, the Dust Bowl, and the Great Depression.

CHAPTER TWO

The Meanest Man in Bakersfield

My grandfather's name was Elsworth Lawrence Hughes, although everyone called him Curly. He left home in Kansas near the turn of the nineteenth century in 1892, riding an early motorcycle. He was fifteen years old, and it is unclear whether he was kicked out of the family home or just a runaway. Regardless, there is no argument that he was incorrigible. Curly's attitude and nickname were likely the result of him being rendered bald at a young age due to a severe bout with scarlet fever, the same disease that had taken his mother's life. It is also clear that no one tried to talk him out of leaving, nor did anyone go looking for him after he left.

The Sequoia Logging Camps

Curly found his way to the Sequoia logging camps just a bit north and east of the California Central Valley town of Tulare. These were rough places suitable for those times, and even at his young age, he fit right in. He was tough to deal with: quick to fight, quick to challenge a perceived slight, unfriendly, and contentious. That about sums it up, except for his gambling and drinking—vices that lived with him for the rest of his life (with no apparent regret, at least not on his part).

He drove out from Kansas on an Indian motorcycle. Some questioned if he was old enough to drive it, some questioned where he got the money, and some questioned whether it was even his. For all such questions, he had but one answer, and it wasn't pleasant.

When he arrived in California, Curly was too young to work at logging, so he washed dishes, did laundry, and worked at any other odd job he could find. Soon he found his way to the gambling saloons that dotted the logging territory, and a few years after the turn of the century, he was running his own establishment, which determined the course of the rest of his life. In California, you could not legally run a gambling establishment without providing food for the patrons. My grandfather knew a lot about gambling but knew nothing about cooking.

Having hired and fired several cooks, he was desperate. This frustration resulted in his first marriage, as it seemed that was the best way to secure a good cook.

Curly's wife left with no regrets after he ran his motorcycle off the road, injuring himself so severely that he was unable to work his saloon. I have been unable to find records of either a marriage or a divorce.

Curly and Myrtle

There was a strong relationship between a successful gambling establishment and great food. My grandmother, Myrtle McCoy, perhaps a bit desperate at the age of thirty and living in relative social isolation as a cook on a Native American reservation in Oklahoma, responded to my grandfather's advertisement for a cook in the Sequoia Forest of California. When Myrtle announced her intent to head for California, her sister, Montana McCoy, the only teacher on the reservation, was apoplectic.

My grandfather wired Myrtle money for the train ticket, so she set off for Fresno, California, the gateway to the giant redwoods of the Sequoias and, at the time, the logging capital of the world. It was the last time the sisters saw each other until my return from Egypt in 1966.

My grandfather was waiting for Myrtle at the train station. He was a strapping man, five feet ten inches tall, broad-shouldered, handsome, and formidable, despite his permanent limp from his motorcycle accident and his bald dome. My grandfather proposed not long after their meeting, and Myrtle accepted. This is how my grandmother, Myrtle McCoy, at the age of thirty, a veritable spinster in those days, came to marry Curly Hughes, a man ten years her senior, a gambler, and a saloon keeper.

On July 8, 1917, less than a year after she arrived in California, Myrtle McCoy recorded her marriage to Elsworth in her family Bible. She was a believer, as her marked-up Bible attests, and as such, she set about to make the best of what God and Elsworth had provided.

To my knowledge, Curly never stepped inside a church, not even for my baptism. His propensity to drink accelerated into severe alcoholism, but his poker winnings never seemed to suffer from his lack of sobriety. Though he was not an educated man, he was astute. He was known as a man not to be fooled with, earning the moniker the "Meanest Man in Bakersfield." However, with all his faults, he always treated my grandmother with respect, invariably referring to her as *Mother*, and never did her harm. He always provided for her, which was a challenge in those difficult times.

There Will be Blood

Though he was not an educated man, Curly was bright and clever, and soon he saw that the lumber boom was about over. Loggers had pretty much depleted the magnificent trees outside of the protected Sequoia National Park, which was established in 1890. Curly knew oil had been discovered along the southeastern side of the San Joaquin Valley, igniting the area's economy and significantly buffering the effects of the depression.

My grandfather quickly saw the change in fortunes of men who took advantage of the *black gold* oozing up to the surface in the valley. As a result, Curly and Myrtle pulled up stakes and migrated to the lower San Juaquin Valley, first to Tulare and then to Bakersfield. These were the days glorified by Daniel Day-Lewis' epic movie *There Will Be Blood*.

My grandfather had no interest in rough and dangerous work, whether logging or wildcatting. His primary objective was mining the winnings of those who did. So, with my grandmother's help, he started and acquired several restaurants and gambling saloons in the lower San Joaquin Valley.

Those years were good for my grandparents. My grandfather ran the saloon and the tables, and my grandmother kept the books and turned out great food. They made a good team, Elsworth and Myrtle. Both were hard workers, and each fiercely protected the other. They did well in the southern San Joaquin Valley.

On January 17, 1920, prohibition became the law of the land. Suddenly, my grandparents' business was reduced to a small restaurant called Pickett's with a few forlorn slot machines and poker tables just outside the city limits of Bakersfield. They kept their restaurant open, but business was slow. My grandmother would arrive midafternoon to begin preparations for the meals of fried chicken, pork chops, grits, and greens. Some said that more than cider was being served at Picketts, but no one could prove it. As finances allowed, they had one or two helpers that cleaned up.

Then on September 24, 1921, Elsworth and Myrtle's only child, my father Harry J. Hughes, was born. It was a rough time and place to be born.

With Myrtle's help, my grandfather kept order at Pickett's, making sure it was spotlessly clean before closing, even though there were many nights when one of the bartenders had to help him home because he was drunk.

These stories bring to mind a memory. I was young, maybe three, when my grandfather took me to his bar on a Saturday morning. The first thing he did was clean the stainless-steel preparation bar, which was about a foot below the mahogany "customer" bar, extending into the service area.

There were wooden racks about every six feet, a couple of inches below the customer bar. I enjoyed using the wooden racks to propel myself along the service bar, sliding as fast as possible. At some point, I asked my grandfather why he had the wooden racks. He looked at me for a moment, then opened a drawer below the service bar. "Roger," he said, pulling out two pistols and slipping one into each of the nearby racks, "In this bar, you never want to be more than an arm's length away from a gun."

Interior View of Turf Saloon, Hughes and Hill Proprietors, Bakersfield, California.

Though prohibition proved a challenge, the family survived, but my grandfather's anger grew. He railed against the prohibitionists, the city fathers, the government, and anyone who looked at him sideways. Many citizens of Bakersfield voiced their disapproval of his behavior, apparently with good reason. He made a point of making those with whom he was displeased stand aside or be bumped off the sidewalks. I learned later from a neighbor that many "good folks" would cross to the other side of the street if they saw him approaching, especially if he had been drinking, and those who owed him money would turn the other way.

In addition to keeping Pickett's open as a restaurant, my grandfather, ever the entrepreneur, fitted his Model T Ford with a billboard sign that read *Hughes and Son Grape Juice and Home Produced Wine*. The emphasis was on "Home Produced Wine," as prohibition allowed individuals to make wine in their homes but set a reasonable limit for home consumption.

My grandfather, accompanied by the boy who'd become my father, would make house calls to consult on making their home-produced wine. He would provide all necessary accouterments for winemaking, including bottles and bottling tools. He even supplied the grapes. Traveling from home to home, he would regularly consult with the home vintners to see them through the production cycle, assuring a quality end product. Some of the city fathers objected to his trade, but it was entirely legal. In addition, my grandparents tended to their fruit and nut orchards, harvested honey hives, and developed some small commercial properties along Brundage Lane, which was becoming a major road into town.

As soon as my father was old enough, he earned money doing chores around the ranch, such as gathering honey from the family beehives, maintaining the neighbor's beehives, and doing odd jobs around the neighborhood. At an early age, he earned a reputation for being able to fix, weld, or mend anything that needed repair, and he developed a respectable garage on the premises to support his passion for all things mechanical.

My grandfather was one of the few ranchers who would harvest honey from wild beehives, and neighbors would pay him to remove hives from their property. Of course, my father was conscripted into the enterprise as soon as my grandfather deemed him ready. Dad was responsible for steadying the three-legged orchard ladder as my grandfather, wearing his head and shoulder protective netting climbed it to retrieve the hive.

One memorable day my grandfather was removing a hive from a neighbor's tree when a bee, laden with honey, dropped from the hive, falling straight into the collar of my father's shirt and down his back. My father started swatting frantically at the bee rumbling around under his shirt. Unfortunately, he lost sight of his principal responsibility during the battle—steadying the ladder! Without my father's support, the wobbly ladder tossed my grandfather to the ground, still holding on to the hive.

The neighbor helped my grandfather home while Dad, filled with fear, trailed behind. Watching through the bathroom window, Dad could see my grandmother bathing Epson Salt onto angry red welts on my grandfather's back, arms, and legs. My father decided it was best to spend the night in the barn.

To my father's great surprise, when he returned home, my grandfather never complained about his handling of the event.

The Mechanic

Those who grow up on a ranch understand the need for self-reliance, and, as one would expect, my father became quite handy at repairing just about anything that was broken. Even before it was legal for him to drive, he fixed the family Model T and appliances. Soon neighbors were bringing him their cars and appliances for repair, allowing him to earn a good income.

My father opened a little repair shop on their small acreage while in high school. Night or day, he could be found in the garage fixing small appliances, broken furniture, and anything that moved. With my grandpa maintaining the gambling establishment, my grandmother managing the restaurant, and the home wine consulting business, they did all right throughout the depth of prohibition and the depression. How well they did was not discussed openly, but my grandparents had accumulated a reasonable nest egg by the time prohibition was repealed.

Pickett's business returned with a flourish as if it had never been interrupted.

The growing tension between my grandfather and the city during prohibition seemed to break out into an all-out war, even though prohibition was over and his business remained in the county, not in the town. Despite the renewed legality of alcohol and my grandfather's proper liquor license, the City of Bakersfield continued to harass his patrons whenever they passed from the county into the city.

The House on Hughes Lane

After prohibition was repealed, my grandparents built a modest home on the corner of Hughes Lane and South Myrtle Street in Bakersfield. My grandparent's house was small, with two bedrooms, two baths, a living room, a dining room, and a kitchen, with a nice covered breezeway. On the other side of the breezeway, there was a guest room, bath, and garage, bordered by a canal which my brother, our friends, and I would navigate for miles (well, it seemed like miles), gigging frogs and netting small fish.

From my earliest memories, their house was filled with knickknacks, jewelry, tools, artwork, and other eclectic items from around the world that my grandfather reputedly won in poker games or which he acquired because of unpaid debts. In the house was a safe filled with jewelry, including gold and diamond rings, earrings, necklaces, watches, and tie pins, resulting from my grandfather's powers in poker.

The most fun we had was perusing the three outbuildings on the property. These buildings contained hard assets won by my grandfather in poker games or taken in for debt collateral. Here furniture was stuffed to the rafters along with a variety of tools, chests filled with treasures (or so it seemed to me) like vases, plates, and silver. I learned from several subsequent experiences that such items usually don't have a lot of value, but they provoked endless musing and storytelling.

Eventually, my grandparents owned a significant number of acres surrounding the house on Hughes Lane. My grandfather subdivided much of this property, and he and Dad built several homes and developed several commercial properties nearby.

I have been told emphatically by scions of the founders of Bakersfield that neither Hughes Lane nor Myrtle Street was named after my grandfather or grandmother. Still, they don't dispute that the nearby streets of Irene Lane and Terry Lane were named after my mother and brother. Their little subdivision had no Roger Lane because it was built before I came along, though I still carry a grudge.

Elsworth and Myrtle

Despite my grandfather's temperament and the challenges of the times, my grandparents reached a repose of sorts. They were successful at their chosen professions—my grandfather ran the saloon and tables and engaged in a host of sundry endeavors, while my grandmother ran the kitchen and kept the books, house, and garden in order. As far as the family and the community knew, there was never a sharp word or disagreement between them.

My grandparents remained married for the rest of Elsworth's life. Upon my grandfather's sudden death in 1950, my grandmother, Myrtle, was left financially secure enough to travel extensively, visiting us in several places throughout the world. Myrtle continued developing and expanding the properties but never remarried after Elsworth's death. She remained a faithful churchgoer throughout her life, as the prayers and notes in her Bible, which sits on my desk as I write, attest.

My Conclusions

The Dust Bowl and Great Depression forever shaped my grandfather and grandmother. Families were torn apart, often scattered forever. Many had no social network, and people frequently drifted away with few or no plans. Relationships were often just accommodations for men and women, survival deals really, with trades spoken and unspoken, which sometimes grew into love. Such relationships were not to be taken lightly, even if they were temporary, as they were almost certainly significant. Through all of this—the struggles, trials, and sorrows—somehow, hope endured.

Undoubtedly, my grandfather and grandmother were bound

together by necessity, and their significant differences were of little consequence given what they faced. They were both extremely hard workers. They were both very bright. They were both savers, and neither looked to someone else to protect them from the ravages of the depression. Given my grandfather's drinking and gambling, I am confident that, but for my grandmother, he would have died much earlier, broke and destitute.

As for my grandmother, she received the protection afforded by the Meanest Man in Bakersfield. Though he devolved deeper and deeper into his alcoholism, my grandmother took control over the modest finances, which protected him. Somehow, she managed as she tempered my grandfather's demons.

I can only believe she was not on her own and that her prayers were answered.

Curly, Harry, and Myrtle in front of the family home in Bakersfield.

CHAPTER THREE

Last Call

The last call at Pickett's was a bit of a cat and mouse game with the Bakersfield police. Although my grandfather's establishment was outside the city limits and beyond the reach of the police force, many of his patrons were not. In fact, squad cars would wait outside of Pickett's at closing time to harass the patrons as they passed from the county into the city. Indulging patrons whose journey home required them to pass into city jurisdiction were best advised to take a circuitous route, while more sober customers traveled directly down Brundage Lane.

Regardless of the time of day, my father's view was that if he was within the city limits, he was subject to being hassled by the police just for driving while being a Hughes. Dad was likely worth following, as he took after my grandfather in many ways. And, like my grandfather, he had a glint in his eye that law enforcement saw as confrontational. To put it simply, when recounting his relationship with the police as a teenager, Dad would say, "All I can tell you is that my dad did not like the law, and the law did not like him. And I bore the brunt of all of that."

That may be true, and I never knew my father to tell a lie, but from bits and pieces I put together from my father and a few neighbors, such as the Machados, it is clear that there was enough blame to go around. For example, Dad was a dedicated dragster and while serious races took place outside of Bakersfield's city limits, plenty of huffing and puffing and showing off took place in town. It is fair to say that the city was strict while the county was lenient.

A Surrogate Father

The Machado family was very kind to Dad, and he returned the favor. A surrogate father-son relationship developed between Andy Machado and my father, as my grandfather spent virtually every evening at the bar, tending poker tables and keeping a watch on the till.

Dad helped Andy with his car and repaired almost any item around his house that needed attention. He also got Andy interested in fishing, one of Dad's lifelong passions. For the rest of Andy's life, whenever Dad returned to Bakersfield, he would take Andy out fly fishing.

When I returned to Bakersfield from Cairo at age nineteen, I moved in with my grandmother, the only family I had in Bakersfield. The Machados treated me with the same kindness they had extended to my father. Andy took me to the same fishing holes he had fished with my father. Some of the best stories I heard about Dad's younger years came from Andy.

Fearless Master Mechanic

Dad's reckless toughness in high school was balanced by his growing reputation as a master mechanic. He was not interested in academics, but he did well enough to get by. It was his mechanical skills, however, that set him apart and earned him an uncommon level of respect from his peers in school and around the neighborhood. He could fix almost anything with an engine, wheels, and a body to encase them. His attention to detail, persistence, and willingness to take on risks advanced his development as a dragster in high school and as a premier mechanic and metallurgist who earned the admiration of the mechanics in his Marine squadron.

His toughness and his love for speed ultimately led to him graduating number one in his flight training class at the US Marine

Corps Air Station Cherry Point during World War II, and then to many decades flying anything with wings in various theaters throughout the world, including Korea, the South Pacific, the western United States, North Africa, and Thailand.

I know quite a bit about his WWII experiences, a bit more of his activities while in Egypt, and only a little bit of what he was up to in Thailand.

Dad's mechanical skills, tenacity, and refusal to back down while still in high school portended who he would become as an adult. Whatever mode of vehicle—vintage or classic, wheels or wings—he could fix it, pimp it, race it, or even raise it from the dead if necessary, or so it seemed to me.

A Tenacious Fighter with a Heart for Service

I frequently saw the effect of Dad's quiet self-assuredness with both mechanical and physical issues. His command presence alone could calm tense situations. In short, things rarely got out of hand when he was around, and on a few occasions, I saw how quickly he restored order. Responsibility for service is ingrained in every member of the Corps. In Dad's case, it certainly was not inherited from his father, who, deep in his soul, was an anarchist.

Dad would never pass by anyone who had broken down by the roadside, day or night. With a great set of travel tools, he soon got them running. If he didn't have a needed part, he would somehow jury-rig a way to get the stranded wayfarer to a service station so no one was left behind. Once retired, he became a member of Good Sam (short for Good Samaritan) Roadside Assistance Club, and well into his eighties, he participated as a volunteer mechanic for the Good Sam RV Adventures tours in Mexico, and, again, no one was left behind.

After Dad's retirement, my parents settled into Atascadero, California, just over the hill from the midcoastal California towns of San Louis Obispo and Paso Robles. Dad's mechanical skills soon made him a local legend with the Paso Robles Estrella Warbirds of America, known worldwide for their restored military aircraft. I am told that the Paso Robles branch would not consider a purchase without Dad's advice. Often, he was able to get a "wounded bird" back home on its own wings rather than having to send it back in pieces. His knowledge almost always proved critical in making a good deal or avoiding a bad one, giving the Paso Robles branch a significant advantage when acquiring and restoring the most sought-after planes.

CHAPTER FOUR
World War II

My Father Enters the War

Hundreds of thousands of young men like my father, descended from all nationalities, stepped forward to face the challenge of the war with Japan. They fought simultaneous battles in the South Pacific, the European Theater, and North Africa. Never before had such a war been fought, with this number of losses and so much hanging in the balance.

The day after the Japanese attacked Pearl Harbor, my father proudly enlisted in the United States Marine Corps.

My grandfather was incensed. No, he was furious! As I said previously, my grandfather was an anarchist to the depth of his being. He was suspicious of all authority and believed that privileged men waged war at the expense of the poor. My grandfather came through the depression a hard man, untrusting of all authority, suspicious and temperamental, quick to take affront, and quick to back his temper.

My grandmother's heart, however, never needed softening. She was the best example of abiding hope and a sense of obligation that I have ever known. Two compelling forces of grit and duty bound my grandparents together, allowing them to survive extraordinary challenges in extraordinary times. Dad inherited the best of his parents' natures, making him a force to be reckoned with.

I'm sure my father would have enlisted no matter what, but he made it clear that he wanted to be considered for flight school. Of course, the recruiters told him that if he had the right stuff, the Corps would need a lot of pilots. This closed the deal for Dad.

My father enlisted without consulting my grandfather, which created quite a row when my grandfather found out. He marched Dad down to the recruitment station and demanded that they rescind his enlistment.

The recruiter's response stopped even my grandpa. "He is a Marine now, sir, and there is nothing you or anyone else can do about it." And he went on, "Let me make this simple, sir, he reports, or he faces a firing squad."

My father reported to the Marine Corps Recruit Depot Parris Island for boot camp, where he graduated at the top of his class overall and was number one in each specialty except for marksmanship. As the number one graduate overall, he should have had his choice of follow-on assignments and been able to choose aviation. But, since these were not normal times, Dad was sent to metallurgy school, not flight school, for the good of the service.

He was beside himself and expressed disappointment to his gunnery sergeant. "Right now," Gunny said, "the loss of planes at Pearl Harbor is so extensive there are far more pilots than serviceable planes. The priority is repair, and since you were at the top of the metallurgy class, that's where you are needed most, and that's where you are going." I can almost imagine my grandfather smirking in the background.

But Gunny was not without a heart. "Don't worry, Corporal, planes are rolling off the assembly line, and pilots are returning home in boxes. Keep at it, and you will get your chance." Such were the times that Dad took this macabre utterance as encouragement.

Regardless of his disappointment, he had no choice. He had one week of leave plus three days of travel time before he had to report for his assignment in Chicago.

He raced home to Bakersfield to gather a few things. To his shock, he received a hero's welcome as the Marine Corps had leaked his number one status to the local newspaper. Even the police officers that once harassed him, many of whom knew him on a first-name basis, wanted their picture taken with him. A picture of my grandpa standing proudly next to Dad in his Marine "greens" appeared on the front page of the *Bakersfield Gazette*. Amazing what a war can do for one's reputation.

CHAPTER FIVE
South Side of Chicago

It was now deep into the winter months of early 1942. Despite reason and common sense, my father decided he would ride his Indian motorcycle to the metallurgical school in Chicago on a route he had never driven, to a place he had never been. His motorcycle was not the same model his father had ridden when he first arrived in California—not by a long shot. I can assure you it was fast because he made the entire journey in a little over a day and a half, rather than the three days he had allowed in the event he encountered inclement weather. He did not stop for anything except absolute necessities. Otherwise, he was *balls out* all the way. (That's an old Bakersfield expression for very fast).

I can see Dad ripping down the highway, sunrise to deep night in my mind's eye. Almost certainly, he took the more southern route to minimize the winter weather travel: leaving Bakersfield on Route 466 to pick up Route 66 in Arizona, which took him through New Mexico, Texas, Oklahoma, Kansas, Missouri, then up to Chicago. Whichever route he chose, all went well, and he completed the journey nearly two days before school started, giving him time to explore the famed South Side of Chicago, renowned even then.

Apparently, after buffing up at boot camp and learning how to defend himself and kill quickly if need be, he was full of himself. Dad related the following story to me for the first time only after I graduated from law school when he felt that the time for discretion with his children had passed. He told me that the first thing he did upon arriving in Chicago was seek out a South Side bar. Wearing his Marine casual khakis, Dad did not need to reach for his wallet as drink after drink appeared before him on the bar, with no accompanying tab. Early in the war, this standard courtesy was extended to servicemen, particularly those wearing their Marine standard-issue greens. South Side bars extended this courtesy to service members without limit.

Late in the night, Dad decided to return to the hotel room he had rented for two days. As he was heading for the alley where he had parked his bike, he was intercepted by a lanky South Side guy (in deference to Jim Croce, I will just call him "Slim") who said, "You've had too much to drink to drive that motorcycle, Marine, and we need you for the war. You can sleep it off on the cot in the backroom and drive safely back to your hotel in the morning."

Now, that is not something most people would want to say to a recent Marine boot camp graduate, and sure enough, Dad did not take kindly to the suggestion. "Who's going to stop me?" he said, heading for the alley. That was the last thing he remembered before waking up early the next morning, laying on a cot in a back room with a sore chin and a formidable hangover.

Getting himself together wasn't easy, but he was happy to find the keys to the bike were in his jacket pocket, where he had put them when he entered the bar. No one else was around, so he gathered himself up and went outside to the alley. Bracing for the cold Chicago wind, he found to his great relief, that his motorcycle was still parked where he left it the night before. Great! His relief quickly faded when he saw that someone had cut the distributor wires.

He was beside himself until he noticed that whoever cut the wires had neatly stripped the ends for splicing. On the seat of his motorcycle was a roll of electrical tape with a note saying: "When you are sober enough to splice the wires, Marine, you'll be sober enough to drive. Semper Fi." I would like to say that the note was signed *Slim*, but that would be stretching the truth. Dad said it was the only fight he ever lost, and I have never had reason to doubt his word. If you are going to lose only one fight, it best be to a guy from the South Side of Chicago.

Six months later, when Dad graduated from metallurgical school, the air war in the Pacific was going full bore. Gunny's macabre prediction of thousands of young pilots being lost at sea or coming home in caskets was tragically coming true. And just as Gunny predicted, the loss of pilots in the Pacific forced the Corps to accept non-officer candidates into flight school.

Such is the elixir of war that my father would greet such news with a mixture of great sorrow and a bloody desire for revenge. In each of these young men was the soul of a warrior, born of a deep desire to join the fight. Now my father would have an opportunity to fly in this war because of an attrition rate that was nearly 90 percent.

What is the elixir for valor? The lust for revenge is a deadly potion that has launched wars and has driven the history of man. "Carpe Diem, young man. This is the moment for which you were born." Surely Dad understood this, and indeed, he mourned the death of each of his fallen brethren, and surely, he would have given his own life to save any one of them. Yet, this moment of tragic loss opened a life that my father could never have imagined.

Just as my father graduated number one in his class from boot camp and metallurgical school, he successfully graduated number one from various flight programs: first, basic flight school, then advanced training in Texas. Finally, in May of 1943, he earned his gold bars as a second lieutenant and was admitted to the elite advanced flight combat school at the US Marine Corps Air Station Cherry Point in North Carolina.

CHAPTER SIX

Top Gun

Not everyone was happy with Dad's acceptance to flight school. Historically, only a few pilots who had earned commissions without having college degrees were admitted to this elite program. As far as I know, Dad was one of the first. Not having a college degree was a great annoyance to his instructors and his classmates, particularly when it became known that he had earned top honors in every program to which he had been admitted.

Apparently this difference between him and the others was simply not to be tolerated. From Dad's first day in the program, he was made to feel that his presence was an offense, not only to the Corps but—in the eyes of the instructors—to the honor of the program. So extreme was the venom directed his way that my father came to believe that his fellow candidates were intent on seeing him fail. Even the instructors joined in the vitriol, giving my dad the least mechanically reliable planes. He learned about this from the mechanics with whom he quickly made friends.

As the top graduate in metallurgical school, Dad spent every free moment with the mechanics and the planes. He poked over, through, and around every part of them. He paid particular attention to those in bad repair, as those were usually the planes he was assigned. As a result, Dad learned the idiosyncrasies of each aircraft and how to avoid or overcome their weaknesses in flight.

Harry's picture from flight school.

The mechanics admired my father. They rooted for him, tutored him on what each plane could or could not do, and showed him how to compensate for the deficiencies. The mechanics seemed to empathize with him: a guy from the same side of the tracks, fighting the odds. They admired his grit and hated the arrogance of the officers who assumed that his lack of formal education made him unfit to fly a Corsair. They also found him to be a highly trained mechanic, almost as good as they were in diagnosing problems and correcting flaws. In short, he was a kindred spirit, and they did everything they could to see him succeed.

Quickly, he established his status as the lead contender to be named "Top Gun," a distinction given with the first mock dogfights to denote the best pilot within each flight school class. (This is not to the same as the US Navy Fighter Weapons School known as TOPGUN that was established in the Vietnam era and immortalized in the popular movies of the same name.) Once he had it, he never let go. He endured taunts, challenges, and cold shoulders. The closer he got to graduating at the top of his class, the rougher things became. Whereas before, he was assigned the weakest of the flyable planes, now he was often assigned planes that the mechanics had not recommended for flight at all.

The idea of a non-college graduate being in the program, much less leading the class, was so vile that the instructors repeatedly reminded the other candidates what it would mean if someone like him led the class.

All the insults, plotting, and even the overt sabotage were to no avail. Dad grabbed hold of Top Gun and never let go, right up through graduation.

In 1942 after President Franklin Roosevelt signed The Navy Women's Reserve Act and created a division of the US Navy commonly known as WAVES (Women Accepted for Volunteer Emergency Service), she volunteered to help the war effort. Assisting in the flight tower, her perch gave her the best opportunity to assess and admire the young Navy and Marine pilots as they vied for the best of class of the Navy Corsair fighter school. From her vantage point, I have no doubt that my mom set her sights on my father early on. After all, he was top of his class, a position he earned and retained from the first day of competition to his graduation from the elite Marine fighter pilot program.

My parents had their ups and downs, some of which were dramatic. They endured some tough and stormy times—and, in accord with my father's greatest compliment, they stayed the course. And that means a lot.

Tailhook

Decades later, while on a family vacation, my daughters—Melissa, who was fourteen, and Erin, eleven years old—asked Dad whether he had ever landed on an aircraft carrier, since most Marine pilots are land-based. Dad had qualified for membership in the Tailhook Association with his carrier landings in flight school at Cherry Point, and had maintained it throughout his time in the Corps and as a Reservist. The girls wanted to know what it was like to land on a carrier. I was nearly fifty at the time, and I am confident that I had never heard this story before.

"We were off of Cherry Point, five of us in our squad. We were the number one squad, and I was the squadron leader, the leader of our class; therefore, I would be the first to land, right after our instructor, who had just returned from the South Pacific, where he'd been assigned to "Pappy" Boyington's squadron. George "Pappy" Boyington was a true American hero and an Ace who received both the Medal of Honor and the Navy Cross. Each remaining member of the squad was to follow in the order of their ranking. Our instructor would approach from downwind at a ninety-degree intersection to the course. Then, at the intersection with the carrier's course, he would make a steep turn into the wind and go hard for the deck."

Dad knew that the landing jockey, the guy with the hand paddles, sometimes referred to as *four eyes* (two eyes and two paddles), would give the landing signals that the pilot must follow. It was vital for the pilot to react only to the paddle signals, as responding to deck movement would put the pilot behind "real-time." That would almost certainly lead to disaster because only the pilot's visual observation of the paddles would communicate the most current information.

As soon as Dad saw the flight leader hit the deck, he was to initiate his approach. At this point in the story, he said, "We were at an altitude such that the carrier looked like a pea in a sea of whitecaps, about the size of my balls in my throat. The instructor made a steep descent at the prescribed ninety-degree angle while we circled above. He then banked hard into the wind, just as he said he would, when suddenly his plane flipped ninety degrees straight into the water, never to be seen again."

Dad told us he was shocked but continued circling and awaiting instruction. He was beside himself and selfishly thought, *Well, I guess I won't be qualifying today.* Then he heard Tower Control say, "Okay, Hughes, you're next." As he related it, the only thought that went through his mind was, "Okay, I guess I am going to die today." He sucked it up, measured his position, and made his turn for the carrier.

Dad continued, "You had to make five successful carrier landings to qualify for fleet deployment. Each of my five landings was successful, leaving me the only pilot to qualify five of five on that day. In fact, my plane was the only one that was still flyable at the end of the day. A major search and rescue effort was immediately launched for the instructor, but his plane was lost without a trace."

By this time, the air war for carrier pilots in the Pacific was nearly over as the Allies had established clear air superiority. The first deployment of pilots was scheduled for rotation home.

Dad, however, was assigned to a new squadron led by "Pappy" Boyington himself, which was scheduled for Pacific Theater deployment. Dad was thrilled—until Boyington filled his squadron with former comrades, bumping out the newly assigned qualified pilots, one by one, until finally, the squadron was one hundred percent returning veterans.

Dad, who was the last to be bumped, was sick with disappointment and had to accept that he would be heading home. How could a young father be anything other than relieved by such news? The streets were full of rejoicing revelers. Strangers were dancing, sharing great relief and heartfelt joy, as democracy triumphed. But the great contradiction of war lurked in the shadows, a contradiction that could not be spoken.

My father had earned a stature through grit, determination, and valor that few others could ever have achieved but for the fortunes of war. Now they were told to go home to the lives they had before the war. Many went home to great promises joyously. Others, like Dad, went home to uncertainty. The sharp edge of steel honed for battle is not easily sheathed.

Most of the returning warriors, who had prepared for the greatest competition known to man, did well in their transition to civilian life. Parades and speeches were the norm. Once the local bad boy, my father received a hero's welcome, and once again, his picture was featured in the local newspapers.

The Bakersfield Pontiac dealer put my father to work in his auto body shop. He and my mother were even featured in commercials as they tooled through Bakersfield in a brand-new Pontiac convertible. Yet, in response to the adulation of his hometown greeting, he felt estranged—not a fraud, but a man out of place.

Harry and Irene

Less than a year after my parents returned to Bakersfield, I was born. Two years later, Dad opened his own auto shop. He did well right from the start, as his new best friends, the policemen of Bakersfield, referred him a lot of business. Interesting how things can work out, just as it is interesting how quickly things can change.

On June 25, 1950, the massed army of North Korea, supported by the troops of the Soviet Union and China, poured into South Korea. The United Nations recognized the invasion as an act of war and called for an immediate cease-fire. The North Koreans intensified the attacks. On June 27, 1950, twenty-one countries of the United Nations contributed armed forces to the defense of Korea, with 88 percent being supplied by the United States.

Most of the first responders were from the United States Marine Corps. Dad was immediately called back into service. He was assigned temporarily to El Toro Marine Air Base in Southern California before being deployed to defend South Korea, and we settled quickly into a rented home in Corona Del Mar. This was shortly after my brother Terry's sixth birthday (June 6) and just a few months before my fourth (August 20).

What now?

Part Two

CHAPTER SEVEN

Big Boys Do Cry

Hawaii

As was often the case with military families, Dad traveled ahead of us to the Marine Corps Air Station Kaneohe Bay, Hawaii with the rest of the Marine first responders deployed to defend South Korea. My mother, brother, and I flew from Long Beach to Oahu on the Pan Am Clipper in August 1950. I recall the wake of the giant plane covering the windows with froth, both on takeoff and landing. Once in the air, Terry and I took turns looking out the window. The land faded away until we saw nothing but blue water, white caps, and dark blue islands that I learned were shadows from the clouds above. I then asked my mother about all the white lines I could see on the blue ocean below. My mother explained they were the tops of waves traveling all the way from Hawaii and beyond. I had more questions, and my mother did her best to answer me, but soon she suggested that perhaps it was time for a nap.

I tried, but it seemed an endless journey. My next memory is of our landing in Pearl Harbor and Dad greeting us. He was anxiously awaiting our arrival. It seemed we had to go immediately to high ground because an imminent tidal wave (a tsunami) would hit the island within just a few hours. This news was more than I could take in, but we rapidly drove into the mountains as we were told. It seemed to me that we waited for several hours high in the sky until the all-clear signal was sounded. In the end, the tsunami threat was a false alarm, but it certainly got my imagination going.

Living With the Native Hawaiians

Virtually all Marines assigned to the Marine Corps Air Station Kaneohe Bay lived on the base with their families to take advantage of cheaper housing, nearby medical facilities, shopping, and base schools. Dad, however, always the rebel, rented a small house about as far away from civilization as he could get. It was almost dead opposite the air base in a little hamlet on the North Shore of Oahu.

My memory of that time is like a dream. The tiny house Dad rented was on about an acre of land shared by a local Hawaiian family. There were several other small homes on the property, all arranged in a square around a large lawn. From the minute we arrived at our house, the family greeted us with open arms, inviting us to local family gatherings and luaus.

There were distinct benefits to living away from the military base. Terry and I had the run of the beach enclave, and the older kids in the neighborhood paid careful attention so that we didn't wander into trouble. Fronting the family compound was a little country road called Kaneohe Lane with a thick grove of pine trees sheltering it from a small cove. I think the cove was Kaunala Beach, just north of Sunset Beach, known only to the locals back then and to a tiny group within the surfing world. Rarely was anyone on the beach.

My mother, Terry, and I would walk the beach many mornings, picking up our favorite shells and always finding new ones we had never seen before. Although it seemed safe to Terry and me, we were not allowed to go to the beach without my mother or father. Despite this restriction, I managed to assemble a lovely collection of local seashells.

To say that the shells were plentiful is an enormous understatement. The beach was strewn with seashells of all kinds, and we would come home with bucketfuls. Many years later, I learned the names of my favorites: Pink Bubble shells, Miser Dove shells, Twisted Serpents, and Knobbies.

We sold the shells in front of the family compound to tourists who arrived daily on busses. They were surprised to buy shells from a couple of *haoles* (non-native to Hawaii) among the Hawaiian natives.

I loved my collection of shells, and I would take them out of my little treasure boxes over the years to admire their deep colors and varied shapes that still enliven my imagination.

I loved our neighbors as well. They were so kind and generous to include us in their family activities. I wish I could reconnect with those who meant so much to me as a child.

On the first day of school, the neighborhood children walked my mom, Terry, and me through the sugar cane fields to our new schoolhouse. Mom introduced herself to our new teacher, who kindly suggested that Terry and I didn't need to wear shoes to school. The children on this side of the island didn't have shoes, except for sandals, which they rarely wore. The teacher recommended that we try going barefoot to see how it felt. Mom stayed with us for the first morning of school and left with our shoes, satisfied that we would not need them, which we did not for the rest of our school days in Hawaii.

An additional oddity that did not become apparent to me until more than a decade later was that Terry and I were the only haoles at the little elementary school we walked to and from daily.

The Greatest Question

Though my life in Hawaii was wonderful, exciting, and exhilarating during this time, I couldn't help but ponder my greatest question—what happened to the war Dad was fighting? There was no sign of a war that I could see. I didn't understand that the war was still half an ocean away. Nor did I understand that Dad would alternate, one month in Hawaii then one month in Japan, where he would fly multiple daily roundtrips to Korea. I knew nothing about the heavy fire he faced as he delivered supplies and troops. Nor did I know that my father would lose many friends who were flying in and out of Korea daily under similar circumstances. Of course, as a child, I had no understanding of these things. I did not know about this until I came across James L. Stokesbury's excellent book, *A Short History of the Korean War*.

Many years later, I learned about the risks and suffering my father and his comrades endured during their monthly rotations between paradise and hell. I did not understand that the North Koreans and Chinese had no regard for the lives of their troops and certainly none for the lives of their enemies. Nor did I know that regardless of their losses, the North Koreans and Chinese simply deployed more and more troops from their endless supply of human fodder. My stories cannot do justice to the dangers posed by this little-remembered war, as my father never spoke of them—never.

My parents on undeveloped Waikiki Beach.

Years later, looking upon this poignant photograph, I can only imagine that while my father contemplated his next deployment to hell, Mom contemplated the unknowable.

The Douglas C-47

During the war, my dad flew the Douglas C-47 military aircraft, which was developed from the civilian Douglas DC-3 airliner. The workhorse for American military transport for more than half a century was known for its versatility, durability, and great fuel range. Even today, this excellent plane remains in service in various parts of the world. It has great internal space and tonnage capacity and converts quickly from passenger to cargo function in record time. But there is another reason for its worldwide usage. The Douglas C-47 proved in Korea and various other places around the globe that it could absorb internal and external abuse from unexpected cargo shifts, lousy weather, and unfriendly fire far beyond any other plane in service.

Harry and a colleague. Any landing is a good landing.

The North Koreans were masters at camouflage. Snipers were concealed along virtually all approach and takeoff routes. The closer the landing fields were to the front lines, the more dangerous were the air operations. In Korea, the C-47 earned its reputation as a great warbird due to its speed, versatility, and durability, matched by no other transport plane of its time. To this day, it still can be found doing yeoman's work where heavy lifting or treetop navigation is required.

Heroes of the Highest Order

Given the losses sustained, the ground they won and lost, only to be won and lost again, and the great price of time, pain, and blood they endured, my father and his fellow warriors should be forever remembered as heroes of the highest order. In tribute, I offer a few particulars paraphrased from James L. Stokesbury's book to give readers a sense of the risks and dangers confronting those engaged in this least remembered of our modern wars and, perhaps, as a result, an understanding of the depth of feeling from which I write.

Intelligence estimates suggest that the United Nation's 270,000 troops faced nearly 700,000 Communist forces. The value that the United States placed on the lives of an individual put us at a decisive disadvantage when fighting an enemy with little or no concern about the resulting loss of human life. Our warriors' frustration in the face of these odds was exacerbated by our country's reluctance to use its superpower strength to prevail in the war effort.

These details cannot do justice to Dad's story, nor those of his colleagues, who raced into harm's way at full throttle and at treetop level to, as Dad would say time and again, "Be gone before the bastards can hear you coming!"

Marine Buddies

As you would expect, the local families welcomed my father's Marine family into the local family enclave where we lived, just as they had welcomed us. The Kaunala Beach house soon became a hangout for a number of Dad's Marine buddies, and Mom was always cooking for a crowd, never knowing how many of these warriors might show up.

As is common in communities of young men and women facing daily risks, large quantities of alcohol were consumed, and many stories were told. Terry and I listened late into the night.

Often the conversation got raucous and apparently very funny, not that I knew any better, but Mom often had to tell them to settle down or take their conversations outside. I did not follow much of what was said, but it seemed a lot of it was amusing, especially early in the night then; sometimes, things got sad and scary too.

It was then I learned that something I had been told was not true. I learned that sometimes, late at night, big boys do cry, and though I did not know why, I cried too.

CHAPTER EIGHT

Who am I? Why I'm Calvin!

Return to Southern California—1953

We returned to Southern California from Hawaii in late fall 1953 as the air war in Korea wound down and an unofficial truce took hold (which is still the status of the Korean conflict as I write). Dad was assigned to El Toro Marine Air Base in Southern California, the only airbase dedicated solely to Marine aviation in the continental United States. Just north of El Toro, the sleepy town of Santa Ana is known mainly for its sea of orange groves. Among the orange groves and palm trees, my parents purchased their first-ever new home, and I entered Santiago Elementary School for the second quarter of my third-grade year.

Marine Work Ethic

My parents' purpose for buying a new home was to save money. The house was purchased bare bones— no landscaping and only partially finished interiors. Translation: Terry and I labored through most of the rest of our growing-up years as indentured servants to my parents. Okay, I am exaggerating, but only a little bit. Through a lot of sweat and struggle, I learned the value of hard work and how to build, maintain, and enhance the value of a home.

Old Hughes Home

Harry and Irene. Bakersfield, California

Terry and I had lots of work to do. Dad was a jack of all trades: rough and finished carpentry; wallboard installation; plastering and painting; digging trenches for irrigation lines; moving dirt for landscaping; digging holes for plants and trees; plus cutting and threading cast-iron irrigation pipes. He was raised on a ranch, so he had his own cutting and threading tools, which were great for developing forearms and shoulders. These were just a few of the tasks we were assigned.

For all this toil, Dad's goal was to "sell up" by making significant improvements to his purchase, such as eye-catching Japanese landscaping, including ponds with small islands and villages, bridges, trails, and exotic fish. At least they were exotic to me.

I don't know that he made a lot of money doing this, but I presume he did better than okay since he repeated the practice every time he bought a house, knowing he would soon sell it. This worked out pretty well once we got the rules straight, and it provided Terry and me with pocket money, well-earned and nice to have.

Two Shysters

My brother Terry was eight, and I was seven. Our first job was to rake up the rocks in the front and back yards and put them in piles for later removal. Dad promised, "I will pay you a dollar for each box load." This was serious money, and our enterprising spirits were born as we worked very hard. Terry, always the smart one, figured out that the landscapers working in the adjoining backyard were doing the same thing. So, one of us came up with the brilliant idea that we would just go next door and ask the landscapers to fill our box with rocks! We would become rich with hardly any work at all.

Dad had been away for more than a few days, and he was amazed upon his return by the number of rocks we had amassed until he saw that there was little progress in the yard for all the rocks we had accumulated. About then, he spotted the landscape workers across the backyard property line, raking rocks into piles in the neighbor's yard. Putting two and two together, he soon marched over in his Marine command strut to have a "talk" with the neighbor's laborers.

Terry and I stood by in terror. The landscaper foreman was a pretty burly guy, but he quickly determined that Dad, who was still wearing his greens, was not to be fooled with, and soon he had his crew loading the rock pile in our yard into his truck to haul off. Dad was a pretty persuasive guy when he got his "green" on. In the end, he got a pretty good deal since the landscapers removed the rocks they had given us and the rocks we had legitimately accumulated.

When Dad turned his attention to Terry and me, our blood ran cold. We shuffled around nervously, trying to look innocent and wondering if there really was life after death, when to our shock and amazement, Dad began to laugh—not just chuckle, but really laugh. "Okay, you shysters, get back to work," he said, shaking his head. Neither of us knew what a "shyster" was, but we knew enough to get back to work. And thus began my innocent man schtick, an art I later developed to perfection as a trial lawyer.

School Daze

School was okay but not very interesting, and I was mostly daydreaming like my future hero Calvin, the little boy in the comic strip whose stuffed tiger talked when no one was around. With little effort, Terry got straight A's in everything he did, while for me, everything seemed challenging.

I remember only a few sparks of academic enlightenment from this time. My most significant discovery was the theory of continental drift. I stumbled upon patterns of the shapes and outlines of the continents that seemed like a puzzle to me.

My third-grade classroom in 1955 had a large globe of the world sitting in a wooden cradle so we could spin the world around. I remember examining the globe carefully one day, moving it gently from side to side. My teacher came over to see what I was up to when I said, "See how the pieces fit together like a puzzle?" pointing out how the eastern bulge of Africa above the equator fit neatly into what I came later to know was the Caribbean Sea. And I went on excitedly showing my teacher how the large western bulge of South America, just below the equator, would fit the same way only backward into Africa. The land fit together like a puzzle, I concluded triumphantly.

I was on a roll, pointing excitedly here and there, when my teacher, nodding somewhat vaguely, said it was time for me to go back to my seat. So I, along with the continents, drifted off to other things.

I have wondered many times if my teacher thought back to our conversation. Probably not. Much later, I learned that the theory of continental drift was initially developed in 1915 by Alfred Wegener. Still, I took solace that his theory remained controversial and little understood until 1968, when geophysicist Jack Oliver produced the decisive treatise of *Seismology and the New Global Tectonics*, that hopefully settled the controversy.

Dyslexia and the Third Eye

I came to understand that my early ability to discern patterns, such as I did with the globe in my third-grade class, was an indicator of a different way of learning common to children suffering from or blessed with the condition now known as dyslexia.

Researching my history in preparation for writing this book included reviewing the voluminous documents and artifacts collected by my mother throughout my parents' lives. She collected an extraordinary amount of material, including such diverse items as a cocktail napkin autographed by Frank Sinatra, rocks and pebbles from the many exotic places my parents visited over the years, and mummy beads sifted from the sands near the Egyptian pyramids.

Unfortunately, none of this memorabilia was organized, confirming my suspicion that my mother was also dyslexic. Searching through the boxes, bags, and piles of stuff felt like an archeological expedition. In this dig for hidden treasure, I found my report cards from every semester, well preserved in an envelope.

Reading the report cards these many decades later was more than a little painful. What emerged was a young boy struggling with mediocrity, whose parents were counseled to steer him into the trades.

I came to see the clear pattern of dyslexia that led to my mother's concern regarding my poor reading and printing skills in grade school. Mom had performed poorly in school as well, but she became an accomplished artist and decorator. So, when my teachers counseled her to steer me toward the trades, she was undeterred concerning my future. However, she had little assistance from Dad or my teachers in charting a course for my development. These misimpressions are understandable but sad nonetheless as many children, including me, my kids, and many millions of other children were not properly evaluated about the challenges of non-linear learning.

I feel I could write my own book on this issue as later, my two daughters self-identified with the same condition. Note that I say "condition," not "affliction," as I came to understand that dyslexia is just a different way of seeing the world, as the excellent book *The Dyslexic Advantage* revealed to me for the first time.

A Miracle Happened

Time went by quickly and somewhat uneventfully until one day, a miracle happened, or so it seemed. Across the street, a new family moved in. Our neighborhood was pretty tight, and my parents, who loved to throw parties, hosted a block party at our house to welcome them. At the party, we met their son, who was around the same age as Terry and me.

The father, it turned out, was a senior executive for a new amusement park that was under construction nearby. I didn't even know what an amusement park was, but you may have heard of it—Disneyland. Yes, Disneyland!

Before the park opened, we were given tours, and as each new portion of the park opened, we were among the first tryout guests. We drove to work with our new best friend and his dad two or three days a week.

We came to know every nook and cranny of the park, but our favorite section was Tom Sawyer's Island. This was an enchanted summer, an extraordinary opportunity to be the first kids in the world to explore the historic amusement park before it opened, and the first to experience the happiest place on Earth.

CHAPTER NINE

Things Were Getting Gnarly

The Grasshopper

After the outbreak of the Korean war, the United States declared that the "neutralization of the Straits of Formosa" was in the best interest of the United States. In support of the declaration, the US Navy's Seventh Fleet was deployed to the Formosa Strait "to prevent any conflict between the Republic of China (ROC)—what we know as Taiwan—and the People's Republic of China (PRC). Little did we know what this declaration would portend for our family.

"We are moving!" Dad announced, coming home to our house on Olive Street in Santa Ana. Having just finished a year and a half at one school, I was ready for a change, so I was excited when he got out the globe, the same globe that sits at my desk now as I write.

"Here we are now, about right here," he said, pointing to a dot. Then, turning the globe counterclockwise to the sun, he rested his forefinger on the Hawaiian Islands. "Do you remember Hawaii?" he asked. Of course, we did, and we informed him so by diligently nodding our heads up and down. "Well," he said with a smile, with Mom standing by with a smile of her own, he started a slow northwestern motion with his finger away from Hawaii, across the Pacific, when suddenly I yelled, "Japan! Are we going to Japan?"

"How did you know that?" my father said, almost stunned, looking at me as if I had somehow cheated. Remember, Terry was the gifted one, and I was—well, I was the challenged one.

"It's on the map, right here," I said, pointing to the word "Japan," putting my finger right over the island nation, feeling a bit rebuffed by my father's tone.

"Okay," Dad said questioningly, "but how did you know about Japan?"

"It is on the large world in Mrs. Schema's class. It's the grasshopper country!" I exclaimed. Mrs. Schema had been my third-grade teacher the previous year at Santiago Elementary School when I explained to her the concept of continental drift.

"Look," I said excitedly, "It looks like a grasshopper. There, see!" I said, almost dancing.

My parents looked at the globe where I had been pointing, then Dad looked at me and shook his head a bit like I had stolen his thunder. If he had let me, I would have told him that the grasshopper was about to leap toward Hawaii, but he gave me a look meaning he had heard enough, and he said, "Anyway, that is where we are going, and I am certainly glad you know the way." I beamed at what I took to be a compliment.

I was quite proud of myself, of course, but clearly, Terry was not, and I knew I was in for it as he had made clear in the past that when talking with adults, he would do the talking.

The Land of the Rising Sun

My sense of life beyond the moment developed with our departure from Santa Ana for Japan at the beginning of my fourth-grade year. Until then, I was just along for the ride. However, this sense of a personal journey came on full force early in our adventure, and it came on hard.

As usual, my father went ahead, leaving my mother, my brother, me, and Fuji-san, the family parakeet, to tag along behind. Fuji-san was more than just a family pet. Dad brought him home from his Marine housing in Japan outside of Tokyo at the end of his Korean War deployment. Fuji's verbal skills, sense of fun and drama, and ability to mix pathos with humor brought our family together.

The plan was that Mom, Terry, and I would travel with Fuji-san hidden in a small purse made of wicker that Mom would keep on her lap throughout our long airplane trip. We flew from Long Beach to Hawaii on the Pan Am Clipper, the same type of seaplane we had flown when we first went to Hawaii three years before. Upon reaching Hawaii, we were to switch the next day to a Navy cargo carrier that would take us the rest of the way to Japan.

Fuji-san

Flying on the Clipper ship was an exciting experience in and of itself. And no two ways about it, flying a second time on the Clipper was more fun and excitement than any kid should ever expect since it was enhanced by Fuji-san traveling (smuggled) along with us. The plan was that Fuji-san would stay in his little wicker basket on Mom's lap since there was no such thing as luggage inspection when flying within the United States and its territories in those days.

Dad named Fuji-san after the famed volcano, Mt. Fujiyama, featured on almost all Japanese travel posters, as Fuji resembled Mt. Fujiyama! His body was blue with a white crown that shot up from the top of his head like a volcano, the result of his having been pecked hard on the head by an older bird. When in Japan, Fuji was Dad's constant companion. When Dad came to Hawaii, Fuji-san did not want for companionship from the other Marines.

Whenever Dad went barhopping with his Marine buddies in Tokyo, which was often, Fuji-san would travel in his shirt pocket, upside down, like he was hanging from a branch where he seemed quite comfortable until Dad and his buddies got to the bar. Fuji-san was then allowed "out of the hanger" to roam the bar at his pleasure.

Dad kept Fuji-san's wings sufficiently clipped to keep him from getting into too much trouble.

To the patron's great delight, Fuji-san would walk around the bar-top, free to roam, to eat up the spillage left behind by the salt shakers, to insult the patrons with his off-color language, and, of course, to beg a sip or two from the patron's drinks. Dad kept a close watch on him, and as you could hear him all over the bar, that wasn't hard to do, especially when he let loose with his choice "Marine" insults. And, there was little chance he would get into trouble as he was loved by all. When he got too drunk, it was back to the hanger for Fuji-san.

His Father Is a Marine!

For our trip to Japan by way of Hawaii, the plan was to keep Fuji-san in Mom's purse throughout the flight. The only problem was covering-up Fuji-san's rather loud and lewd bird noises. I was assigned the task of providing cover for Fuji as over the years as I had perfected my parakeet imitations. If Fuji-san started with any racket, I was to launch my own squawking and other birdlike sounds. It worked like a charm with one significant exception. Over the years, living with Marines, Fuji-san developed a rather foul mouth; excuse the pun. So, if Fuji-san got going with his foul language, Mom was ready to say sternly to anyone who seemed to care, "What do you expect? His father is a Marine!" Fortunately, the subterfuge wasn't needed.

This time when we landed in Pearl Harbor, there was no tsunami approaching, but an unexpected mad rush waited for us as soon as we disembarked.

CHAPTER TEN

Anchors Aweigh!

Having traveled with the sun, our plane landed in Oahu's main harbor in midafternoon. As we disembarked from the Pan Am Clipper, we were met by a good-looking young Navy ensign, who told us that we would be boarding immediately as potential storm conditions were developing west of Hawaii. This was a significant turn of events, as Mom had planned to do major shopping at the Pearl Harbor Navy Exchange.

The ensign only knew he was under orders to get us to our ship as soon as possible. Mom, who was nothing if not clever, looked pleadingly down at the young man with her big blue eyes and coyly said that there were some things she had to purchase at the PX before getting on an all-male ship for five days. She said that she would assure the captain that he, the ensign, had been heroic in accommodating her needs while getting us to the ship as fast as humanly possible. Fortunately, Fuji-san was quiet throughout this exchange except for a few expletives that our ensign didn't hear or chose to ignore. The ensign, caught between two forces, hesitated for just a moment, then said, "Okay, let's go!"

He then took charge, getting our baggage stowed into his van, and we raced off to the Exchange. When we got there, Mom, Terry, and I began racing up and down the aisles: I pushed the cart as fast as possible while Mom grabbed things she had marked on her list, barking orders to Terry to do the same. It turns out that Mom's list was considerably longer than any of us expected. The ensign was getting nervous and somewhat wide-eyed as he saw a growing train of carts being filled. Finally, he said with his best authoritative voice, "Ma'am, we simply have to leave for the ship!"

My mother stopped, drew herself up to all of her formidable near five feet ten inches of height, and said slowly with a voice that brought an icy mist to all who could hear, "Then I guess you better start hustling . . . ensign!"

He looked at her for but a second and then started throwing things into the cart as fast as my mother gave the orders, clearing the aisles and yelling at anyone in the way, "ship leaving port, ship leaving port!" Waiting customers parted before us as if Moses himself had spoken. Soon our carts were divided up among several cashiers frantically tallying the tab. Thank goodness we paid in cash! Then waves of volunteers raced our bags and boxes to the van. Our ensign had the doors open for loading, waived us in, and soon we were on our way, too nervous to laugh.

We rushed well past the speed limit with emergency lights on until we reached shipside. Other crew members standing by, clearly waiting for us, jumped to get our stuff on board. As soon as the last bag cleared the boarding ramp, we felt the ramp rumbling in response and the gangplank clanging loudly as it was raised just behind us. We appreciated the racket.

We were greeted at the top of the gangplank by a young officer who welcomed us aboard and informed us that he was assigned to show us to our cabin, but Mom said, "Excuse us for just a moment, officer." Then without waiting for a response, she instructed Terry and me to turn and salute the ensign who had assisted us so gallantly. He was watching from the pier. As Mom waved kindly, our young man couldn't resist a small smile as he returned our salute, and we pulled away from the dock, proceeding to sail out of Pearl Harbor.

My mother came from a very poor family in Cincinnati, Ohio. Although she had only a high school education, she traveled the world with my father, and wherever they went, they made incredible, lifelong friends, from shopkeepers to royalty. To this day, I am not sure where her poise and confidence came from, but there is no doubt she possessed both.

Most likely, these qualities came from being the youngest child with three older brothers, the smallest of which was six foot four and the tallest, like her father, a barber, was almost six feet, eight inches tall! She was the princess of her family. They sacrificed a lot for her, and she was always well protected.

In for a Rough Ride

It was soon apparent that we were in for it. Our captain quickly introduced himself, immediately directing one ensign to take our purchased goods to storage and another ensign to take us and our suitcases to our cabin. He ordered the ensign not to leave us until he was sure everything was tied down.

Then he said, looking our mother directly in the eye, "We are now underway, Mrs. Hughes, and we are in for a very rough ride. Do not let your children out of your sight and pay close attention to instructions and notices given over the ship intercom." His voice made clear that it was not a suggestion; instead, it was an order. And then, again, said, "Do you have any questions?" in a voice making clear that questions would not be welcomed.

Being a good judge of men and circumstance, my mother said nothing more than "No Captain, and thank you. Your men have been thoughtful and very courteous." The captain nodded, then turned and left for the bridge. And that was as it should be.

Everything was strange; everything was abrupt. The coming storm had everyone on edge, but there seemed more to it than that. Of course, the coming storm could undoubtedly account for this, but a little bubble was coming to the surface of my eight-year-old brain. Why were we the only family on the ship? That seemed strange to me.

The oncoming storm quickly pushed aside all other concerns. The waves built up over the next few hours, but things seemed manageable, though we had no porthole and no visitors other than a nice young ensign who stopped by occasionally to check in on us. The ensign gave us a tour of our level, showing us our assigned restroom, set aside exclusively for us. By this time, we couldn't walk down the passageway without using our arms to brace against the walls, yet we never suffered from seasickness. This was exciting and fun for Terry and me, but for the first time, our mother showed a bit of nervousness.

By five o'clock the next morning the typhoon had moved nearer to our course such that we were at its outer edge. We were informed that we were changing course again—this time to the north so that we would circle in from the Aleutian Island Chain, along the Kamchatka Peninsula (Russia!) and then south to enter the Sea of Japan. We were told this should allow the ship to avoid the worst of the storm. On the night of our second day, we changed course again to go farther east to gain the protection of the Korean Peninsula. This is why we had been in such a hurry to leave port.

Then, late in the evening of the second day—a new crisis. At the height of the storm, a young sailor trying to secure a wayward line was engulfed by a rogue wave and washed overboard. We learned later that there was no question that the ship could not be stopped or even slowed significantly in such a storm as losing forward momentum would present an intolerable risk. This meant we could not circle back. We also learned that in the sea we were experiencing, returning to the exact location where the sailor went overboard would be impossible.

Then, in the midst of this crisis, a seaman recovered a wayward line tied onto a railing. To his shock, when he pulled up the rope, it carried a significant load. The load turned out to be the missing seaman, dangling and twisting over the side and being roughly tossed about! We later learned that the sailor had been trying to retrieve the wayward line when suddenly the ship, hit by a rogue wave, rolled hard to portside. Engulfed in the water, the sailor wrapped the line around his arm and held on for dear life.

When the ship righted, he had gone overboard, dangling below the deck level. Somehow, he had managed to create a sling as the rolling ship tossed him back against the hull hard. Soon a process was improvised, pulling the rope up when the sailor was swinging out and holding steady when the ship rolled to port so the sailor could get his legs out to cushion the blow when he hit the hull. The system worked, and our sailor was retrieved mercifully and quickly.

Of course, all Terry and I knew about this adventure was that something serious was going on. Hearing all the commotion, Mom had somehow stayed up on events as they unfolded. The next day was Sunday, the third day of our journey, and the day broke with sunshine. Though the sea still rolled impressively, the sky attested that the worst was now behind us, and everyone's mood lightened.

Before this adventure, I only recall going to church a few times. But the ship's captain announced that there would be a special nine o'clock church service the next morning in the mess hall for those wanting to give thanks for the safe recovery of our seaman. Our mother told us we would be attending and that we would be dressing up as best we could for the occasion. Frankly, I do not remember attending any church service before this, although I am sure my grandmother must have dragged us to church once or twice. But, in no way could we be considered churched. So, Mom's plan was that we would sit in the back, keep quiet, and behave ourselves.

As you might imagine, getting the three of us spruced up in such tight quarters was not easy. My mother did have a little curtain she could pull for privacy, but Terry and I were in each other's way from the beginning, and our tempers grew thin. Once we were ready, we realized that we had never ventured near the mess hall because of the storm, and we had no idea where it was.

Finding it proved more than a bit of a challenge. The final hurdle, however, was that even though the weather was bright and sunny, the swells were still huge, maybe even larger than at any time in our journey, so navigating the halls was difficult. Going down the stairs to the mess hall was a lot of fun for Terry and me but terrifying for my mother, who was in heels, low heels, but heels nonetheless. Late as we were, we found our way with the help of a young sailor and arrived on time—barely!

To our embarrassment, we were among the last to enter. The makeshift chapel was arranged such that when we entered, we found ourselves up front, right at the makeshift altar. My mother froze, desperately looking for seats in the back, but of course, the chaplain saw her dilemma and, quickly cutting off her escape, gestured to a few sailors to provide us with front row seats, just two feet from the altar! My always-poised mother was a bit flustered, just a bit, but she was.

As the service went on, the pitch and roll of our ship intensified until we could hear the noise of chairs sliding and rocking. Suddenly, a big roll caused the side of the cross near me to lift significantly off the altar. Without thinking, I lunged toward the altar. As Mom frantically tried to grab me, I pulled away from her grip and reached out to steady the base of the cross.

After the service, the chaplin came up to me to say that I had exhibited great courage, but the truth is much different. In retrospect, I realize I just acted out of instinct. Our father had instilled in Terry and me at a very early age, "When something needs to be done, do it!" He would say, "What are you waiting for, an invitation? Move!"

We traveled southwest, hugging the shore of South Korea, trying to wait out the typhoon on its course to the north. It was frustrating knowing how close we were to Japan, but wait we did.

CHAPTER ELEVEN

Land of the Rising Sun

After waiting out the typhoon, the storm clouds lifted, and, on the horizon we enjoyed our first glimpse of the Land of the Rising Sun. The western edge of the rugged mountains of Honshu, magnificent in the cresting morning sun, pointed us on a southwestern course to Japan's famed Seto Inland Sea. I watched, mesmerized as we passed the southern tip of Honshu, rounded to the north, and entered the sudden tranquility of the Inland Sea. A short sail north brought us fully into what may be the most significant inland harbor in the world.

We sailed deeper. Twisting and turning my map, I tried to make some sense of all the frenetic energy around us. Soon I abandoned the map and just looked wide-eyed at all that lay before me.

It had been some time since we'd seen my father, but long absences were not unusual for the family of a Marine. Even so, the reunion of our family was a poignant reminder of just how precious was our time together.

Everything was Different

Almost immediately, we saw Dad waving from dockside. It was not difficult for him to pick us out, as we were the only civilians, and the sailors were busy securing the ship. Soon we were reunited. Dad told us that our luggage would be delivered later, but for now, he was anxious to provide us with a tour of the town of Iwakuni and the little village on its outskirts where we would be living.

Everything was different! The streets, neat and clean, were tightly packed with little shops, sliding bamboo doors, and windows without glass. Pennants, bamboo birds, and whirling little fans danced with the slightest breeze; vegetables and fruit were on display, neatly stacked; kids ran up and down the dirt streets trailing red, blue, and orange kites, as little bamboo pinwheels whirled frantically. People made room for our little car everywhere we went, though driving required great care. Did I mention that everyone was driving on the wrong side of the street?

Soon we were outside of a small village, which I came to understand was across from the entry to the base. Rice paddies with green sprouts sprung out of the water; it was pretty, but the smell was odiferous in the extreme due to the use of human waste for fertilizer. "Don't worry," Dad said, laughing as I covered my nose with my sleeve, "You will quickly get used to the smell," and so we did.

Just before the entry gate to the base, we made a sharp left turn onto a little dirt road. The road was just a few feet above water level and took us toward a small group of little bamboo houses, which I have now learned to call a hamlet. Just before we reached the hamlet, we turned to the right toward two small houses lined up one after the other. We stopped before the first one. I was surprised but stoic, which was my usual expression when faced with the unknown. This would be our home; I did not know for how long.

Our Japanese neighbors were extraordinarily kind, as were those in the nearby village. They smiled, bowed, and welcomed us into their shops and homes. It took me years upon our return to the United States not to bow when introduced to new neighbors and friends. Our house was only a five-minute walk from the small group of homes where our tutor lived. Mioko-san was beautiful and gracious. She was very interested in learning English and my parents were anxious that we learn some Japanese. So, several times a week, we rode our bikes to her house for tutoring.

Terry and Mioko-san. Photo taken by Roger.

I had never seen anything so perfect as those little houses. Each had sliding partitions and an interior court with a garden; precise, perfect, restful, and at peace.

Everywhere we went in Japan, we found friendship. Could it be that Terry and I had no limits on where to roam? We rode our bikes to nearby little shops, and it was embarrassing how we couldn't leave without receiving a little gift, though we had no money for purchases. We did not get lost because everyone knew who we were, and when we asked for directions, we were quickly shown the way home, as all knew where we lived, and if the way was tricky, a youngster was assigned to guide us.

A Potential War Zone—What the Heck?

Dad was stationed in Japan because of the threat the People's Republic of China was imposing upon the remnants of the Republic of China. The Japanese and American forces stationed in Japan were on alert. Positional forces (not combat forces—unless attacked) were reinforced to react to hostile actions by other nations (meaning the People's Republic of China) that threatened Formosa's right to unimpeded access to air and sea travel within the international waters of the Straights of Formosa. President Eisenhower assigned Marine air and land forces from the United States Kaneohe Naval Air Base to reinforce and support existing air and sea resources at the Iwakuni Marine Air Station, Iwakuni, Japan. It was a relatively short flight from the Marine airbase in Japan to the Formosa Straits, so the message was loud and clear to the People's Republic of China (PRC) that interference with the Republic of China (ROC) was unacceptable.

The boundaries and major cities of the Empire of Japan at the time it entered the First World War in 1914.
Image via New Zealand Ministry for Culture and Heritage.

Things were getting tense over the Straits of Formosa, and once again, Dad would be in the middle of an international conflict. The proximity of Taiwan, China, and Japan, combined with the limited availability of strategic sea routes, left no doubt about why. Yet, much was unclear. If my father was being assigned to another potential war zone, what the hell were my mother, brother, and I doing in this mess?

Good questions, to which I can provide some facts and some suppositions.

The Facts

1. The long absences from home during the recently concluded Korean War had taken a toll on Dad. He lost many friends during his one-month-on, one-month-off, to hell-and-back missions.
2. Though the new assignment was limited to a show of force and support for Formosa, at any moment, the mission could turn into a full-blown war with China.
3. Such a short time after his Korean combat deployment, military protocol would have allowed my father to decline the new assignment.
4. Dad was a top-ranked and highly decorated Marine pilot.
5. His superiors and others he worked with respected his skills, courage, and repose under fire and needed his presence in the new theater.
6. His reputation and command presence would be a morale booster for his fellow pilots.

So, he chose to go, but with conditions.

The Rub

The rub for my father was that in response to the president's order, the Marine commander of the Formosa operation determined that dependents of Marine aviators having to fly in potential combat conditions would *not* be allowed to have their dependents in residence. Not an unreasonable decision given the risks the pilots would be facing.

But Dad's view was that his long absences during the Korean Conflict had taken too great a toll on his family, and it was time for others to take his place.

The Work Around

Noting that US citizens were not prohibited from visiting or living in Japan during this time, the commandant reasoned that we would not be in conflict with his order if Mom, Terry, and I lived off base. Clever, but this left open the question of medical and educational support to such civilian dependents.

Therein Lies the Rub

How would Mom, with two small children, survive without the benefits given even to civilian workers providing base support and their dependents?

The Solution

I believe an unofficial solution, dubbed *The Look Away*, was worked out just for us. There may have been others as well, but I was unaware of any other off-the-books dependents. How much was known, by whom it was known, or when it was known remains unclear, and the rest is just conjecture. This, however, explains the incongruity of our voyage from Hawaii to Japan as the only civilians on a commissioned Navy ship, as described in the preceding chapter. It also explains some of the oddities of our exploits in Japan that follow.

The Look Away

Our living accommodations in Japan were unique. Base housing was generally available for authorized personnel but was not available for us. Aside from the small house next door, our house sat alone in the middle of the rice paddies. The two houses were as isolated as could be, and the house next door was seldom occupied. On the few occasions when it was occupied, strange Caucasian men who kept to themselves, never saying hello or even making eye contact, stayed there.

All American civilian employees and military dependents not subject to the commandant's prohibition were afforded full base privileges. However, benefits for our family were achieved only by Machiavellian subterfuge. We were never officially checked in, even when getting a shot at the clinic!

Though Mom was meticulous about keeping records, she kept no memorabilia from our stay in Japan. This is the woman whose stash from our travels was a family joke. She would pick up pebbles from famous places; she took photos wherever we went; she collected worthless coins, knickknacks, matchbook covers, you name it. However, aside from our report cards, which I could happily do without, there are no keepsakes from our time in Japan. As for our trip on the Navy ship, I can only find one photo that was taken with my camera, before Mom tucked it away for the rest of the voyage. "You made me haul souvenirs from all over the world. I have boxes and boxes in the attic. You kept everything. Why are there no records of this one trip?" But my questions were posed long after her death.

All of this did not seem unusual to me at the time. After all, we always lived off base. Dad seemed to dislike military housing, whether in Hawaii or Santa Ana. But some things were immediately strange, even to Terry and me. First was the ritual that Terry and I would have to go through to get onto the base when Dad was not present. We complied with our father's request and took strict precautions when we needed to go on base. This included attending school, appointments at the infirmary, and going to the hobby show. He told us to approach the gate and wait until the Marine on duty was occupied checking the credentials of traffic entering the base. He said that if no one was coming, we were to go slowly toward the gate until the guard turned his back, and then we were to proceed through. Upon reflection years later, it became clear to me that we were not "officially" present. Some type of accommodation must have been reached to encourage Dad to re-up for this high-risk theater assignment. I'm sure that no Marine guard would miss anyone going through the gate, even if they were just kids.

Roger and Terry sailing to Japan on a Navy Ship

The Clincher

We became used to the strange treatment. The clincher, however, is what happened when a typhoon appeared to be approaching Iwakuni directly. All Marine pilots, including Dad, were required to ferry aircraft out of harm's way, apparently leaving Mom, Terry, and me to fend for ourselves in our little house in the midst of the rice paddies.

Yet, that was not to be. When Dad was leaving for his mission, a Marine Corp van pulled up. Mom was waiting with us—all packed—and we got into the van and drove up to the camp gate. The guards snapped to, as well they should. I later found out we were being chauffeured to the camp's guest house in the base commandant's van.

It was a lovely place, and I liked it a lot. At some point, when the storm was reaching its height, the base commander himself braved the storm to check in on us. I remember him being a very nice man, and he assured us that the house, the roof, and the windows were all typhoon-rated. The commander also told us that an automated generator would kick in if the electricity shut down, and power would quickly be restored. Then he bid us good night by saying that if anything rough happened, someone would be right over.

CHAPTER TWELVE

Shadows on a Wall, 1956

I stood staring,
At shadows on a wall,
Not understanding, not really,
Though I had been told.
Could it be, could it really be,
That these were shadows of children,
like me.

Not long after our arrival in Japan, Dad had arranged for a short vacation. It was quite an experience. We journeyed first to a small village on the Inland Sea just North of Iwakuni. A small boat took us to what I know now to be the Island of Miyajima.

At the time of our visit, Miyajima was a delightful small village with exquisite facilities, including hot spring baths and beautiful, soulful Japanese gardens. Today it is a world-class resort. Nevertheless, I would not trade our experience in our small cottage for any five-star hotel in the world. I remember this time as magical, a dream with restful, beautiful, magical gardens. Even Terry and I stopped our quarreling!

But, the shock for Terry and me was our first exposure, and I do mean exposure, to the hot baths of Japan. Men, women, and children of all ages shared the same large steamy pool—with no clothes. I didn't know how to act or what to do. Fortunately, the steam from the boiling waters hid any reason I might have had for embarrassment. And soon,

I was totally, completely relaxed, an experience I had never before enjoyed. I didn't want to leave the pools.

We spent a few day days traveling through the inland sea, seeing beautiful and sometimes terrifying shrines and volcanic rock gardens with gurgling hot springs. We returned each day to our little hotel feeling as if we'd been to another world, which I guess is what we had done.

Itsukushima Shrine is a Shinto shrine on the island of Itsukushima, best known for its "floating" torii gate.

On the last day, we left the islands and drove a little way north to the town of Hiroshima. The town had been fully rebuilt since the day the world turned to fire and the heavens melted before God's eyes. Of course, I had no idea what we were about to see, though Dad tried to prepare us for our visit to the Shrine of the Shadows.

I chose not to show pictures in this book of the shadows of children at play at the most destructive moment in human history nor of the resulting carnage. The images are too disturbing to me, even to this day. I understood what happened, but I did not understand why. Dad didn't try to explain except to say that it was important for Terry and me to understand that war is a terrible, terrible thing. I looked at him with tears starting to form. "You need to know," he said simply, and then again, "You just need to know."

I am passing his wisdom on to you: you just need to know. That knowledge inspired me to write the poem at the beginning of this chapter.

We were not in Japan too long before things got hot and the Chinese and American fighter pilots began nerve-wracking flybys. Dad was on constant alert and often in the air, claiming our space over the Straits of Taiwan. Soon, Mom, Terry, and I were on our way home as things were getting too dangerous for us to stay. So, once again, we said goodbye to our father.

Part Three

CHAPTER THIRTEEN
Leaving Santa Ana

Young adolescents do not just get bigger; distinctively different bodies emerge from these growing years. More extensive physical and personal changes now occur than at any other time of life. While the physical changes are the most obvious, profound changes are taking place in mental, social, emotional, and moral development.... These are the years when lines of character are graven.—John H. Lounsbury, *Understanding and Appreciating the Wonder Years*

Not to take anything away from Dean Lounsbury's excellent and informative article, but he left out that for many boys, and indeed for many girls as well, the *wonder years* are better described as the *terror years*. Yes, the TERROR YEARS!

First, the Bad

In Japan, living in close quarters, Terry began to bully me. I mean, really terrorize me, at least it seemed so to me. Occasionally he would sneak up behind me and say something to cause me to startle and turn around, unaware that he was timing a blow to my unsuspecting jaw, nose, or eye. I was a sitting duck. There was not much I could do about it as Terry waited until our father was out of town before launching an attack. My poor mother would throw a fit, but she was ineffective with both Terry and me when Dad was out of town, which was often. And, not wanting Dad to be greeted by a litany of woes that occurred while he was gone, Mom instructed Terry and me to say, "Everything went fine, Dad!"

Upon our return from Japan, we moved back to the house on Olive Lane that my parents had purchased two and a half years earlier. Terry continued to exercise his pugilistic practices. In other words, I was his punching bag. There was one benefit—I learned the art of ducking, parrying, grabbing, and holding. I also learned to use my weight advantage and everything else I could think of to get him to the ground. Then, I would run, for hell was a-comin' if I didn't quickly find sanctuary.

Put on the Gloves

If a ruckus broke out when Dad was home, his solution was to "put on the gloves," which always worked out to my detriment. Dad would haul out the puffy low-impact boxing gloves for young boys. He would strap them on, saying, "So, you want to fight? Go ahead— settle it." Dad knew that using the big padded gloves (practically) assured no severe damage would result. Dad did not realize that his solution, which seemed reasonable to him, gave Terry all the advantages. Terry's reach was an advantage, and his height gave him an advantage, so he would wait for an opening, letting his reach and height edge take their effect. At the same time, the gloves minimized my weight advantage and my grappling skills. As soon as Terry saw an opening, using his long reach—*boom*.

I rarely got a lick in, as he would jump around and dance away after landing a blow. Finally, I would get mad and jump him, causing the referee, Dad, to step in and pull me away with the admonition, "This is boxing, not wrestling."

"*Aargh,*" I would mutter under my breath. Sooner or later, Dad would call off the fight declaring it a draw. "Good fight, good fight," he would say, but it didn't feel that way to me. It is true that no severe damage ever resulted from all of our flailing, though I am confident I received many more blows than I landed. The best I can say is that I learned the art of sparring.

From the Land of Rising Sun to the Edge of Night

I got along okay at Roosevelt Elementary School, though nothing remarkable happened. In fact, I don't remember much of anything about my sixth-grade year, except that the pretty little blond-haired girl I was smitten with moved away. Every day, however, was an adventure for me, at least in my mind.

I sat in class, reliving memories of shells along the many beaches I had roamed. Their colors and shapes danced before me, as vivid as when I first picked them up from sandy beaches, marveling at their colors and shapes. I lay in bed at night, feeling their swirling conical pinnacles closing slowly with each spiral until suddenly they turn inward as if swallowed into eternity. I swear these angels of the sea still sit on my desk as I feel the roll of the deck and the gray mist of the sea settling on my cheek. I drift off to rice paddies and pinwheels and kites and gurgling hot springs, aware that the shadows on the wall are never far away.

I wanted to be high in the banyan trees again, stealthily perched within deep green branches, such that I could see breakers crashing against the rocks just past the white band of sand. I remember it all vividly: Clouds reflecting off flooded fields as a storm passes over our isolated little home; narrow alleys and dense shops; rolling decks and roaring engines. All are around me as my mind brings forth these fractional visions, a kaleidoscope accompanied by a cacophony of music, wind, and surf, all bantering for my attention.

Tap, tap, tap on my desk. "Roger, Roger, are you listening?"

"Huh? Uh, I guess not," I said, trying to come back to the present, but not for long. Soon, again, the wind was lashing my face. Again, I was riding my bike wherever I wanted to go, unaccompanied. Kimonos, brilliant with every color, adorned the little shops. Exotic prints of delicate cranes and flowers all danced before me in soft pastels or blazoned with sharp dragons and warriors, clothed with brilliant reds, as orange fire swirled to the heavens. There was no room for the present when all about me swirled memories, competing for attention amid crashing waves, stormy skies, and thundering planes, all intertwined within the misty land of my mind.

"Roger, Roger, hello! Are you there?"

No, no, I am not! I try to be! Really, I try to be!

"Roger is a good boy," my teacher told my mother, "but he is a daydreamer. Perhaps if he shared his experiences with us, that would help ground him a bit." Well-intended advice, but how could I share my experiences with new classmates? Their friendships were formed long before I got there and would last long after I left. I tried my best, I did, and certainly, some of my classmates were friendly to me. But after traveling the world, I found myself now as a "stranger in a strange land."

My last year of grade school was pretty uneventful. I received mediocre grades but was no trouble to anyone, and my tussles with Terry were becoming less frequent and less one-sided, which was good news. Perhaps there was a correlation?

I enjoyed playing summer Little League baseball, but I lost interest when neither parent came to any of my games, and I was happy for summer to end. Mostly, I floated through misty summer days, enjoying calamities and near disasters, surviving torrential rains pouring from the garden hose; and most of all, saving the day with my verve and swashbuckling heroics as I stormed or protected my castles in the sky.

Beyond the Edge (or, better yet—My Poor Mother)

Somewhere during sixth grade and certainly fully blown by my seventh-grade year, my poor mother lost control over Terry and me. Of course, this was only when Dad was absent, which was most of the time, as he was often on extended flights or temporary assignments.

For the most part, Mom was never one to impose discipline. She accepted in good faith our sergeant's "Yes ma'am!" avoidance strategy. Mom saying "Boys" was a hypnotic cue to tune out our poor mother. Our reactions were not necessarily intended to be mean, but there was an element of *Who is going to make me?* not uncommon for service families. Unfortunately, this ancient, instinctive hierarchy has ruled the behavior of adolescent boys since Eve first told Cain, "Wait until your father gets home!" And so we did.

So, we reached an angle of repose with our mother. She was okay as long as the piles of clothes, games, trash, and everything that didn't move were picked up, both in the yard and in our room, and all was spotless before our father opened the door. Mom would keep us advised of Dad's ETA. In Mom speak, "Your Father will be home any time," translated to "about thirty minutes," and generally, that schedule seemed to work.

Our messiness was not a problem when Dad was home, as he disapproved of conditions that were less than "Marine Clean." However, when Dad was returning from an out-of-town stay, things could get a little ripe, depending on the number of days he was away. We pushed the clean-up schedule to the minute, and we adjusted the actual arrival time based on the modulation of our mother's tone.

However, even Terry and I began to panic as Dad's ETA would draw near. The veil of complacency would lift, and suddenly, we would see our room through our father's eyes! The floor was wantonly strewn with books, clothes, leftover snacks, and pieces of various games. Panic was followed by frenzy. We redoubled our pace and then went into overdrive. Now we worked as a team, Terry and me. No arguing, no grumbling, we rose to the challenge as the Spartans of old to clear the bedroom floor.

This was when we were at our best! The balls and gloves parted as if Moses himself commanded restoration of each errant sock, each misplaced baseball, each wantonly mislaid book. Board games found their way to their appropriate shelf, stacked such that all the whatevers and mystery things returned magically to their appointed place. We were on fire!

Renascent closet hangers and hooks came to life, born again for their intended purpose as if compelled by Mickey's magic wand. Festive shirts and rugged pants now hung smartly in the closet. Shoes, those we could find, were in line on the closet floor because we knew these were the first things our dad would see. We did well!

But now, the field of battle shifted to the backyard. Dad took great care to replicate the style of the miniature gardens of Japan. He snuggled a miniature garden up against the far-left back corner of the yard. Dad formed the pond into a near figure eight with the smaller oval high up near the summit. Water trickled down through bonsai trees and over little rocks fast enough that we could hear the sound of the running water from our bedroom window on a hot summer day. It was wonderful just to sit and enjoy this peaceful corner of Japan in Santa Ana.

It is hard for me to remember the carnage rendered during our backyard battles, but the miniature garden was off-limits. We would, however, have to step into the little garden to pick up and clean errant remnants of our battles. I must confess that Terry and I both became skilled in launching small cannonballs (mud balls) at toy soldiers that had taken refuge in the garden, so one of the last chores was to be sure the miniature garden would pass the inspection of the gods.

So spurred on by Mom's continued warnings of our father's expected return, somehow a transformation would take place. As I write these words, my heart breaks for single mothers and single fathers charged with raising young boys and girls through adolescence. For those who are able to stay the course and bring their children to stable, productive lives, all I can say is, "Blessed. Blessed are you."

Then, while the battle might be over, the first order of business upon Dad's return was the dreaded inspection. Really! Despite trying as hard as we could, never were we able to pass on first review; a small snippet of a gum wrapper here; a toy overlooked there, a hedge not trimmed to Marine perfection. We expected this, and the punishment was light so long as a good faith effort was evident, and occasionally Dad uttered the words, "Good job."

Junior High Terror

If grade school was isolating, junior high school was sheer terror! The two-block walk from our house, in the exact opposite direction of Roosevelt Elementary, might as well have been a thousand miles. In fact, Willard Junior High School might as well have been on another planet.

I walked to my first day of classes at Willard, noticing that the sidewalks were different: rugged, cracked, and marked with what we now call graffiti. Our immediate neighborhood was pretty much the same. Still, I found out that our White middle-class neighborhood joined in almost perfect balance with the nearby Hispanic and African-American communities along the divide of Flower Street, a four-lane thoroughfare. I had no clue that such a divide existed, as I rarely ventured outside of our immediate neighborhood, and, for that matter, I had no sense of what racial divide even meant.

The classrooms had an undercurrent of hostility. Walking the halls was intimidating. Hallway fights were not uncommon, and recess was often a nerve-racking experience. In fairness, this experience is typical for many incoming seventh graders regardless of how homogenous the population. But attending Willard Junior High upped the ante from anything I had experienced before or since. These were the days of corporal punishment, and the practice was dispensed regularly, supposedly to achieve a semblance of order in a pretty harsh environment.

However, I could not have been too intimidated, as it was during my one year at Willard that I received the "tennis shoe" punishment. As you may have guessed, this punishment was applying the bottom of a tennis shoe with force to the bare butt of a perpetrator. In my particular case, the shoe left a temporary waffle mark on the target and an indelible mark on my psyche.

This draconian instrument of pain was reserved for the Physical Education instructors to inflict. My crime occurred at the end of PE when, after shower time, a towel flipping war broke out. Now, I was a guilty flipper, I admit it, but I was just having fun as one of the guys. Somehow, I was singled out from the gaggle of towel flippers, probably because of my size, for the terror of the tennis shoe. As I said, I was guilty, but I was only one of many, so I thought the whole matter was an injustice. The humiliation stayed with me for a long, long time, and I resolved that I would do nothing for the rest of my prep experience that would result in my standing out, a pledge I found impossible to keep. I learned over time what an extreme contradiction I was: an introvert, for the most part, who just could not help acting out.

Then Cometh the Reaper

A year after our return to Santa Ana, our family was dealt a blow that makes my anger boil to this day. President Eisenhower announced his "New Look" strategy. Based upon the assumed deterrent power of our country's nuclear delivery system, Eisenhower decided that conventional military forces could be drastically reduced.

The first and the hardest branch hit by the reduction in force, or RIF, as it was called, was the United States Marine Corps. The Marine Corp protected commissioned officers who had attended particular military academies, while officers without a college degree were exposed to the RIF. Worse, the officers closest to retirement without a college education were the first to go. Though Dad was a highly decorated Marine who had flown in two wars and the Formosa conflict under enemy fire and was less than a year away from vesting, the Corp unceremoniously handed him discharge papers.

Thank you very much for your service, Captain Hughes. Please don't let the door hit you on the way out.

Think about it. At eighteen years of age, Dad left his trade to join the United States Marine Corps the day after the attack on Pearl

Harbor. He served his country faithfully with highest honors in every program, only to be shown the door as World War II ended. Fine, and though unexpected, he started his own auto body shop in Bakersfield, California. He soon was doing well when the Korean conflict erupted, and he was called, not asked, back into service. His family was disrupted again, and soon Dad was flying into hostile fire in Korea, one month on, one month off.

Then, he was assigned back to the States for two years and then to Japan, where he flew missions in close contact with and constant harassment from Chinese MiGs. In 1958 he was reassigned to El Toro Marine Base just in time for Eisenhower's announcement. I was entering seventh grade.

Of course, everyone was anxious to see how the ax would fall. The reality was harsh and arguably misguided, as the nation's military forces soon had to gear up due to the increasing communist activity in Southeast Asia. All of this was traumatic for members of the armed services, but what came next went far beyond traumatic to what can only be described as treachery.

Treachery

A lot of effort was made to find positions for the best and brightest officers and men who would survive the deep RIF that was coming. Dad was highly decorated for his service under fire and for sacrifices made in taking on overseas assignments, many of them in high-risk conditions. He was known for never shirking from a responsibility regardless of the sacrifice.

So, a scramble was on to find positions for Dad and the many other heroic officers facing the harsh and lamented cuts. Fortunately for my father, he was appointed the chief pilot for the commandant of the Marine Corps, the highest-ranking officer of the Corp. This highly prestigious position would ensure that Dad would survive the coming RIF. But relief turned to bitter disappointment just weeks before his report date; Dad received notice that his orders had been rescinded by direct instruction of the commandant himself. The rescission occurred when the commandant belatedly discovered that Dad had not followed a regular officer's career path. And that was that.

Dad's receipt of the notification that his services were no longer required was a rough and emotional experience, and though he buried it deep and never talked about it, I know it changed his love for the Corps forever.

Dad pressed hard, looking for work, stoically attempting to get on with one airline after another. Having been deluged with applications from ex-military pilots over the preceding years, the airlines were not hiring. He flew for a while for a non-scheduled airline, meaning that when they were booked, they flew. Otherwise, flights were canceled, and then he was not paid. He even tried selling insurance door to door, and I helped him by handing out flyers. He was stoic about his hard luck, and he pressed on, but the pressure clearly wore on him. He drank more, and my parents' arguments grew more frequent and much more intense, which I think wore off on Terry, who took his angst out on me.

To put it politely, it was a gruesome time. Then, for us, there was a miracle! Dad was accepted into the Federal Aviation Administration's Flight Inspection Program for the Utah, Nevada, and Arizona territory. We breathed once more, and besides, I was ready for a change, but there is no doubt that some wounds did not heal.

CHAPTER FOURTEEN

Stranger in a Strange Land

My memories of Salt Lake City are a montage of emotions shrouded in loneliness, beset with conflict, angst, and fear. In other words, I was a typical teenage boy. I suspect, however, that my angst was enhanced by my having to come of age in a foreign land. Yes, after Hawaii, Japan, and Southern California, there could have been no more foreign place for me than Salt Lake City in 1960.

After experiencing a kaleidoscope of cultures, Utah presented an incredible culture of sameness. Sameness in architecture (single-story houses with either red brick or wood siding) and sameness in housing developments laid out in an ingenious but rigorous and unforgiving matrix of streets and addresses. All were meticulously set forth with an east/west and north/south numbering system (no street names, just numbers) that I had just learned to understand before we left the state four years later.

The issue of *sameness* I experienced in Utah overwhelmed me. I found it to be present not only in the architecture but also in the culture, the race (Caucasian), and, of course, in the religion practiced by the vast number of its populace. Most of the kids at school had known each other for years, and almost all attended the Church of Jesus Christ of Latter-Day Saints (LDS). This is not meant as pejorative as, over the years, I have had many wonderful LDS friends, partners, and neighbors. However, with few exceptions, it was only after leaving Salt Lake City that I really got to know them. Don't get me wrong; I am quite confident that if any of my 1960s Salt Lake City classmates had moved to Santa Ana, they would have experienced the same sense of isolation.

I floundered in this culture, struggling helplessly most of the time, clumsy and awkward and out of place. Those in school with me at the time would likely say, at best, "What a strange guy," or just as likely, "Oh yes, what a dork!" I would not argue with either description. I was a dork, really, in all respects, for which Salt Lake City was only partially to blame. Having changed schools, often more than once every year, in different countries, each with vastly different cultures, it is understandable that I would have difficulty fitting into the culture of Salt Lake City. Our neighbors, however, were kind and helpful, but I suspect that in private, they would nod, understanding that I was a fish out of water in this unique and strange land.

I had enrolled in Wasatch Junior High, a brand new, state-of-the-art school, just after our arrival in Salt Lake City, knowing no one. My strategy for getting along at school was a good one— keep a low profile. Yet, it was not to be. It turned out that class *fashionistas*, as we now call them, set the standards for each season. In telepathic conformity, students quickly mimicked their decisions, just as a school of fish instantly changes color in some type of metamorphic magic act. All of my classmates knew exactly what was expected. For me, it was too late. My pre-school clothing purchases had been made, and that was that. So, feigning indifference, I soldiered up, and it didn't really bother me until my non-conformity rendered me infamous.

The campus was set on a slope from the east. It had snowed heavily the night before, one of the earliest storms of the season, and during recess, a rather intense snowball fight broke out. I joined in and perched myself at the high point of the campus, looking down at the corner door.

I was killing the crowd below, as I controlled the high ground.

Suddenly, a man in a suit stepped out of the door just as my magnificent snowball with its astounding arc glanced off the side of his head, knocking his glasses off.

Now, as shocked and horrified as I was, I knew this shouldn't be a problem because there were hundreds of guys throwing snowballs. Unfortunately, as you may have guessed, all of the fashion minions were wearing gold—gold shirts or gold vests or gold sweaters—while I was wearing a plaid Pendleton shirt. I stood out like a gypsy at a country club wedding.

The gym instructor grasped me from behind and marched me off to the principal's office, and on the way, I made the fatal mistake of saying, "How do you know it was my snowball?"

I got suspended for a day, and upon my return, I had to go to the principal's office for a lesson as to why one should not throw a snowball at the principal. Fortunately, Dad never found out about the incident, as Mom believed in the right to remain silent. It was an unfortunate introduction to my eighth-grade classmates.

My only other memory about eighth grade was equally bad. Eighth-grade biology was taught by a very conservative Mormon who did not believe in evolution. Apparently, this rejection was part of the Mormon doctrine at that time and, for all I know, may still be the Church's position. Our textbook, however, taught evolution and our teacher went to great lengths to discredit the textbook. I took exception to the teaching and pointed out the evidence described in the book. His response was to ridicule me. "So, you think your ancestors were monkeys?" he said, laughing at me.

"No," I said, not giving up. "But I think we had common ancestors, as it says in the book."

Things went from bad to worse, but I didn't back down, and neither did he. I was soon called into my counselor's office and was told I was being transferred to another biology class. I was shocked and dreaded any additional notoriety. This is the first time I recall being punished for a belief, and the counselor, to his credit, told me that my position was rational and arguably, based upon scientific evidence. This was the first time I felt empowered by logic. I am sure the experience had a significant impact on my future.

CHAPTER FIFTEEN

The Best of Times, the Worst of Times

Charles Dickens wrote *The Tale of Two Cities* in 1859. It begins with one of the most remembered paragraphs in English literature:

"It was the best of times, it was the worst of times, it was the age of wisdom, it was the age of foolishness, it was the epoch of belief, it was the epoch of incredulity, it was the season of Light, it was the season of Darkness, it was the spring of hope, it was the winter of despair, we had everything before us, we had nothing before us, we were all going direct to Heaven, we were all going direct the other way."

This is a good description of my four years in Salt Lake City, Utah, at three different schools: eighth grade at Wasatch Junior High School, ninth grade at Olympus High School, and my sophomore and junior years at Skyline High School. For better or worse, somehow, these were the years I began to emerge from the shadows.

The Worse

I was mostly miserable during my first two years in Utah, and admittedly much of my misery was self-inflicted. Terry did well, of course, graduating at the top of his class at Olympus High School with a full scholarship to the University of California, Santa Barbara, leaving behind many friends with whom he stayed in touch for the rest of his life. It took me a while to make friends, and I didn't settle into any deep relationships.

I have given some thought to the discrepancy between Terry's and my ability to make new friends. I wasn't mean. I didn't make fun of people, and while I made some good friends, they just didn't deepen like Terry's friendships. I now understand that my experience was not uncommon for the "close in time second child," especially in junior high school. The senior sibling is anxious to break away, leaving the younger sibling to fend for himself for the first time. The younger brother, used to floating along in the older brother's wake, suddenly finds himself on his own.

Simply put, it took time for me to learn how to fend for myself, socially and academically. Most of my jokes fell flat, or worse, they were downright embarrassing enough to make me uneasy thinking about them even now. I also had a stubborn streak, again a younger sibling trait, which often landed me in trouble. While the older brother learns to lead, accommodate, and facilitate, the younger brother learns to speak out without considering the consequences. At least, that was the nature of our development—Terry was the thinker and strategist, while I acted like an impetuous troublemaker.

This trait got me into serious trouble in ninth grade. I argued with my history teacher about multiple-choice questions I thought were incorrectly marked wrong. Apparently, the defense of my answers was misinterpreted as a lack of respect, resulting in me being kicked out of the class. Really! The school transferred me to a different class for defending an answer that was marked wrong on my test when I was certain I was right. Perhaps this was the beginning of my interest in debate. Though it didn't always work out when I argued with teachers, this burgeoning skill provided me with a state championship in debate and, much later, a long, satisfying career as a trial lawyer.

Like any younger brother, I was not nasty or disrespectful, just hardheaded. After all, if you weren't hardheaded as a younger brother, you might as well fade away into the woodwork.

Thinking about it over time, I concluded that it was just who I was. I was not hostile or demeaning, but there is no doubt that I had a streak of stubbornness that stayed with me, especially when I thought I was right, which was, most of the time—a trait that often landed me in trouble. "Mister Hughes, you have made your point; now sit down!"

As I complied, I am sure my face said, "Well, one of us is stupid, and I don't think it is me!"

I can almost see my grandfather Elsworth, the meanest man in Bakersfield, smirking in the shadows. This stubbornness got me in trouble many times until I finally learned to control my facial expressions and my tongue. Also, I learned the hard way that a bit of graciousness when making a point makes for a much softer landing if one turns out to be wrong.

My new history teacher was thoughtful and considerate and had the courage to tell me that my disputed answers were correct.

During this school year, I developed a bad habit of doing as little as possible to get by. I didn't care enough to study, and since my parents already thought I was academically slow, I got little pressure to change my poor habits. On the other hand, Terry continued to get the highest grades in his class, resulting in his appointment as the writer of an editorial column for the school newspaper entitled "Hughes Views." My grades were not terrible, just a bit over average, for which my parents were grateful and relieved.

Miss Penelope J. Jones (or Penny As She was Known)

In the fall of our first year in Utah, Dad was anxious to renew his enjoyment of bird hunting. He purchased a 16-gauge shotgun in Japan with hunting scenes intricately engraved into the wood stock and engraved in the silver plating on the breach. I loved looking at the swirling patterns, the birds breaking into flight, and the pointers at the ready.

Upon our respective fifteenth birthdays, Terry and I received our own 16-gauge shotguns, both Winchesters. The fields around Salt Lake

City abounded with quail and pheasants. In the fall, we could be found in those fields, that is, if we weren't fishing Little or Big Cottonwood Canyon. I became an excellent rifle marksman, but I never got the timing required to take down a bird exploding from the brush. In truth, I didn't mind gutting a trout, but bringing down a pheasant or quail bothered me a lot. It just did.

If you are going to do any serious bird hunting, a good bird dog is essential, and that is how Ms. Penelope J. Jones, otherwise known as Penny, came to be a member of our family. Although Dad was careful with money, he did invest in an excellent breeder and outstanding trainer.

Penny was brilliant and took to training quickly. Terry and I spent a lot of time reinforcing her training, including several tricks, such as holding absolutely still as we placed her favorite treat (a piece of cheese) on her nose. She would hold point until we said "okay," and then—snap, the cheese would be gone in the blink of an eye. Penny was very well disciplined as long as we were looking, but she had a mind of her own when we weren't. Although we tried, we could not break her from this lapse in discipline.

Worse was Penny's penchant for running once she passed some secret boundary known only to her. The boundary seemed to define the difference between obedience and freedom for Penny, and when she reached the boundary, run she would. The back of our home on the eastern hills of the Wasatch Range provided a 180-degree view of the rugged mountains to the east, the south, and west of Salt Lake City. If our attention drifted from her, she was off in a heartbeat, running the hills and foothills above our house. It seemed she would run forever. But, eventually, for her own reasons and in her own time, she would return, tongue dragging, her tail dripping blood from thrashing through the brush.

It was frustrating, maddening, and nerve-racking. We would follow Penny with our binoculars, running as fast as she could go. We soon learned, however, that she would always come back. We just had to wait her out. She never displayed remorse, no matter how harshly we told her what a bad dog she was. She would walk around the yard with her enormous tongue dripping, her chest heaving; then, after draining her water bowl as fast as we could refill it, she would plop down on her pillow and go quickly to sleep.

Penny the Fierce Defender

Terry and I taught Penny many tricks, and rarely did the teaching take more than one repetition. She loved to show off for a treat, and with only a few repetitions, she nailed the trick. One particular trick enthralled and somewhat alarmed our guests. One of us played the good guy, and the other was the bad guy. The good guy would yell, "sic 'em," pointing at the other. Penny would chase the bad guy and lunge to knock the "bad guy" down, growling and mouthing him without ever drawing blood. This was a game that Terry and I fostered and which Dad encouraged, saying, "You never know." Years later, Penny's aggression proved to be a great asset in Egypt as she protected our home.

Penny and Fuji

The worst part of integrating Penny into our household involved making peace between Fuji-san and Penny. And, as you might have guessed, Fuji-san was the aggressor. He tormented Penny every waking minute, whether or not we were in the room. "Bad dog, bad dog," he squawked, flapping from one safe perch to another as Penny barked ferociously just outside of snapping range. It soon became apparent that Fuji and Penny could not share the same perch. So, Fuji-san went off to live with Grandma in Bakersfield.

CHAPTER SIXTEEN

A Collection of Stories

You must have surmised by now that my time in Utah was full of anxieties: I was unsure of myself, out of place, and often had a contrarian bent. In other words, I was like many young boys on my way to becoming a young man. The adjustment was not easy. The preceding Utah chapters give a brief view, just a smidgen really, of my most memorable moments in Utah, but a few stories keep beating on the stage room door; they cannot be denied.

First in Line—Somnambulism

Dr. Long and his family, our uphill neighbors, welcomed us from our first day in Utah until the day we left. Remarkably, their friendship endured even when they were victimized by my somnambulism. Yes, I was a sleepwalker—big time.

As a child on sleepovers, my parents warned our hosts that they might find me walking about in the dark or, worse, thrashing about, bumping into things, and not knowing where I was. When I awoke on my own, I would start out okay, trying to find a light switch or a bathroom, even though I had little or no notion of where I was. When I was at home, things were not much better. I still would not know where I was or who I was fighting with or running from.

Experience taught me that I should start with my hand on a wall, any wall, and then keep going in one direction, usually knocking pictures askew or upsetting stuff along the way, but all the time with the urge to pee becoming more and more insistent. I would bang my toe, head, or knee into something unknown until finally, I would find a light switch and, gratefully, a bathroom.

Fortunately, I usually found my way with no great adventures. Mom was a deep sleeper, but Dad, the Marine, was conditioned to hear noises that went bump in the night. My parents had been told the standard advice: "Never wake a sleepwalker." If Dad heard my bedroom door open and the bathroom light did not quickly turn on, he would get up with his flashlight in hand to find me, ensuring that I came to no harm. It didn't happen often, but sometimes I would walk outside. Dad would continue to follow me, flashlight at the ready to keep me from any harm. The mental image of Dad patiently following me in the dark until I made my way home comforts me to this very day, and I have come to see it as an accurate analogy of our heavenly father.

Most of the time, I would make my way back to my bed unharmed and continue sleeping uninterrupted. But one night in Utah, when Dad was out of town, I woke in a small closed room in the middle of the night. Frantic, I thrashed about, trying to find my way. Everything seemed strange when suddenly a door swung open, exposing a beam of blinding light. Quickly, another light, a hall light, came on, revealing Dr. Long and his wife, our next-door neighbors, staring at me wide-eyed, almost as wide-eyed as I was staring back at them.

With the benefit of his professional training and his experience as a parent, Dr. Long quickly figured out that I had been sleepwalking. After calming me and settling me down, Dr. Long and his wife graciously escorted me home, much to Mom's surprise, as Dad was out of town.

It was good to know that Dad had helpers, but after this experience, he put chain locks near the top of each door that opened to the outside.

Our Neighborhood Friends and Trout Fishing

Our family made many friends in our neighborhood, including a very nice family whose name, regrettably, I cannot recall. In addition to being friendly and welcoming, when these neighbors learned of Dad's love for fly fishing, they invited Dad, Terry, and me to their family cattle ranch somewhere in remote central Utah for the fishing expedition of a lifetime. It was an extraordinary opportunity that only a few would have the privilege of enjoying. Mom was invited as well, but she politely declined. Not so Dad, Terry, and me. We accepted immediately.

The Short Cut

Days before our trip, our neighbors explained that there were two ways to get to the ranch. One, the safe but slow route, involved a long circuitous drive through southern Utah, followed by an extended circle back into the central Wasatch Mountains. The other route was a "shortcut." Our neighbors warned us, "It is manageable in some parts, but in others, it can only be described as rough. As long as you take your time and stay on the jeep tracks, you should be fine, and you will save more than a half-day of travel."

Our neighbors went on to point out that if we chose the short route, we should be prepared for some rough going and that the thing they called a road was made up mostly of dirt, sand, cobble rock, gravel, and stream rubble which, after our adventure, I simply referred to as "a rough track."

That was all Dad needed to hear. He wanted the challenge of the shortcut.

We were on our own getting to the ranch, but, fortunately, our neighbor provided precise directions, which I have now completely forgotten. In honor of our neighbor's privacy, and subject to my poor memory, I provide only a rough description of our route:

Head east out of Salt Lake City on Highway 40 over the Wasatch Mountains, then turn south and head past Park City.

Keep going a long way until you see a state mileage sign corresponding with what is written on your envelope.

When you pass the mileage sign, look for the first bar gate on the west side of the road.

When you spot the bar gate, open the lock with the combination written in your envelope, and drive through.

Lock the gate behind you and head to the ranch.

That was the end of our instructions, except for some words of advice: "Once you clear the gate, there is only one way to the ranch. It's about an hour and a half drive once you leave the paved highway, and most of it is rugged. It is unlikely you will meet someone coming the other way, but you never know, so give a honk before entering a blind turn."

On to Our Adventure

Dad gave Terry and me our estimated departure time— "Early, early!" meaning "Butts out of bed at three a.m. sharp" in Dad's vernacular. We packed the car the night before, including our fishing gear, icebox, and sleeping bags, and each of us had a small bag for personal items. Everything else, we were told, would be available at the ranch. Dad, however, had his own rules. He never went on a road trip without a selection of emergency tools, including a selection of hand tools, a block and tackle, and a small generator. So, all Terry and I had to do was get comfortable and hopefully doze a bit.

Sometime later, we turned south, driving past the now famed Park City Ski Resort, which at that time was just a few rope tows and two short chair lifts, but not much more. So, given there was nothing to see in the dark, I managed to sleep most of the trip.

Before we knew it, Dad woke Terry and me, telling us to keep an eye out for the mileage flag that would signal the bar gate was close by. Sure enough, both came in quick sequence. We jumped out of the car as soon as it stopped moving, anxious to confirm we had the right gate. One by one, we were stilled by the impossible beauty of the moment. After driving for hours in the arid high plains, the majesty of the eastern side of the Wasatch Mountain Range was breathtaking. The sun on our backs sent long shadows rippling across the desert tundra, and we looked like three elongated clowns.

Dad quickly brought us back to the moment.

"Well, we might as well find out if we have the right three numbers to the combination and whether the bar gate actually works." I had not considered such uncertainties and immediately began to contemplate what we would do if we couldn't find the right gate. We were not expected at the ranch until midday or early afternoon, so help would be a long time coming if it ever came at all! Worry, worry, worry! Looking back on this scene now I would think: *What would Calvin do?*

As far as I could tell, neither Terry nor Dad wasted any time on such questions. Instead, Dad walked up to the bar gate and turned the combination as Terry and I stood by. The lock clicked, and the bar gate released without a hitch. I must say, there is nothing like hearing a locked gate opening when you are in the middle of nowhere. Even Terry was smiling.

Ahead of us—the high desert of the eastern face of the grand Wasatch Mountains—all was magnificent but formidable. Twenty miles away, the mountains were waiting for us.

It did not occur to me to wonder how Terry and Dad felt about this roadside moment when the desert opened to the glorious splendor of the morning. Such things were not shared in our family. My feelings were euphoric, the moment etched within me—an unspoken memory I cherish to this day.

The Road In

The road to the mountains that sprung straight up from the floor of the desert was the longest, straightest dirt road I had ever seen. The desert calm and the beauty of the snow-topped mountains lured us on, even though the mountains remained out of touch and mysterious.

My blood stirred as we picked our way through fallen trees and broken boulders on this rugged mountain road. At the very top of the track, we discovered a cutout, so we pulled over and enjoyed the view of the valley below. I admit to a touch of vertigo as if we were in flight. I wondered who constructed such roads in the wilderness and believe my fascination with these unknown men and women sparked my future interest in the construction industry.

The High Country

We knew from our neighbors that a series of valleys lay ahead of us, each attaining a higher altitude than its predecessor. We also knew that the last summit would bring us to the base ranch. So, we traveled on, Dad maneuvering around massive boulders and burled, knotted cottonwood trees, while I wondered how the massive boulders that dotted the meadows came to be.

We made good time despite the terrain, and I enjoyed the ride. We rocked along in the wagon, sometimes traveling the valley floors and occasionally looking down into the valley below. Terry remained in the front seat, leaving me the option of moving from side to side as the scenery beckoned. At some point, I settled into a calming rhythm, punctuated with moments of trepidation ("Watch out! The boulder is going to fall on us!"), but I would quickly settle in again.

Where Giants Came to Play

Tight against the canyon wall, I looked up as high as I could. My eyes followed deep cracks in the rock walls that must have met astonishing resistance from the devil himself. Moving to the other side of the station wagon, I looked into the valley below, where wildflowers danced among the boulders that spread helter-skelter across the meadow.

Surely, this is where giants came to play. The valley gave evidence that nothing is permanent—not the canyon walls, not the massive boulders planted in the meadows, nor the large cottonwood trees, crushed and broken, perhaps a missive from the gods. But despite the evidence of carnage all around, amid the craggy abyss, fallen trees, and giant boulders, somehow, beside the river, flowers still bloomed.

It was not until many years later, when I first saw Picasso's work and the work of other cubists, that I came to understand the canyons of Utah.

The High Valley Ranch

Almost by surprise, we found the ranch house and its outbuildings on a high plateau. We arrived, thankfully, while it was still early afternoon. We enjoyed a welcoming greeting from the ranch manager after he quizzed Dad about how we managed to get here by the high northern entry in a station wagon. After giving the Pontiac a good going over, including the stowed tools, he gave Dad an appreciative nod, saying with a slight smile, "Well, I never thought anyone could manage the northern entry in a station wagon, but here you are, and in pretty good condition too."

He gave us a tour of the ranch while telling us what we needed to know, how to stay out of trouble, and most importantly, that dinner would be served when the triangle bar rang, adding, "It's best not to be late." He was rightfully proud of the property and his role as its manager.

Soon we were sitting on comfortable camp chairs beside the river whose upper branches we came to fish. I considered hiking along the river's edge but was too stiff from our journey, so I stayed put. Almost immediately, I nodded off, only to be roused after what seemed a short time by the clanging of the triangle bar. Given the hordes of hungry cowboys rushing in, it was apparent that if I didn't hustle, I would be late for supper.

I have no recollection of the meal, but I am sure it was good. On my way back to the bunkhouse, I was as near to sleep as I could be while still standing. I was brought up short by the pale turquoise of the early evening sky and then watched the shroud of dusk give way to the glory of the stars. One by one, it seemed, then more, and more again till soon, the canopy of heaven was open before me.

The moment stirred memories of passages long ago: to Hawaii, the Orient, the high camps in the Sierra. Later, much later, I would reflect on this moment and other evenings as well; nights in the mountains of Alaska and the isolation of the deep desert of Giza; on the beaches of Mali, Thailand, and King Garden Bay; sailing on the Red Sea; and hitchhiking on a lonely road in Yugoslavia in the middle of winter, wondering if I would live to see another day.

Though I have forgotten much, I remember this night in the Wasatch Range, in the midst of nowhere. Everything was different in my surroundings, yet the heavens remained the same. I was not acquainted with God during most of these adventures, but I saw His Glory in the night skies. Nothing compares with these evenings.

The Awakening

I slept like the dead until the ranch's triangle bar rang. Was it an emergency? No. Was there a fire? No. It was just early morning at the ranch, and we were being called to breakfast. What happened to the night, I did not know. One moment, my head hit the pillow, and the next, I was being assaulted by this terrible noise. Where were my clothes, my boots, and my flashlight? Mysteries all.

Dad, of course, was already up and dressed, and he encouraged me along. Terry was no more than a half a step ahead of me, but ahead of me, he was. This morning, however, I really didn't care. After a huge ranch breakfast, I saw our horses, saddled and waiting, tied to the corral rails. "Take your time. We're in no hurry," said our wrangler to whom we were introduced the previous day and who was assigned to guide us to our four-night camp and fetch us back.

When we were ready and mounted, our guide turned to us. "We've got about an hour and a half ride ahead of us, all upstream, plus or minus, and the fish will be there no matter what, so we want to go safe and sure. Any questions?" he said as we mounted up.

"Yes, sir," I said. "What's the difference between a river and a stream?" I thought it was a reasonable question until Terry snickered, shaking his head.

But our wrangler didn't skip a beat as he settled into his saddle. "Well, a river you have to boat over, a stream you can ford, but a creek, well, if you can piss over it," he said, turning up trail, "then it's a creek, not a stream." I thought Dad and Terry would fall off their horses laughing as we settled into line. I was embarrassed, but I still thought it was a reasonable question, even after the joke entered our family folklore.

We moved along the trail, keeping more or less on a constant, comfortable ride. Here and there, however, tough spots required maneuvering around or over rocks, obstructions, or fallen trees. The cottonwood trees, which had owned the canyon floor since we left the ranch, gave way to pines. Time went by fast as it wasn't a rough ride, and the morning chill had dissipated, leaving us with a comfortable, slow dance in our saddles with the sun at our backs.

Our wrangler pulled up at a middling high point of the day, "We're out about ten minutes or so from the camp. If you listen, you can hear the rumble of the upper falls and see the mist." Sure enough, as we stilled our horses, we could do both. "That's one of the falls that feeds the streams where you will be camping," he said, nodding to the northwest. "See it tumbling down from on high? That's the mist I showed you earlier."

Sure enough, looking as directed, we caught glimpses of the falls cascading down until the mist disappeared behind a curtain of high pines. "There are four falls altogether, but it's too rugged and dangerous to climb, and there ain't no fishin' that high anyway. Behind them trees," our wrangler said, pointing just below the bottom shroud, "there are more rainbows than you could possibly want, small, ten to twelve inches at the biggest but great to eat. Downstream, lying under the banks of the meadow," he nodded, "you can catch some big fish. Fourteen to twenty inchers ain't uncommon."

We went a bit farther up the trail along the eastern bank of the larger stream to where we could see the intersection of the plateau and the stream. There, we crossed over. The current was manageable; the smaller stream from the northwest approached from the higher elevation but clearly had less force and speed. The larger stream, darker in color, coming in from the east was slower, wider, and the water, though definitely clear, had a green tinge to it picked up from the moss channels that tracked the stream's flow.

Sparse mountain grass covered the infield of the meadow that was dotted with multicolored flowers. At the broadest upstream side, three sizable boulders backed up to the rough terrain above, in a configuration of boulders that reminded me strangely of Mr. Clean, with his massive bulging head in the middle, and two smaller boulders, one on each side, hunched in as protective shoulders. This spot was where we would make camp, as others had done before.

The campsite was a bit rustic but restful and nicely elevated, giving good views of the merging stream and river just at our camp. The sunlight danced on the surface of the merging streams while below, refractions of orange, amber, and green played with the light of the sun.

The depth of the combined streams varied from just a few inches at the fringe to two or more feet midstream, with pools four to five feet deep, formed by mighty boulders, fallen trees, and sudden bends up and down the river. I couldn't contain myself any longer. "Three days and two nights, now playing at camp roustabout!" I said, raising my arms high, "A story of soaring spirits and sore butts!" Neither Terry nor Dad seemed amused by my wit, but I thought I saw a slight grin from our wrangler.

In the middle of the clearing sat a firepit and grill. The boulders provided good protection from the wind, though there was little to speak of upon our arrival. The provisions carried by our pack mule included some rather rustic fold-out chairs for relaxing while engaging in the two most regenerative pastimes known to man—watching the shadows subsume the day and telling stories.

There were three additional, very welcomed luxuries that I remember clearly. First, someone, some time ago, had fashioned a runnel that diverted water from the stream above directly to our camp, so there was no need to trek to the stream to wash the dishes or fetch water. Second, there was an ingenious refrigerator. Yes, a refrigerator—that was cougar-proof! The runnel, when open, filled a rock pit with cold clear water in which sat a perforated metal box just a few feet away from the fire pit. The runnel streamed water into and around the box, keeping our goods fresh and cold. A heavy iron bar was welded onto an iron hinge that could be swung over the top of the box to the opposite side of the pit, clearing the box by just an inch or so to where it could be secured to a sister pipe. With a bolt in place, we had a cougar-proof refrigerator right at our campsite, not to mention cold, clean drinking water delivered to our doorstep. Pretty neat!

Downriver and downwind, about twenty feet back into the bush and out of sight, was a rustic privy. "All the comfort of home," I pronounced, "except for the TV."

We settled in, and as soon as we had the camp set up to Dad's liking, we started fishing. Our wrangler gave us a few tips before heading back to the ranch, but I was too excited to listen much, except to hear him suggest a "woolly worm for fishing up to midafternoon and then just trust any hatch you see for dry flies." Picking the right spot took time and attention, but choosing the proper nymph? At that, Dad was the expert, and we would always defer to him.

The last tip I remember very well. Our wrangler told us, "The stream undercuts the banks where the meadow grass is. The bigger fish will be waiting under the stream's edge." But he warned, "Approach carefully," looking at Terry and me, "or you might find yourself in a sinkhole. Don't panic if you do, as the hole won't be so deep as to swallow ya up, but . . ." he said looking directly at me, "you might not be happy if a mountain lion or a bear amble by while you make a ruckus trying to get out of your hole."

I was getting a bit weary of his picking on me by this time, so I responded deadpan, "Don't worry. If I do, I will just put him to sleep with one of your stories." He guffawed, and that story also stayed in the family folklore for years.

Then, assuring our camp was ship-shape, he asked if we had any questions. Since there were none, he quickly mounted his horse and turned down the trail saying over his shoulder, "See you early on the fourth day."

Ready to Fish

We were ready even though it was early afternoon and not the ideal time for fishing, but Terry and I wanted to try anyway. As taught by Dad, we began to turn over rocks in the stream to determine the *bug du jour*. With the information acquired from our bug foray, Dad made a few selections from his substantial cache of flies that he had brought with him. Just in case he guessed wrong, he was prepared with his fly-tying kit to quickly come up with the right fly on the fly. (Oh, please forgive me).

I hiked downstream for a while, foregoing several good spots, looking for the series of ponds our wrangler had described. Soon enough, the trail veered away from the stream to a high point, and there, below, just as our wrangler described, I saw two nice-sized pools, tiered, one after the other.

Water from the shallow upper pool spilled over the slick side of a boulder, funneling the stream toward the far bank of the lower pool. The boulder seemingly served as a flume, channeling the flow (not to mention flies and worms) to the far side of the second pool, where the current partially undercut the overhanging bank of the meadow, just as our wrangler said—"a moving buffet table."

I was the first to arrive back to camp. I started a small fire as the sun was low in the sky. I gutted and cleaned my trout and put him on a string that trailed out into the runnel along with two smaller fish, three fish being the limit.

Soon, Terry and Dad joined me. Terry looked irritated, seeing me back at the camp before him. "Give up, did ya?" And sure enough, he pulled a couple of good-sized rainbows, ten to twelve inches, out of his creel.

"Not bad," I said. Then slowly leaning over, I pulled my beautiful sixteen-inch rainbow out of the runnel. Dad whooped, and even Terry exploded with a few choice words. Of course, I had to tell of my exploits, and I luxuriated in the details.

It was a great trip, and never until now have I admitted that the catch was the result of a mistake. Inadvertently, I had let my woolly float under an underwater log, and it took me more than a few seconds to figure out that the tugging I experienced was the result of my hooking the biggest rainbow I ever landed. Believe me, I had no idea how to land a fish on the wrong side of a log, so I let it play out until we were both exhausted. But please, keep this story to yourself, as I might have exaggerated a bit—but just a bit.

We started a small fire and cooked the fish we caught. I do not recall many details of the trip as a whole, but I remember this night clearly. That was the biggest trout I had ever caught, and I also know there were no leftovers. We cleaned up quickly as the evening darkened the sky. We sat by the small fire, listening to the soft song of the stream rippling through the night. I am confident there is no more calming and comforting sound in nature than that of a running stream.

The small fire in the rock pit (covered by a spark screen, of course) allowed our mellow mood to carry us into the starry night. Our reverie was occasionally interrupted by streaking fire in the sky, once again proclaiming heaven's majesty. Not long afterward, we slept.

It was a trip of a lifetime.

Skiing the Mountains of Cottonwood Canyon

Skiing the many incredible slopes of Utah was an experience I will never forget. Less than an hour from our house was the Cottonwood

Canyon ski area and the Brighton, Solitude, and Alta ski resorts. None were the biggest or the best of the nation's ski areas at the time, but long after we left Utah, all were developed into world-class resorts.

The Solitude resort was a small ski area with one significant attraction—discounted ski passes for church groups. The passes were offered for less than three dollars from 3 p.m. to 10 p.m. As a result, it was a great place to meet pretty Episcopalian girls, all of whom were a lot of fun. I was not the first young man to join the Episcopal Church Youth group for these benefits.

Solitude was the only resort that offered night skiing anywhere close to Salt Lake City. Best of all, we could get out of class at 2:20 p.m. and be on the slopes within an hour. We would bomb down the hills as fast as we could go, then, if we were lucky, we would go back to the chairlift and snuggle up with one of the cute Episcopalian girls—only to ward off the cold, of course. We would race down the hill and back again, skiing our brains out, as the hill at night was always virtually empty of skiers.

One Bad Experience

I only had one bad experience skiing in Utah, and it looked worse than it was. It was spring, and I was full of myself, skiing in shorts and no shirt, blasting down a lower run at Brighton, heading for the lodge in somewhat slushy spring conditions, when I entered the shadow of a tree line. Immediately the sludge turned to hard ice, and I was suddenly moving much faster than my skis. Unwillingly, I found myself on their tips. Then, again unexpectedly, I was out of the shadows back into slush, causing my skis but not my body to slow rapidly. The result—I was flying, yes, flying until I looked up just in time to see a rapidly approaching pine tree. Bam!

That was it; lights out.

When I regained consciousness, I looked up at the blue sky with a circle of people looking down on me. Mothers were covering the eyes of their children.

I struggled to my feet, shaking off the cobwebs. Unbelievably, my skis remained on, and since nothing was broken, I prepared to continue downhill. But it seemed I had lost a pole until I realized that I held the handle of the pole I thought I had lost, but it was now less than two feet long. The pole had snapped about a foot and a half below the grip. "No worries, poles can be replaced," I muttered to myself.

People continued to stare at me, looking wild-eyed. Apparently, the pole shattered when I hit the tree, taking a good chunk out of my side. "It wasn't so bad," I thought. But blood was dribbling down from the wound, running onto my cut-offs, then down my right leg onto the snow. I was okay, and, amazingly, my skis were still on. So I skied off, a bit wobbly, but knowing I'd had it worse.

I didn't realize until I got to the bottom of the hill that, in addition to my side wound, when I landed after my short flight, my right ski came down on my left shin, just about an inch below my knee. The ski proceeded to scrape about a two-inch swath of skin from just below my knee all the way to my boot, leaving a substantial trail of blood behind me, in addition to what was dribbling from my side. All of this explained why women were sheltering the eyes of their children.

"He's in shock; get ski patrol," someone said, and I now think she was right. But, at the end of the day, my sunburn was the worst of it.

And Then There Was Debate

My closest Utah friends came from debate. Being called out in various assemblies with my debate partner Jim Telviti to receive trophies provided some minor notoriety and helped soften my earlier reputation of being a bit odd. Jim was a year ahead of me and clearly one of the brightest people I ever met in school or life. Being within his reflected glow worked favorably upon me, and I was privileged to call him a friend. He was brilliant, while I had a flair for the dramatic. So, we worked it out. I wove the story together and provided a little pathos while Jim was the dagger in the heart.

Together, we made a compelling team, and we did very well throughout various competitions, developing a reputation in our little world and even a bit beyond. In Utah, debate was a big deal, then, as it is now. On several occasions, we were called forth at assemblies and statewide competitions to accept trophies. These accolades raised my reputation, and I became someone of interest. But what happened to Jim?

The topic selected for the state competition in the spring of 1963 was "Resolve that the United States Should Divest Itself of All Land and Property Not Necessary for Conducting Federal Business as specifically prescribed by the Constitution of the United States"—a hot topic in the very conservative state of Utah, mainly since a substantial portion of undeveloped land in Utah was owned by the United States Government.

Jim felt that there was no rational basis for restricting the United States government from owning any amount of land that it acquired lawfully. And I agreed with him in principle but was eager to debate anything. Jim's view was that the proposition was so irrational that it was not subject to debate. His mind was made up, and he declined to participate, leaving me high and dry, but even still, we remained good friends.

When I was left without a partner, our debate teacher reached into her reserves and came up with a major talent from the sophomore class. My new partner and I ended up winning the state competition. I became somewhat of a cause celebre among the very small percentage of our class who cared about such things.

In any event, my debate power did nothing to help me get a date to the prom or any other date for that matter. My friend Sherry Mast, whom I really wanted to ask to the prom, ended up going with Jim, the bum, but I got over it. And Sherry fixed me up with her really nice friend, and we had a good time.

Interestingly, I began to develop a number of friends who happened to be girls—not girlfriends, but friends. Many were from debate, several from other classes, and all of them were fun and cute too. But maddingly, it was clear that while they liked me a lot and they greatly enjoyed my company, they clearly thought of me as no more than a really great friend. None of them considered me, even for a moment, as a romantic interest. I was a great guy. They had no qualms about discussing the guys they were dating and their pros and cons as dating material right in front of me. They even asked my opinion of them. Of course, I had nothing good to say about any of the guys.

The Power of the Pontiac Tempest

Some might say that my elevation from dork status to friend corresponded with Dad's reversion to his hot-rod days. After a trip to California, he drove home to Utah in an almost new, white Pontiac Lemans three-speed convertible, which he purchased from his close friend Johnny Barber through Barber Pontiac in Bakersfield.

Now, this was a hot car! This was not just a *hot* car in Utah. It was a knock'em dead, turn-their-heads car that turned my life into something good.

To my surprise, Dad let me drive it. Not on dates, at least not on nighttime dates, but I could take it out during the daylight hours. Then, shortly before my junior year was over, Dad was promoted to senior pilot for electronic flight facilities inspections (or some such title) for California and Nevada—meaning we would be moving again, this time to Los Angeles. When the ladies learned of my pending departure, they decided to stage a goodbye picnic for me on the Great Salt Flats just outside of Salt Lake City, and to my great surprise, Dad suggested I take the convertible.

I was stunned by Dad's offer, and I was shocked by my friends' suggestion of a goodbye picnic. It touched me greatly. So off we went the following Saturday, me driving the hot-rod Pontiac convertible, top down, traveling down the highway toward the Great Salt Lake Flats with the gals singing to the radio.

We knew the Salt Flats pretty well, and we found a great spot in the middle of nowhere to lay out our blanket and picnic lunch. Turning on the car radio, we danced in circles. Each of my friends wanted to dance with me. For once, I felt like a king. So, as the sun was setting below the western mountaintop, there we were, in the midst of the salt flats, all whirling slowly and rhythmically. Thank you, ladies. It was a sweet goodbye.

By the time I dropped off each of the girls, I was getting apprehensive about what Dad would say because it was well after dark. However, when I got home, he only said, "Did you have a good time?"

"Yes, sir, sure did," was all I said.

"Good" was his only reply as he held out his hand out for the keys. This was the first time Dad really surprised me about my expanding freedom. The second was two years later in Cairo.

CHAPTER SEVENTEEN

3300 Manhattan Beach Blvd., California, 1963

We arrived in Manhattan Beach, California, during early summer after an interminable drive over Highway 50 to Sacramento, then down Highway 99 to Bakersfield to see my grandmother and, of course, Fuji-san. The trip through the desert driving the Tempest "balls out," as Dad liked to say, was exhilarating and, to my amazement, Terry and I were allowed to share the driving, but only through the desert, with Dad taking over when we entered the mountains. We packed food so we would stop for nothing but potty breaks, gassing up, and roadside stops for eating our sandwiches and other goodies Mom packed for the trip.

We left SLC "early, early," meaning, as you already know, no later than 0300 in Marine talk. Mom, the artist, demurred from the driving since the scenery fascinated her, and she continually sketched in her artist notebook. Every moment captivated me. I did not shut my eyes except to blink. The desert west of Utah is primarily flat and barren, with a few forlorn mountain ridges that had sprung up for no discernable reason. Yet all were beautiful and compelling in their own way, awaking in me a desire to be on my own, walking through spaces untouched by civilization, a passion I later explored when we reached Egypt a little more than a year later.

We made the trip in just over fourteen hours, stopping for one quick meal and several potty breaks. This was before interstate freeways were fully developed, so going through the mountains slowed our pace considerably, and we would have made it quicker but for Mom. In her subtle way, which we knew was not to be denied, she would negotiate a vista stop to absorb a view or even render a quick sketch or take a photo that might later appear on canvas.

We all knew she had a gift, and we never quarreled with her desire to capture a unique charcoal rendering. We guys would sigh and grimace, but all of us knew that on the few occasions she asked for something, it was to be.

Soon, we were in Bakersfield, where we spent a few days with Grandma and Fuji-san. With the possible exception of Penny, all of us felt Fuji's absence, though we knew he and Grandma enjoyed each other's company. We spent only a few days, as all of us were anxious to see our new home. Soon we were coming into the LA basin. The smog was terrible, but we left it behind as we approached the beach cities. We exited the 405 onto the Imperial Highway and then headed west for a close look at the FAA facilities and surrounding airport operations where Dad would be stationed. It was riveting. The airport was massive, the most impressive transportation hub I had ever seen, especially with the newly finished elevated, circling restaurant designed as a spaceport. The stop allowed us to put down the top so we could enter Manhattan Beach, which was just a few miles away, in style.

Surf City USA

We headed due west on Imperial Highway and Beach Boulevard, straight into the sun, along the southern edge of the airport with the ocean dead ahead. Rolling sand dunes, ice plants, seagulls, and the smell of the ocean, all a piece of heaven, endless sand stretching north and south, as far as the eye could see, and ahead, through the misty veil, lay the Pacific Ocean. We had arrived in paradise.

To reach our destination, we made a ninety-degree turn to the south on Vista Del Mar, a jog onto Highland Ave, another jog to the

Pacific Ocean, and a final turn to the south. Success, we had arrived in Manhattan Beach and the famous Manhattan Beach Blvd or Surf City USA, home of the Beach Boys.

I had never heard or seen such a thing. People seemed to be surfing the sidewalks! Surely Annette Funicello had to be right around the corner. I am sure my mouth was hanging open, but it dropped even further when we pulled up to the apartment my parents had rented, 3300 Manhattan Beach Blvd, Manhattan Beach, California, home of "Surfin' USA."

Our three-bedroom apartment occupied the entire third floor, offering views of the Pacific Ocean from our living and dining room windows. Just two blocks west of our apartment was a broad concrete walkway shared by pedestrians and skateboarders, as I learned to call them. Finally, after a wide strand of white sand, there was the vast, blue Pacific Ocean.

Wave after wave broke upon the shore. Surfers abounded, paddling out, waiting for the best wave, catching just the right one, and surfing back to the shore or bailing out to catch the next. Terry and I were stunned, never having seen such things except for our time in Hawaii. But in Hawaii, there was little surfing except for the local boys, and I was too busy climbing trees to notice.

Since Terry would be heading off to start summer school on full scholarship at the University of California, Santa Barbara, I was given the first choice of bedrooms. The choice was easy. I chose the bedroom with a private bath and a great ocean view.

I feel faint just thinking about this miracle. My parents had the master suite, half a floor up, with the same great ocean view as the living room. It was hard for me to take it in. I immediately walked two short blocks down to the boardwalk. By then, the sun was about half an hour from setting. Lots of suntanned people walked by or wove themselves in and out of the crowd on boards with wheels. Guys not on skateboards were either carrying surfboards balanced on their heads or were in the water catching wave after wave after wave.

If this wasn't heaven, I would gladly take second best. I sat on the backside of a sidewalk bench. Soon my parents and Terry joined me as all of us silently watched the sun enter the sea.

Getting a Job

The first order of business for me was to find a summer job, as there had been no allowances for the Hughes boys for some time. I scoured the neighborhood but had no luck. There were no country clubs nearby, so caddying was out of the question.

About a week and a half after our arrival, after looking every day for a job, I became depressed. I expanded my job search to Sepulveda Boulevard, a main thoroughfare along the south coast. I finally came to a huge department store. As luck would have it, the manager of the lunch counter concession in the department store, Mertz, had just fired her cook. I told her about my work at Woody's Smorgasbord in Salt Lake City, caddying and working for Dad when he was a landscaper. But I hit the lottery when she asked about cleanliness. "Ma'am, are you familiar with the term *Marine clean*?" I asked. She smiled, saying, "I don't know what it means, but you're hired."

During the first few days of work, Mertz would inspect the counters, the floor, and splash boards. By my second week, she would just walk in and say, "Marine clean?" and I would answer her with a smart, "Yes, ma'am, Marine clean." Soon I modified my response to, "Yes, Ma'am, Captain, sir!" She would smile, and we both knew she didn't have to look.

I had one embarrassing but funny experience when working for Mertz. Once every summer, the department store had a parking lot sale. The parking lots were filled with goods, and we set up an outdoor barbecue for Mertz with all the condiments on a table that folded out. At the end of the day, I cleaned our tables, but I still had to wash down the condiment jugs sparkling clean, then carry them back to Mertz's sparkling clean pink Cadillac. She gave me the keys so I could load the jugs into the trunk. I loaded everything up and closed the trunk just as Mertz walked over. But the trunk didn't shut; it just kept springing up a few inches. I gave it a few quick bounces as Mertz yelled, "Stop," which I was going to do anyway.

Thinking the worst, I opened the trunk. It was immediately apparent that I had not secured the condiment pumps by pushing down and turning the spouts counterclockwise until they locked. We both stood, looking in the trunk in abject horror. The bottom of the trunk was sprayed with ketchup, mayonnaise, and mustard. I looked over at Mertz with terror in my eyes. She looked at the mess and then said, "Marine clean!" over her shoulder as she walked away, tossing towels to me while shaking her head. We laughed about it a lot, and she enjoyed telling others of my misfortune. *Marine clean* became our store motto.

The summer went by slowly because I didn't know anyone. I would take Penny for walks along the beach every day. While I saw the same people, none seemed friendly enough for me to walk up and start a conversation with. So, I anxiously waited for my senior year to come.

And come it did.

CHAPTER EIGHTEEN

Mira Costa High School, 1963–1964

In late August 1963, I walked into a pre-enrollment program for new students at Mira Costa High School. The school was abuzz with energy, like any high school, but it was all new to me. If there was any sense of conformity, I couldn't make it out, although I did notice a lot of suntanned guys with blond hair that I later learned could have been manufactured by bleaching. Bleaching! Really? All seemed fit and confident. The girls certainly were sure of themselves, a bit sassy, laughing and kidding around. It was as if the sun in Manhattan Beach never went down. Even after all these years, I still think that was the case.

It seemed as if I carried no baggage from my previous years. My debate experiences in Utah gave me a confidence that I had never before experienced. Walking up with Jim during assemblies to receive awards and trophies helped shake off my *somewhat odd* reputation, as in Utah, debate was a big deal. In fact, I was accelerating intellectually. I was thinking for myself, expressing my own thoughts, and, thanks to debate, I was beginning to enjoy just being me. Most importantly, I developed more than a few great friends during my last years in Salt Lake City. All this gave me more confidence as I approached my senior year in a new high school.

It was a completely fresh start. As a man of mystery, I drew attention. Upon the day of my admission to Mira Costa, the admissions counselor offered to take me on a tour of the facilities and asked if I was acquainted with Mira Costa's highly regarded football program. I said no, but I was interested in learning about the school's debate program. He looked at me as if I had asked him about Martian agriculture.

"No," he said slowly, "we don't have a debate program, but let me introduce you to our football coach."

As he walked me to the field, I said to myself, "Really, there is no debate program?"

The coach was gruff, as you would expect of a football kind of guy, but he did his best to engage me in his program. I did not realize then, but apparently, somewhere along the way, I had subsumed my father's longtime disdain for "jocks," as he called them. The conversation ended quickly.

On the way back to the office, I once again raised the question of a debate program. "Well," the counselor said, "We don't have a debate program, but we have a great theater program," he enthusiastically proclaimed. "Mrs. Sally Reed came to us last year from Stanford, where she mastered in Theater Arts," he said, almost unable to control his enthusiasm. Thanks to our debate teacher at Skyline, I knew what a master's program was, though I had no clue who Stanford was, but I did my best to match his enthusiasm. "Thanks to our new director, we have an up-and-coming drama department that is second to none."

I wondered why he kept saying "Stanford," and I must now confess that I had never heard of Stanford before that day, but I perked up a bit by the mention of drama, which in my mind was about as close to debate that I could get in the land of eternal sunshine.

So, On With the Show and My Introduction to Drama

I enrolled in the drama class without further fuss, and I am sure this decision and my debate experiences shaped the rest of my life. Mrs. Reed was masterful in getting all of her aspiring thespians involved in one or more of our productions. We put on three major productions in my senior year and several small ones. The major works were: *Cheaper by the Dozen*, adapted from an autobiographical book by Frank Bunker Gilbreth, Jr. and his sister Ernestine Gilbreth Carey, released as a film in 1950; *The Boy Friend*, written by Sandy Wilson in 1953; and our final production, the Pulitzer Prize winner, *The Skin of Our Teeth*, by Thornton Wilder, which opened on Broadway in 1942.

December 6, 1963 edition of Mira Costa High School paper *La Vista*.

Though I was the leading man in two of the three major works and stage manager for the third, my parents did not attend any of my performances. As with all of my debate competitions and award assemblies, I was on my own. I don't know what to say about it other than my parents didn't understand their role as support to their sons.

Thanks to Mrs. Reed's profound talent as a director and coach, as a motivator, and, yes, as a disciplinarian, all three productions were a great success. At the end of the year, Cal State Long Beach hosted a theater competition for local high schools, and our school received the highest accolades.

The Craft (Challenging Students Builds Confidence)

I had my doubts at the beginning of the year as to my skills as a thespian, but my nerves turned to near panic when Mrs. Reed took our class into Mira Costa's new state-of-the-art auditorium. The stage lights provided only dim light when we entered the theater, while the rest of the auditorium was dark but for a faint glow coming from high above the exit doors. We quickly learned the source of the glow was the lighting control booth that seemed to hover above us, waiting for direction. Turning back toward the stage, as our eyes became adjusted, we saw rows of seats disappearing into infinity. Then Mrs. Reed spoke into the darkness with her firm voice, "May we have stage lights, gentlemen," and lo, there was light! We were then marched up to the stage; boys stage left, girls stage right, a direction that created some confusion until the girls sorted things out. The thrill that approached near panic was tangible.

Surely this introduction was for show, I thought. Regardless, it was effective as each of us wannabe thespians clung to every word Mrs. Reed spoke from that moment on. No doubt the theatrical entrance she engineered had a purpose. I know I lost more than a little of my swagger, as did each of my fellow thespians. "Take a good look," Mrs. Reed said, "Take it all in. You won't ever get used to it, but you will come to manage it," she said. "Even the most seasoned performers tell me that the thrill never leaves them when the lights come on."

Taking center stage, Mrs. Reed requested that we join her as she asked for stage light. We gathered around her, hovering like little chicks as she introduced us to our first one-act production. I think it was a Bird Cage production, originating at the famed Bird Cage Theater in Tombstone, Arizona, although I'm not sure. Mrs. Reed had the wisdom to start with a one-act play with many components that would accommodate a large cast. Scene changes were minimal, accomplished by quick breaks under dim light.

Of course, it was a spoof, and, as Mrs. Reed explained, a good spoof could accommodate a limited number of flubs if managed with aplomb. On our first read-through, my friend Ken Thompson was asked to read the leading role of Slim, a disguised Texas Ranger trying to catch an infamous cattle rustler. Tall and lanky, Ken was perfectly cast as the hero of the production. The ranch owner, Betsy, was about to go out of business due to a rash of cattle rustling at the ranch she had inherited from her father. I played the antihero, the bulldog tough ranch manager who was having no success in stopping the nightly loss of cattle. These failures were about to put Betsy out of business. You could tell immediately that I had the villain role, as I wore nothing but black for the whole performance.

Mrs. Reed's motives for doing a one-act spoof quickly became apparent. First, it was complex enough to engage all her students in meaningful roles. Second, it was silly enough to allow for missteps, and third, Mrs. Reed knew that audiences were more forgiving of comedies than serious drama. "Now it is time to see if you are ready to put in the hard work, and beware, comedy is harder than drama. The tempo is overstated and larger-than-life, body movements are critical, and facial expressions are exaggerated, right down to the tilt of the chin or the *slow* turn of the head. The challenge for you," she said, "is that comedic dialogue must be precise in tone, delivered with subtle body movements, down to a melodramatic lift of an eyebrow. All productions require coordinated movements precisely timed, but with comedy, everything must be delivered at a faster pace."

It seemed an invitation to chaos, but, amazingly, our cast members quickly stepped into their assigned roles. As our rehearsals went on, I realized this play was an unstated tryout for future productions. Mrs. Reed wanted to determine which of her students could, and would, quickly absorb direction and which could immediately immerse themselves in their part. She needed to distinguish students who were serious about their craft from those who were just fooling around.

The most fun of all was that we were allowed interplay with the audience. Our audience immediately supported our work, bestowing lots of laughter, but unintentionally, I got the show's biggest laugh. The denouement of our play was a late-night scene. Ken (the hero) and a sidekick were on the lookout for cattle rustlers when suddenly, all dressed in black, I rushed out from behind a side curtain to confront and put an end to our hero. Ken and I were to engage in a mock fight which we had practiced many times. Of course, in our many rehearsals, the fight ended with Ken knocking me out with one mighty swing.

Unfortunately, when I made my rushed entrance, my adrenalin was racing faster than my feet could carry me, and it didn't help that I was wearing cowboy boots with very slick leather soles. The result— I tumbled flat out in front of Ken, right at his feet. Ken, expecting a faux fight, was dumbfounded, but I quickly went into action, grabbing his feet like a mad dog, chewing and growling at his boots. Ken caught on right away as he started beating me with his hat until he and his sidekick got me under control.

The rest of the play went as planned, and, all in all, it was a success. There was a lot of talk the next day at school as to who the villain was, and I quickly became known to everyone in the school. To my surprise, Mrs. Reed lectured the class about my ingenuity, saying that she would use it forever as a lesson of what to do when things go unexpectedly wrong.

We were flying high the night of the first of many cast parties. Mrs. Reed had clearly mastered the director's art of inspiring, challenging, and, when necessary, disciplining, "putting down the hammer," we called it. She demonstrated all of these talents at one time or another as she managed a group of unruly high schoolers through no less than three major productions and several smaller productions. For me, drama offered an extraordinary and sudden entry into my senior class.

Some might think Mrs. Reed asked too much of kids in high school, but she believed deeply in all her students. She told me years later that the most challenging chore for her was finding space on the stage for all of her talented students and then motivating each of them to believe in themselves the way she did.

Those who stayed the course developed talents that served them well for the rest of their lives. Sadly, many of their lives were cut short by the then-unknown terrible disease of AIDS. I miss each and every one of them, though I was far away when they succumbed.

Ah, the Ladies

To my great fortune, what the Utah ladies predicted when I left Utah came to be. At the end of our last gathering at the Salt Flats, my friends marveled at how they could have missed what a catch I was. They assured me that the girls in my new school would not make the same mistake. For the first time in my life, I seemed to be of some attraction to the ladies! Suddenly I had no trouble getting dates, and they talked about me in a good way. "Who was the guy dressed in black?"

Cheaper by the Dozen

As a result of our first play, the cast and stage members came to know each other well, and we became a tightly knit circle. To my shock, Mrs. Reed offered me the male lead of Frank Bunker Gilbreth in the well-known play, *Cheaper by the Dozen*. The play was a great pick by Mrs. Reed. First, it had many parts to accommodate a large cast; second, given our early work, Mrs. Reed was comfortable that she had the right talent to do justice to the great range of parts demanded by the work.

As silly as it sounds, I did not anticipate how each cast member was entirely dependent upon the words and movements of every other cast member. I thought it was enough to master my movements and my dialogue. I quickly came to understand how every word and gesture was intended to trigger some action, no matter how small. It is not just dialogue to which thespians must respond. The things that can go wrong in such an environment are unlimited.

I was nervous as hell about assuming these responsibilities, and I found out that I had every reason to be. Accepting a major role in a theater production is much different from engaging in a debate. Both are challenging, of course, but I was not expecting how each moment on the stage must be honored, revered, and coordinated. Through Mrs. Reed, I learned that neither the collective effort of all nor the brilliance of one makes a successful play; instead, it is the collective sinew of the entire body that allows a play to come to life.

I was not prepared for any of this, yet I was being asked to assume the lead role. Mrs. Reed understood my concern and my phobia about memorizing my part, and she suggested that it would be much easier if I had someone to prompt me as I worked on it. Mrs. Reed did not suggest, however, that it would be helpful if that someone was pretty, kind, and pleasant as well, but I wouldn't put it past her to think of that. And that is how I met Ellen and how we became an item throughout the rest of the year.

The play went very, very well, so it was on to the next production—*The Boy Friend*.

Reality is a Cold Teacher!

To my shock, Mrs. Reed offered me a role in our second major production, *The Boy Friend*. I politely declined even though I knew that declining a role was not a good thing to do. "The part is perfect for you—an old man who is somewhat of a letch."

"Is it a singing part?" I asked timidly.

"Just a bit of singing," she admitted, "just a few lines." That was all I needed to hear. No singing for me, and I stuck to my guns until Mrs. Reed finally relented.

Thankfully, Mrs. Reed did not hold a grudge, and she gave me the position of stage manager and assistant producer. All came together exceedingly well, and Randy knocked the role out of the park, doing a much better job than I ever would have done.

Many years later, I realized that the combined experiences of a debater, a thespian, and a stage manager turned out to be excellent preparation for a trial lawyer. All three endeavors require inexhaustible energy, intellect, resourcefulness, tenacity, and stamina. All three practitioners must control their surroundings, whether they are seething hot, surprised, or elated; they must be able to control the moment, whether practiced or unexpected. All three professions require enormous preparation, research, and, of course, nerves of steel. For example, an actor who delivers the wrong line; an attorney whose friendly witness blurts out, "I guess I had that wrong;" or a stage manager whose prop cannot be found thinking, *Oh shit, what am I going to do now?* all need to meet calamity with calm problem-solving. In short, combining the art of the stage with the art of forensics is outstanding preparation for any aspiring trial lawyer.

So, the fun was on. Drama made up for my just getting by in the classroom. Stage management broadened my thinking beyond the page, and the discipline of the law endowed me with a career.

Discipline, Discipline, Discipline

Mrs. Reed soon welcomed my suggestions as stage manager during *The Boy Friend*, but she made clear that changes in a scene would take place only with her prior approval while ad-libbing would earn her wrath or worse. "Every member of a production depends upon certainty. Ad hoc changes, even seemingly simple changes, are a disservice to all involved in the production: cast members, script prompters, stage crew, and lighting technicians are only a few that depend upon precision in a performance. So, know your marks, know your turns, know your gestures, and know your pace, then repeat and repeat again until perfection is effortless. Anything out of the ordinary, even a stutter or a change in profile, is a disservice to your fellow cast members. So, effortless perfection is the goal."

However, no matter how disciplined or well-rehearsed, the unexpected is bound to happen in debate, the theater, and in the courtroom. To paraphrase the great F. Lee Baily, "No matter how prepared you are, how skilled you are, and how right you think you are, the unexpected will happen. You are like a pilot of a plane whose instruments suddenly stop functioning. In such moments, you just have to fly the plane the best you can."

Poor Mrs. Stubey

To my shock, in my senior year, I was put into a high-level English class taught by a very nice and very interesting middle-aged lady named Mrs. Stubey. How I got into the advanced class, I did not know, but later I found out that it was based solely on my IQ; indeed, it was not based on my academic performance.

I was a puzzle to Mrs. Stubey and a challenge. She was a wonderful teacher, warm and inspiring, a little bit ditzy, and she was as perplexed by me as I was by her. I learned that her class was a college prep course, and, again, I thought this must be a mistake. Mrs. Stubey informed me early on that she enjoyed my contributions to class discussions and the content of my writing. Nonetheless, she told me in writing and in person that I had to do something about my spelling. Mrs. Stubey said, "it really disrupts your work and greatly distracts your reader, and Roger, no matter how good the content of your writing, you will not get the grades you deserve if your work is filled with so many spelling errors."

Of course, no one, including myself, knew anything about dyslexia in those days, as I only learned about it decades later.

So, I struggled along, and even though my teachers came to understand that I was intelligent, they just assumed that I was not motivated. After years of getting mediocre grades or worse, no matter how much I tried, I figured my grades were a losing battle. This befuddlement continued even through my college years, so I focused on those things I was good at, such as debate and drama, both of which I pursued with single-minded intensity.

My papers in other classes came back with comments similar to Mrs. Stubey's, "Very interesting," or "I liked your analysis, but really, really, you need to clean up your spelling." It was frustrating and demoralizing, and I got no support from my poor parents, neither of whom had more than a high school education. They just accepted the evaluation that I was slow—imaginative and fun to be around—but slow. How the dyslexia gene skipped over Terry, I do not know. He always earned exceptionally high grades; he was appointed editor of the school newspapers and garnered academic honors and scholarships.

Trouble at Home

In November of my senior year, the unimaginable happened—John F. Kennedy was assassinated. I was crushed and devastated beyond words. I admired him greatly. He was an inspiration, and for one who focused on rhetoric, he was a master and became my early idol. I was in my high school civics class when the news was announced. We watched, over and over again, the caravan in Dallas, the sudden lurching forward of the president and his beautiful wife trying, we learned later, to retrieve parts of his skull that had been blown apart along with our world. Even Dad, who had never voted for a Democrat in his life, was stunned into silence.

I brooded for many days and carried the deep sorrow for decades to come, as did much of the rest of the nation, but as far as I could tell at the moment, life went on. Vice President Lyndon Johnson stepped in, appropriate in his sorrow and courage, and though bruised deeply, the nation went on, but our world would never be the same.

In the spring of 1964, I became active in California politics, supporting the California Fair Housing Initiative, which was designed to prevent discrimination in the selling or renting of private homes or apartments. I spoke in favor of the initiative in various town hall meetings and was by far the youngest person to speak. The Republican representative speaking against the initiative gave me a dismissive response as I nailed him with the flaws in his logic. He was angry. My civics teacher was in the audience. He said nothing to me or the class about my comment, but to my shock, I got an A in his class, one of the few A's on my report card.

It was this incident, however, that revealed Dad's prejudice. My parents never discussed race in my presence. Dad's prejudice was not on the surface, probably because of his leadership position in the Federal Aviation Administration. He framed his opposition to the bill on the principle of property rights. It was his stated position that no one had the right to tell him who he could sell or rent his property to.

I responded, just as I had in my public statements: "No one can force you to sell your property, but if you choose to sell it, you can't discriminate as to the buyer based upon race. That is what the Bill of Rights and the Constitution is all about."

BOOM, that was all it took; his bigotry spewed forth in all its ugly forms. For the first time in my life, I did not back down from my father. I left the house, or I was kicked out, I am not sure which. I slept on the couch of the teachers who lived in another unit in our building for a few days. It was then that Mom stood tall. For the first time known to heaven or man, she enforced a sub rosa détente, and I was back in our apartment with the understanding that the subject would not be discussed again.

I have come to believe that bigotry is a disease. You are not born with it, you catch it from others, and it is only when you are confronted with the truth that you can be cured. I am pleased to say that ultimately Dad was cured of this disease.

Not Knowing How to Say Goodbye

I carry two sorrows that will never be erased, and I doubt I'll ever be forgiven. My first romantic sorrow arose when I left Manhattan Beach and Ellen, and then the second, two years later, when leaving Cairo and my girlfriend Dewi. I now realize that the many, many moves and the frequent changes I endured as a young man brewed in me the inability to deeply connect in friendships and in love. Love was an emotion that did not awaken in me until much, much later in life. I made many friends, but as with most expatriates, great friendships were for the moment, and should one be fortunate enough to reconnect sometime in the future, such relationships might quickly be renewed. But as for romance, such things were much more complex, much more poignant, and unfortunate. All I can say is I am deeply sorry for the pain I caused.

Part Four

CHAPTER NINETEEN

Arrival Cairo, Egypt, 1964

We stood on the exit ramp of the TWA Boeing 707, the setting sun dominating the western horizon and elongating our shadows on the tarmac. All was ablaze with a golden radiance greater than any I had encountered before or since. The tarmac rippled with 120-degree waves of heat, causing the golden terminal to dance before my eyes. *What was this land we were entering?* I asked myself.

It was August of 1964, and it seemed we had just walked into a world so different as to impair the sense of who we really were, much less of where we were. Once again, each member of our family—Mom, Dad, Terry, and I—found ourselves in a strange, new land. Knowing this would be the opportunity of a lifetime, Terry had elected to leave UC Santa Barbara and accompany us. A week earlier, we had celebrated my eighteenth birthday in Rome, just a week after reuniting with Dad in Washington DC. He'd spent most of the summer there preparing for his four-year assignment to the United States Agency for International Development (USAID), where he would work with flight inspection in Cairo.

Over dinner in Rome, Dad described the scope of his responsibilities during his four-year assignment to Egypt. He slipped into the clipped professional briefing style he always used when discussing his business. It went something like this:

"I will be training a seven-man Egyptian team in the use of ground and air navigation facilities for the purpose of upgrading the United Arab Republics's civilian flight control program. These guys are the top of the class of Egypt's Flight Facility team. Upon successful completion of the four-year program, we will turn over all equipment, including two DC-3s filled with navigation apparatus, to the Egyptian Civil Aviation Agency as a gift from the people of the United States."

To be fair, Dad could be informal or even highly colloquial as appropriate for the moment, but when addressing the troops, such as Terry and I, he reverted to command speak, as I liked to call it.

Herb Stanley

Herb Stanley, head of USAID, Civil Aviation Agency, Cairo, met us on the tarmac along with a small group of embassy and USAID staff members whose job, I quickly learned, was to usher us through the "Welcome to Egypt" protocol. I was immediately taken by Mr. Stanley. I liked his short, rotund appearance and his gracious, friendly mannerisms. I was captivated by his warmth and charm, the perfect fit for a Chief of Civil Aviation Agency Operations in North Africa. All in all, he was a man of stature.

"Welcome to Egypt, a land of immense historical importance," Herb effused as he ushered us into the magnificent two-story reception hall, where he continued his monologue. "And yes, a land of mystery and intrigue," he said somewhat whimsically. Then, looking directly at me for reasons I could not discern, he continued, "Oh, how I would like to be a young man again on my first visit to the Orient."

Herb Stanley was on loan from the Federal Aviation Administration to USAID, Africa, and Dad would be reporting to him for the next four years. Over time I learned that Herb was a keen observer and an equally keen listener. He possessed a sharp intellect, a dry sense of humor, a deep understanding of the Orient, and he was a master at distilling complex matters into iconic, often hilarious metaphors that were always spot on.

Whatever his motives, Herb quickly had me in the palm of his hand as he played up the moment. Along with his undeniable warmth and infectious charm, Herb fascinated me with his encyclopedic knowledge of his territory, his understated persona, and his keen understanding of events. He proved to be a good friend, not only when we were in Cairo but even years later in Alaska, of all places, where he retired from the FAA as chief of air traffic control of the Pacific region. Herb was a wonderful man, and he and my parents became and remained close friends until Dad's death forty years later.

Cairo International

The Cairo International VIP lounge was two stories high with large tinted atrium windows that softened the sun streaming through the western facade, turning all that it touched to a warm, golden glow. Immense oriental and Middle Eastern paintings, stonework, and woodcarvings competed with the setting sun as it illuminated all that it touched. So vivid the light and capacious the room that it could not be taken in from just one position. To appreciate the great room, we needed to move about as you would in a museum. The stone carvings, the paintings, the vases, and the sculptures all adorned the two-story-high interior, which was ablaze in the brilliant, luminescent golden light of the setting sun.

But we had little time to take in the impressive adornments, as we were rapidly ushered into the embassy's private lounge.

Cairo International, US Embassy Private Lounge

Nothing in my upbringing prepared me for such indulgence, luxury, and solicitousness. Certainly, we were not used to being pampered. Moreover, I was not prepared for the opulence of the official American Embassy Lounge of Cairo's new International Airport, where we were ensconced as we awaited our luggage. To put it mildly, this new world was extraordinarily different from anything I had ever experienced.

"This is a safe room," Herb said. "It is monitored and vetted for listening devices with each staff change, and it is maintained by embassy security personnel twenty-four seven." I noticed the few discrete but intense men at the corners of the room. We expected this based on our earlier briefings in the States, but the reality was unsettling nonetheless since the warning was obviously real.

Without exception, wherever we lived throughout the world, our family always secured off-base housing, and the same would be the case in Cairo. I never gave Dad's penchant for privacy much thought, but I soon came to understand that he was careful with whom he made close friendships. But, when such friendships were formed, they were for life.

"Irene," Herb said to my mother, to whom he was paying solicitous attention, "prepare yourself for an impressive greeting from the embassy staff. Extensive and dreadfully boring briefings are lined up for you. But don't fret, as torturously boring as they are, everyone goes through them, and at the end, there will be no test," he said, clearly trying his best to put Mom at ease, to no avail.

"What kind of briefings?" she asked, looking skeptical, a look with which our family was quite familiar. Herb responded jovially, "As the wife of a career Marine officer, I am certain that what they have to say will already be familiar to you." Of course, he was spot on, as wives of Marine officers were undoubtedly well acquainted with protocol and formal affairs.

"I understand this is your first trip to the Orient," Herb said, continuing to apply the balm, "and I know State thoroughly briefed you, but there are some unique subtleties that you might want to brush up on to comfortably navigate this part of the world." Herb was smooth, but so was Mom, and I could see that she felt a pinch of patronage in Herb's comment. So, drawing herself up to her five feet, ten-inch height, she gave Herb a look of studied equanimity, saying that she looked forward to the briefings.

Sensing a subtle change in my mother's demeanor, Herb again applied the balm saying with a smile, "Having navigated the Marine

Corp social scene, it is certain that you will have no trouble here." And, I was sure he was right. Mom graciously accepted Herb's offer of repose, and she and Herb were forevermore the closest of friends.

"Now," Herb went on, "you will find that Cairenes of all levels of social status are very fond of Americans who show them friendship and respect. As to servants, I say the same. They are grateful and helpful, and some are honest to the core, but you should be very careful not to tempt them. So, lock up items of any significant value. Rarely, if ever, are there break-ins, as the authorities deal severely with thieves, but you should expect that small items may go missing. It is just the way it is." Mioko-san was the only household help we ever had, and we would trust her with our lives, so, obviously, this would take some getting used to.

"Most importantly," Herb went on, "from the very first moment, understand that in-house help are debriefed regularly by the Egyptian secret service, so whether they love or despise you, they will have to report. Finally, for tonight," he said, looking at Terry and me, "assume all telephone conversations are monitored and perhaps recorded. So, you should report any strange events to your father."

All of this advice was imparted in the "clean" briefing room while we waited for our luggage to clear customs. There was no doubt in my mind that Cairo was going to be a fascinating station.

"Don't worry too much about all of this," Herb said, speaking to all of us now. "You will be thoroughly briefed over the next few days, so just relax and enjoy the surroundings, but do understand," he said in a serious voice, "the likelihood of there being listening devices in your hotel room is high. So, relax and just assume your verbal communications are not private. If you have a need to speak confidentially, just take a walk."

Really, I thought, relax and assume that whatever you say will likely be recorded. You will get used to it. And so, we did, and somehow it all worked out.

Malesh

I didn't know what to think. The energy of nighttime Cairo was spinning around me, vibrant, potent, and possibly dangerous, so I just laid back, taking in all I could see. Of course, the release of the new James Bond movie, *Goldfinger,* which Terry and I saw right before we departed from the States, left us "jacked" and ready for international intrigue. And this ancient city seemed ready to oblige.

Exciting yet chaotic, mesmerizing yet electric, the city seethed with energy yet maintained its balance. Cars wove in and out, dodging buses, trucks, pedestrians, camels, and donkeys, all sharing the streets and seemingly indifferent to the cacophony of horns, as arms shoved into any car window if the driver dared to slow down. All seemed chaotic, almost frantic, but our driver managed expertly, maneuvering safely through what appeared to me as the "City Deranged," an appellation I affixed to Cairo's nighttime traffic many decades later after reading Max Rodenbeck's brilliant book *The City Victorious*.

As unnerving our nighttime adventure, one apparent gesture stayed with me all these years. It was a gesture of tolerance, delivered by an arm extending out the window of a car or truck, or from the driver of a cart, a palm lifted gently up to the heavens, translated verbally into Arabic as *Malesh*, meaning "never mind," or "no big deal." It is extended as an apology for an affront and is almost always accepted.

Yet, I wondered how Cairo could function with chaos seemingly ruling the night. Perhaps I found the answer in a dance.

The Mystical Dance

Shortly before arriving in Cairo, I read from one of the tourist books given to us by the State Department about the whirling dervishes. Famed throughout the Middle East and many other areas of the world, the members of this sect often entertained at nightclubs and special dinner parties. The dervish dancers, however, are much more than entertainers.

The dancer's purpose is to accomplish cosmic unity, accelerating faster and faster until the dancers, their faces, and their frocks were no longer discernable from the blur of the dance. Then the pace of the dance slows, inappreciably at first, until the bodies and faces are again nearly motionless.

I came to understand that though the physical dance concludes, the spiritual dance never ends, as it is through their dancing that the mystics enter into the presence of God. We joined the dance when we entered Cairo proper, and through the apparent chaos of the night, we were delivered to our hotel, Cairo's gem, the Nile Hilton. But where we were in the dance was yet to be determined.

Welcome to Cairo—Irene and Harry on the left; Roger and Terry on the right.

Spy Versus Spy

The first thing Terry and I did when we checked into our room on the twenty-second floor of the Nile Hilton Hotel was to go straight to the balcony. Terry and I were to share this room until our permanent housing was secured, which would not be easy, but the view was incredible.

In the distance, across the Nile to the south, we could see golden lights bathing the three pyramids of Giza and, barely discernable, the much smaller, enigmatic Sphinx. I am not sure how long we stood at the rail, but certainly, it was for some time before we realized there was work to do. We needed to check the room for bugs, not living bugs, of course, but electronic bugs. After all, that is what James Bond would have done.

We found no bugs, but our search was cut short when the plaster cast hieroglyphic over the dresser we were inspecting slipped from its frame with a tremendous crash that brought our sleuthing to a quick and shameful end. Yikes, the right lower corner had cracked.

Unbelievably, the incident went unreported. Of course, if the room was bugged, we never found out. So, at least for the moment, we gave up our lives as counterspies and reverted to being tourists, peering out from our balcony, overlooking the Nile and the Island of Zamalek. We both had binoculars, and we spent several hours just seeing all that we could from our room. It was a mystical time.

I do not believe that either Terry or I slept that night. Images of whirling dervishes and complex, mysterious edifices were spinning around in my head. I spent the night wondering what the future would hold.

CHAPTER TWENTY
The Portico

We created more than a bit of a stir as we drove along the eastern esplanade of the Nile, top down with Dad at the wheel of our Pontiac Lemans convertible. Just before we reached the famous Shepheard Hotel, we turned into Cairo's Colonial District, one of the oldest districts of "modern" Cairo. We found the major embassies here, with the exception of Great Britain's. Their diplomatic privileges were revoked as a result of the 1954 Suez Crisis.

These were "interesting times" to be living in Egypt, so we were told.

Trade unionists, communists, and members of the Muslim Brotherhood all haunted the shadows. Still, the Brotherhood ruled the night, and they remain a powerful faction even up to the date of this publication. All of these factions claimed an exclusive right to the loyalty of the masses.

But Cairo, as Max Rodenback wrote in *The City Victorious*, ". . . (i)n its confusion longed not for a slogan but for a savior." The people turned first to the stately General Mohammed Naguib, a highly respected army officer "untainted by foreign affection," to "quickly and rightfully establish order." But these turbulent times were unsuited for a thoughtful, temperate leader such as General Naguib. Soon, the general was put under house arrest by supporters of the charismatic Gamal Abdel Nasser, who took over as president in 1954.

Throughout my time in Egypt, I never heard the name or any reference to General Naguib though I did learn of him many decades later. Sadly, he lived out his life in isolation, under guard at his country estate.

Under Nasser's rule, in 1958, Egypt united with Syria to form the United Arab Republic with Cairo as the capital and Nasser as president. Syria's self-determination was undermined under the United Arab Republic, and the country seceded from the short-lived union after a coup d'état by the Syrian Ba'th Party in 1961.

When we arrived in Egypt in 1964, Nassar still touted the professed union between Egypt and Syria. The unified flag was still being flown, and the new name of the United Arab Republic was required in official documents. The two-star flag adorned every major street corner, light pole, store window, and government car. Despite Nasser's pretense, though, the union clearly was a facade.

History was not on my mind as we drove along the Nile Esplanade, top down with the Lemans convertible causing heads to turn, followed by waving salutes and cheers. No doubt the cheers were for the Pontiac, but to be clear, everywhere we went, with or without the Lemans, we were greeted by friendly, accommodating, and solicitous Egyptians. For me, it was a great time to be an American in Egypt.

Quiet dignity subsumed the moment when we turned into the sedate, historic Diplomatic Quarter. Gravitas and permanency oozed from behind these gated walls. Stern guards, garbed in the formal uniforms of their country, stood by at attention. I reacted as the architects of these formidable compounds intended: I was in awe.

The American Embassy

We approached the American Embassy, surrounded by formidable stone walls topped by wrought-iron spear points. Two Marine guards, dressed in colonial blue trousers and dark blue jackets, snapped to attention as we approached and delivered a crisp salute to my father.

No identification was required, and no salute was returned. The significance of this preferential treatment and lack of response did not sink in for me until months later.

Once waved through the main gate, Dad drove past several fine out-buildings, neatly set back from the main drive, including the historic two-story library, which attracted scholars from all over the world, and the Marine House where the guards were quartered. Sadly, these two structures were burned to the ground shortly after our arrival as the result of very serious solidarity riots in the Belgian Congo.

The main office of the United States Agency for International Development (USAID) was physically connected to the American Embassy by a somewhat awkward adjunct attached to the back corner, where Herb spent most of his time. Dad maintained a small office next to Herb's. Still, he spent most of his time at the new facilities constructed at Cairo International, which were designed to house teaching facilities, maintenance equipment, and hangers for two newly refurbished DC-3s. The hangers even had room for the Pontiac Tempest.

The Program

I do not know Dad's official charter, as prescribed by the United States Agency for International Development (USAID). My very simple understanding is that he was responsible for shepherding Egypt's fledging Civil Aviation Flight Control Programs into the twentieth century.

Modern flight control programs in 1964 relied upon the accurate electronic interface between ground radar, also known as the tower team, and the inflight team. My father's USAID team was responsible for overseeing the training of Egypt's civilian flight control personnel, the training of Egyptian pilots in the rigors of inflight navigation, and the maintenance of ground control, planes, and related equipment. Dad considered the safety of those who would depend on his trainees, whether on the ground or in the air, his first and foremost responsibility—as one mistake could be fatal.

The initial work took place in the classrooms, but when the candidates were ready, their classwork was split between ground and air. The pride of the program was two thoroughly refurbished DC-3s. The planes were filled with state-of-the-art navigation equipment that allowed flight technicians on the ground to compare their readings of height, speed, latitude, and longitude against the readings produced by the ground-based facilities. The ability to simultaneously compare ground control data with inflight data was the bedrock of modern air navigation at that time. Of course, this was before the advent of satellite communication, which radically changed the world of navigation.

After the four-year training program, the DC-3s would be gifted by USAID to the United Arab Republic (UAR). No doubt pride was at stake for the pilots, but fear certainly played a role as well, as one word from my father was enough to bounce a candidate.

When not in the air, Dad spent his time at the brand-new Cairo International Airport facilities. He told his recruits, "Take good care of this equipment, and at the end of the program, the planes and ground equipment will be America's gift to your country."

As you might guess, most of Dad's time was not spent in classrooms. "The evenings are for book learning," he would say, "but the days are for flying, and there is no better teacher than the sky."

The Marine Guards

I remained impressed by the attention the Marine guards paid to my father when we approached the Embassy's main gate. After all, there was no outward sign of Dad's prior service. I later learned that his arrival was highly anticipated due to the status he had earned at Cherry Point during World War II and his exploits during the Korean War, where he and other DC-3 pilots employed the tactic of be-gone-before-they-know-you-are-there.

The embassy entry guards were expected to know all civilians attached to the embassy, and this, of course, included Dad. Still, there was no doubt that the Marine guards treated him with the utmost respect, saluting him each time he approached the gate. What puzzled me, however, was that Dad would return the salutes only with a nod. When I asked Dad about this protocol, he said simply, "I am no longer on active duty, so it would be inappropriate for me to return a salute." I later came to understand that there was more to it than that, mostly the resentment and hurt that always lingered about the way his time in the Marine Corps had ended.

Our Briefing Officer

Soon after our arrival in Cairo, Terry and I were scheduled for what I understood would be a full day briefing (meaning lectures) by the embassy's family liaison briefing officer. To put it mildly, I was not looking forward to a day of lectures, but to my surprise, the time was well spent, informative, and even more than a bit entertaining.

I remember our briefing officer as tall and thin, possessing a marshal demeanor tempered by a wicked sense of humor. Her great skill in driving home important facts by using her pointer as a sword impressed me. She even transferred her weight forward when attacking the pull-down map of central Cairo, much like a fencer executing the aggressive and deadly *fleche* movement. It was something to see.

"The area within a short walk of Tahrir Square oozes with historical gravitas," she said. "The Egyptian Museum of Antiquities draws tourists and academics from all over the world. Visitors frequently come to explore the Folklore Arts House, the Mogamma Government building, the headquarters of the Arab League, the historic Kasr El Dobara Evangelical Church, the campus of the American University in Cairo, founded in 1919, and much more. These are just a small representation of what you will find in or near the square," she gushed.

Not for a moment did I find her dissertation boring. "This is just a small portion of the history that awaits you," she continued, wielding her telescoping pointer in a way that threatened various landmarks on the map.

"After you become acquainted with the major landmarks around the square, which you will be doing this afternoon, you can expand your adventures to include the Island of Zamalek, the Nile Esplanade, and on and on. So, mark your map with points of interest which you can check off as time goes on."

In fact, time went by quickly, and I filled my notebook with high points, good suggestions, many pithy phrases, and more.

I kept the map and my notes long after I left Cairo, but sadly, over time, much was lost.

Staying Out of Trouble

The remainder of our morning session was learning lessons primarily devoted to staying out of trouble. These lessons stuck with me for the rest of my life. They might be of interest.

"Lesson One. Keep only the amount of money you might reasonably need for your current excursion with you when out and about. I am certain your father has your passports under lock and key, and I can see that your wallet with your embassy ID is in the travel pouch inside your pants. I assume you know that the cloth covers steel webbing capable of withstanding the swipe of a knife blade," the briefing officer advised. I knew that, of course.

"It is intended, however, that you use only the loop that best matches the color of the pants you are wearing, while the other loop should be tucked away. If you don't match the color, you might as well put a sign on your chest saying wallet down here, with an arrow pointing to the loop." I felt more than a bit foolish as I had put my belt through both loops, and yes, the tan loop stood out dramatically on my black trousers.

"Lesson Two. Keep a throw-away wallet with a few bills in it. If you are accosted, pull out your wallet and throw it as far away as you can while running in the opposite direction, yelling 'Haraami! Haraami!' which means thief. Almost certainly, the thief will run after your wallet, giving you time to head for the hills.

"Lesson Three. Don't get me wrong," our briefing officer said. "Cairo and most of Egypt are very law-abiding, but sometimes young men venture into places they should not be, particularly the port cities," she said without any hint of condemnation. "I am sure you young gentlemen would never go to such places, but if you inadvertently wander where you should not be, or if you get into any type of trouble, the best advice I can give you is to get to a taxi and get out of there! If you can't readily find a taxi, go to the nearest hotel or shop and ask them to call the number of the American Consulate Office, which should be in your wallet.

"Lesson Four. When crossing traffic in Arab countries, remember there are no rules *except for one*: vehicles must yield to pedestrians, so walk slowly and deliberately, and drivers will make room for you. If you stop or even hesitate, that will be an invitation to speed by you. If you wait for someone to yield, you will likely be standing around for a long time," she said with a smile.

"Lesson Five. When taking a taxi, which you almost certainly will do, first write out the address on a city map. Know the distance and have your destination written out in Arabic. Always ask the driver for the expected time and expected cost, and have the driver repeat the name and address of your destination with confidence. These precautions will reduce the driver's likelihood of taking you for a longer ride than necessary.

"Lesson Six. Make sure you have the phone number of the embassy in your pouch. If anything goes wrong, call the US Embassy, explain you are a US citizen, and ask for assistance. You will quickly get the help you need.

"Lesson Seven. Most important," our briefing officer said directly, "don't leave a group at night unless you know exactly where you are going.

"Lesson Eight. Finally, please remember that there is safety in numbers."

Yikes. Travel, as described by our briefing officer, was not nearly as carefree as I thought. I memorized my notes in my travel diary, and I took her advice to heart, except for the admonition to travel in groups. I simply could not resist traveling on my own. I found myself in a few challenging circumstances due to my own stupidity, but whether by fate or good fortune, kindness or mercy, I managed.

In return, I was blessed with a lifetime of memories.

The Heart of Cairo

During lunch, Terry and I were each given a map of the city, which included our hotel, the embassy, and, of course, Tahrir Square—all the significant buildings and parks within walking distance of the heart of Cairo.

As soon as we were finished eating, our briefing officer arose, saying, "It is time for you to put this morning's efforts to work, and if you stick close to Tahrir Square, the Nile Promenade, and the immediate surrounding sites, you will be fine."

Then, with a bit of a smile, handing each of us a small pouch, she added, "And if you get in trouble, in your pouch is a simplified map of what we reviewed today and, very important, my card with my direct phone line, which will be answered twenty-four seven, just in case you go awry. I mentioned it in the lecture, remember?" Watching us, she added, "The pouch is intended to be carried inside your pants. Remember to use the loop closest to the color of the pants you are wearing."

She then paused. "If you run into any trouble, day or night, hail a cab and tell your driver to take you to the American Embassy or Consulate or call my direct line any time day or night. The number is in your pouch."

"But now, your father will be waiting for you here at four o'clock, and that's *Marine time*," she announced, mimicking Dad's stiff briefing style to a tee, "so you have three hours to yourselves."

"Tomorrow morning, be here by nine thirty, as you will be taking your driver's license test," she said, leaving both Terry and me a bit stunned. Terry, of course, stepped in quickly, telling me, "Just focus on today!" and, as usual, he was right. The moment required all of our attention since we were stepping into the adventure of a lifetime.

On Our Own

We left the embassy with great anticipation and more than a little nervousness. Tahrir (Liberation) Square was only a short walk from the embassy, but the transition was startling.

We left behind the shade, tranquility, and security of Embassy Row, which was formidable and guarded. We passed the buildings housing international organizations, which I recall because they had teams in our softball league.

Suddenly, we were at Tahrir Square, standing before the front gate of the American University of Cairo (AUC), where I would spend my freshman and sophomore years of college. Our briefing officer had informed us we would be touring the school the coming week and suggested we undertake a quick walk through the grounds to understand the gravitas of the school we would be attending.

Many years after I left Cairo, the main campus of the American University was moved to Heliopolis, a suburb near the Cairo International Airport. Though I understood the need for the move, as it facilitated a four-fold increase in enrollment, I lamented the loss of the energy and excitement of Tahrir Square.

Already we had to make hard choices on our first unaccompanied walk around Cairo. We chose Tahrir Square only because we knew we would get a guided tour of AUC the following week.

From our perspective, the country seemed stable, and those whom we met were friendly and hospitable. But, unapparent to Terry and me, sedition and treason roiled below the surface, stirred by the blood of martyrs for causes, ancient and new. Little did we know that the world would become transfixed for decades to come by events unfolding in Egypt during the years we were there.

Khedivial Opera House, oldest opera house in Africa, destroyed by fire 1971.
Image via Wikimedia Commons.

Mogamma Al-Tahrir, Tahrir Square by VascoPlanet Cairo.
Photo by Vyacheslav Argenberg.

Egyptian Museum of Antiquities by Egyptian Photography.
Photo by Ahmed Alattar.

CHAPTER TWENTY-ONE

The Test

Dad had made clear when we arrived in Cairo that we would not have access to the Pontiac Tempest, as the Cairo traffic was notoriously bad, so I had no idea why we would need a driver's license. We were not accustomed to questioning Dad, but Terry could not resist, "Dad, I thought we wouldn't be driving? What's the deal? Why are we getting our license?"

"I want you to have a license, just in case," Dad said casually.

"Just in case of what?" Terry followed up as I listened intently.

"Just in case, that's all," Dad said, closing out the discussion.

Huh? I thought. I was more than a little nervous about taking a driver's test, as I had heard and seen enough horror stories of driving in Cairo. Terry pushed the subject a bit, but Dad said simply, "No choice! I don't expect you will be driving, but you never know when it might be necessary."

So, the next morning, with Dad at the wheel, we made our way to the Department of Motor Vehicles. Don't forget, Dad was a former drag racer and fighter pilot, so I was not surprised that he didn't break a sweat, and I was greatly relieved to see Herb curbside directing us into a private alley off the busy road.

"I just wanted you to be as comfortable as possible when taking your test," Herb said with the near omnipresent twinkle in his eye, communicating that he was very much enjoying the surprise. But even Herb's presence did not quell my nervousness, as the traffic coming to the Department of Motor Vehicles had been the typical horrific, swirling mess. We went inside.

An officious, stern officer was waiting for us. Herb seemed to know the officer. As they exchanged pleasantries shaking hands, Herb identified him as the test administrator. He gave us a firm look and a brief nod. "First," he announced sternly, "the written test!" Terry and I were told we would each be shown three different street signs, and we had to identify their meaning. I was near panic, as I had paid little interest to street signs and wasn't at all certain that I could pass such a test.

The administrator held up a traditional-looking stop sign in Arabic with a large hand held with the palm out, toward the driver. "Stop," I said somewhat tentatively, thinking there might be a trick.

"Good," came the authoritative reply.

Next, he showed us a vertical arrow with a sharp, ninety-degree bent to the right.

"Right turn," I said with growing confidence.

"Yes," he said again, and I was feeling much better, and then the third sign, administered with a bit of a sly smile—a circle with four curved arrows peeling off to four different quadrants.

"Roundabout," I said with some trepidation.

"Good," came the reply with a slight nod, "You passed the written test."

I almost fainted. Terry passed as well. That was much better than expected, but still, we had to drive.

We were shown outside for the dreaded driver's test, and Terry went first. He was directed to the Tempest. Thank goodness we would have a car with which we were familiar. "Drive to the sign ahead," our administrator instructed Terry. The sign was only ten feet or so ahead. "Good, now back in reverse to the same spot," so he did. "Good!"

The administrator then directed me to do the same. That was it; we both passed! I was greatly relieved and more than a bit surprised at the ease of the test, but only for a moment, as I saw Herb's hand linger a bit during his goodbye handshake when he thanked the administrator for his efficiency.

We then returned to the Embassy for additional lessons from our briefing officer. When we arrived, she was waiting for us and expressed delight that we had passed our tests. I wondered how she knew we had passed. She then took us into the briefing room for our final lesson, asked if we had any questions, then told us our dad was waiting downstairs to take us home.

CHAPTER TWENTY-TWO

On the Wall

Cairo, Egypt 1964

It was near dusk, Thanksgiving Day 1964, when the embassy called Dad. Anti-American demonstrations were expected that evening with a strong potential for violence. Americans were being warned to *shutter up*, a euphemism for "stay indoors with protective shutters in place." Such precautions were required for all embassy family residences, though this was the only time in my two years in Cairo that they were issued.

The demonstrations were in response to the United States providing assistance to the Netherlands, which was evacuating Dutch refugees under siege in the Belgian Congo. The rescue efforts brought about widespread protests across Africa, including Egypt. As a career Marine, Dad was no stranger to trouble, so we complied.

Heavy shutters bordered the windows of our three-story villa in Maadi (a garden community approximately ten miles south of Cairo), which Dad had rented during our initial stay at the Nile Hilton. Up until then, I had not given them much thought. Nor had I given much thought to the locked armoire in my parent's bedroom on the second floor of our villa. I supposed that its purpose was to protect my parents' liquor and cigarettes from pilfering, perhaps from Terry and me.

My suppositions evaporated quickly, just after the embassy called my father. As soon as he hung up the phone, Dad directed Terry and me to shutter and latch all of the windows and doors of our three-story villa. When finished, we were to move the heavy furniture up against the shutters. Next, we were to put Penny in the backyard, where we knew she'd raise a fierce defense if any intruder penetrated the perimeter, an unlikely possibility given the canals and the thick thorn hedges surrounding the back and front yards. Though Penny had never bitten anyone, Terry and I trained her to put up a fierce show, a loud ruckus of barking, snarling, and other menacing behavior if a stranger appeared. Once Penny was properly introduced, strangers turned into fast friends. It only occurred to me then that Penny's training had been intentional.

When we finished securing the shutters, we quickly made our way to our parent's second-floor bedroom, unsure of what to expect. The cupboard door to the large armoire was open. In addition to cartons of cigarettes and alcohol (which did not surprise me), there were various weapons, including Terry's and my 16-gauge shotguns, several of Dad's scoped hunting rifles, and boxes of ammunition and ammunition aprons.

Dad handed out the shell aprons and shells (tied together in packs), which we quickly placed into our aprons. I had no idea that any of this made the trip to Cairo, but there was no time to consider such surprises now. I watched Dad measuring Terry's and my reactions. Having learned to hunt in Utah, Terry and I were no strangers to weapons, and, certainly, we were accustomed to taking orders. So, we fell in line.

Just hefting my Winchester 16-gauge shotgun was oddly comforting, and having spent many weekends in the fields surrounding Salt Lake City hunting quail and pheasants, neither Terry nor I was nervous. In fact, the weight of our shell aprons and the heft of our shotguns had a calming effect.

We then headed to the open stairway, which led to the third floor that housed my bedroom and bathroom, which were at the backside of the house. A large patio partially covered by an overgrown trellis was in front of the third floor. A three-foot wall, wide enough to sit upon, surrounded the rest of the patio. Its only purpose was to provide protection.

Mincing no words, Dad quickly briefed Terry and me on what he expected of us: Terry would take the right corner of the front parapet wall, and I the left. From our positions, Terry and I could easily see the front yard, the front gate, and the street, but Dad made it clear that no matter what, we were to keep very still with our eyes just above the ledge of the wall unless he directed otherwise.

"Your shotguns should be out of site, faced away from each other, with the safeties on unless I tell you otherwise," he said. In the background, I could hear rhythmic chanting, rough and edgy, and though I didn't know what it was at the time, I could hear the pounding of wooden staffs on the street. The unnerving sound grew closer.

Dad's last directions were straightforward, something like: "Keep your weapons out of sight unless I direct otherwise. Keep your safeties on unless I tell you, *Safeties off*, and last, if I order you to rack your weapons, stand up quickly, rack them with authority, and immediately crouch down and move fifteen feet away from your position."

I knew exactly what he meant. There is no sound like a shotgun shell being moved into position for firing. His last directive was a bit unsettling, "Don't show yourself and keep out of sight unless I give the order to fire, and if I order you to fire at will, you are on your own until you hear otherwise from me."

I am aware that many self-defense experts recommend not racking your weapon if an intruder is in your home, and that is probably good advice, as it gives away your location. However, racking your shotgun before the perimeter of your home has been breached, in my view, may still be the best deterrent, as the chilling sound may convince the intruder to flee. But what do I know about such things? This was the first and only time in my life I was confronted with such a menace.

Dad was high up in the deep shadows of the trellis now. He had the best view of the street, but I could barely see him even though I knew where he was. Dad gave us one last direction before he disappeared into the foliage: "If I give the order *Direct fire*, don't think; just shoot to kill. But no matter what happens, keep as low as you can. No matter what, don't fire unless I give the order." I agreed.

The source of the banging on the pavement and the chanting were now visible. A large crowd stood directly before our house, thirty to forty robed protesters, disciplined, standing in orderly rows, pounding the street in unison with six-foot wooden staffs.

They began crowding up against the entry gate. "Stand and rack," Dad directed. We racked, covered, and moved as directed. They left quickly.

Twice, the protestors came back; twice again, we racked, ducked, and moved. The third time they continued to pound the pavement for some time, yelling Arabic words we did not understand, but they didn't approach the gate again.

Finally, they left, and thankfully, they did not return. We remained behind the wall through the night. I nodded off more than a few times, but each time I awoke, I could see Dad watching from the shadows.

We learned the next day that mobs burned the 100-year-old American Library to the ground and did significant damage to the Marine House. Welcome to Cairo.

The "mob" was clearly not a mob, as they knew exactly what they were doing. The library and the Marine House were not technically part of the embassy. Therefore, according to international law, their burning was not considered a direct attack on the United States. The same mob burned a small part of the entry gate to the American University, but again, this was not an attack on the United States.

Two days later, except for the sad burned-out remnants of the library and Marine House, all seemingly returned to normal. The street crowds were as friendly as ever. While non-American students spoke their condolences quietly, fellow American students gathered in private to discuss our Thanksgiving Day experiences.

We learned from discussions with our friends that our home was the only residence singled out for aggressive demonstrations. When I asked naively, "Why did we get singled out?" One friend responded, "You don't know?"

"Know what?" I replied.

"Don't you know that your father is the head spook of the Cairo branch?"

My dad was a spy? "No, I *don't* know that!" I replied truthfully, but from then on, my eighteen-year-old mind was never the same.

The Rest of the Story

Dad was many things. For much of his life, he partied, drank, and argued too much; and certainly, he was away from home too much. With the exception of his grandchildren, for whom he showed nothing but unremitting love and kindness, he certainly disciplined too much. But through it all, he was a serious man who loved and served his country well.

CHAPTER TWENTY-THREE

On Thin Ice

Our first winter break since arriving in Egypt found Terry, our friend Jack, and me traveling deck class from Alexandria, Egypt, to Piraeus, Greece. Jack was the perfect traveling companion; he was very bright, with an excellent sense of humor, and, most importantly, he was easy to get along with.

This trip turned out to be an adventure of a lifetime. It is an understatement to say that it did not turn out the way we planned, and certainly not how we had sold the trip to our parents.

Jack's father had recently accepted a Fulbright Scholarship for studying and teaching at the University of Cairo. He was a renowned archeologist and the author of many well-known books on the archeological treasures of the Levant, a large area in the Eastern Mediterranean region of Western Asia.

What better way for us to spend our four-week winter vacation than tracking his works in the Greek Peninsula and Peloponnesian Islands?

How we got from the Greek Islands to summiting a mountain pass trying to get to Geneva with a broken accelerator in the midst of a snowstorm is odd. Let's just say it sort of worked out that way. To appreciate our predicament, you have to hear the whole story.

Alexandria to Piraeus

The weather in Alexandria was clear and mild on the day of our voyage, which was fortunate as we were traveling deck class to save our funds. We had secured passage on a Greek freighter at a reasonable fare, but as we were about to board, we learned that we could travel deck class for one-third of the price, and since we were frugal young men, we changed our accommodations.

We sailed out of Alexandria with warm and sunny weather lifting our spirits, but by noon, the temperature had plummeted. Deep cumulous clouds with dark underbellies had set in. We were prepared, however, for all eventualities. We dug out tarps from each of our bags and used them to pitch a canopy with sharply angled sidewalls to shield us from the elements. We lashed our tarps to nearby crates, so our makeshift tent was ensconced among several storage containers. Finally, we positioned smaller crates around the perimeter with our Marine duffel bags (supplied by Dad), securing the sidewalls to the floor, creating a formidable redoubt against the elements.

Several other deck class passengers gave hearty approval of our ingenuity while sharing a drink or two. But in the end, we knew to be careful with casual acquaintances that we would likely never see again.

All our preparations were well worth the time. By midafternoon, the wind came up, and the rain followed hard. We moved freight around a bit more as the storm picked up, but all seemed well. The rainwater was diverted by our homemade runnels that Jack ingeniously devised using freight and canvas. Though it was somewhat of a miserable night, we were dry and were afforded some sleep.

The morning dawned bright and clear, and Terry and I effusively praised Jack's engineering powers. No water had reached us, and though we had rocked and rolled more than a little, we were wedged in like babies in a cradle.

Athens

We stood at the rail as we entered the harbor of Piraeus. The port was somewhat seedy, dirty, busy, clogged with traffic, and unsettling, typical of many of the world's busiest port cities. Above the chaos, on the hills in the distance, the sun was glorious as it reflected off the impossibly white houses vividly contrasted by the intense blue water.

Soon we disembarked, locating the bus that would take us closest to the Athens Youth Hostel. The bus ride from Piraeus to the hostel was uneventful. Almost immediately after exiting the bus, our way to the youth hostel was disrupted by a march of Greek Communist Party members. Protestors waved large red flags with hammers and sickles and chanted anti-American slogans venting anger over America's growing presence in Vietnam. The street seethed with protesters and counterprotesters.

We pressed into a nearby shop portico to let the protest move on.

Today, living near Berkeley, such things are commonplace, uncomfortable, yes, but nonetheless, you adjust. But here in Athens, in December of 1964, it was like nothing any of us had ever seen. When the protestors passed by, we continued on our way to the hostel, where we checked in. Then, the second part of our education began.

We made our way to the café on the sidewalk in front of the hostel. Here the youth of the world gathered. Conversations were serious and fun, profound and frivolous, heated one moment, then jovial the next—all in a multitude of languages.

Those gathered in the café exchanged all types of information in the spirit of comrades. "The skiing in the alps is absolutely fabulous," one offered. "How much does it cost to get to . . .?" was answered a multitude of times. "You just have to try the Baklava at . . ." was added to the wealth of information. And it was here at such a table, we learned that Europe lay open before us and that for three dollars we could travel freight class on a train from Athens, through the middle of Yugoslavia, to Venice in twenty-four hours. At this point in time, my brain exploded. "And you can rent a small Fiat station wagon and go anywhere in Europe in a matter of days, just for a few dollars a day," a new friend added.

Wow!

The next day we purchased our cheap tickets to Venice and boarded the train. To save money, we traveled in freight class with the chickens. We shared a boxcar with other frugal passengers, sleeping on crates, but otherwise, we spent our time hanging out and buying food and drinks in the lounge car.

Venice was magnificent, but it was a bust for three single young men on a budget. The streets were empty, very few restaurants were open, and worst of all, the youth hostel was empty.

So, what now? On to Geneva

I wanted to see the Swiss Alps in all their glory. Since Jack and Terry were not skiers, I had a little convincing to do. I referred to the rest of the sidewalk chatter from Athens and reminded them that we could see the Alps for practically nothing. We could rent a Fiat station wagon here in Venice, put the car on a train that would go through the Alps, then drive the Fiat into Geneva, which was only a few hours from Munich. And what self-respecting young man could resist the Biergartens of Munich? Finally, Jack and Terry were all in, but the list of things we did not know was long indeed.

We rented the "acclaimed" Fiat station wagon, stowed it on a flat car, and boarded the train that would take us through the Alps to Geneva.

The train took us in and out of mountain tunnels, edging up against the sky, and laying low as misty clouds and snuggling fingerlets stretched deep into the crevices and valleys of my mind. Nothing in my travels, not the mountains of Utah, Colorado, or Japan, nor the magnificent Sierra Nevada, compared to what towered above, below, and around us. All was stunningly beautiful.

Geneva

Our train arrived in Geneva in the midafternoon. We retrieved our car as light snow began to fall and darkness closed in. We quickly gained altitude in our rented Fiat wagon. The highway was well-engineered, allowing us to make good time.

It was a pitch-black, moonless, starless night when suddenly, the engine stopped running. It idled regardless of how hard Terry pushed down on the accelerator. He had no choice but to pull over onto the precious narrow shoulder of the curvy mountain road. Cars raced by, paying little attention to the 130 kph (80 mph) speed limit. Now we were in complete darkness except for the intense strobe of headlights from passing cars that blinded us and intensified the whiteout conditions caused by the snowstorm.

Thankfully, Jack was familiar with European cars and had a clear head in a crisis. He opened the engine hatch and soon realized that the accelerator cable had snapped. The engine, which was in the back of the car, under the luggage compartment, was not responding to the movement of the pedal.

I am not sure who came up with the solution. We concluded that if we removed the floorboard of the rear luggage compartment, someone could manually operate the lever to which the cable should have been connected. Concerned about exhaust coming back into the car, in another burst of ingenuity, we rolled down the front windows and opened the back hatch so that the exhaust did not come back into the car. Brilliant!

With the hatch open, however, the noise was horrendous. So, I sat in the middle seat to relay accelerator instructions to Jack. He was straddling the engine to operate the carburetor manually while Terry managed the driving.

Off we went, and all went well. Folks who passed us by were dumbfounded, laughing and pointing, but giving us a friendly wave or thumbs-up.

In addition to my communication responsibilities, I was the

navigator. No great task while we were in the mountains, but as we entered Geneva, things got dicey.

I tried to memorize the directions while things were somewhat under control, but it was hard to see the street signs through the thick, heavy snow. Then, disaster struck.

As we entered a roundabout in central Geneva, whether out of fun or due to Jack having become deaf from the city's noise, we were in trouble. When Terry yelled "slow" as we entered a large roundabout, which I dutifully relayed to Jack, Jack yelled "Go!" and poured on the gas.

Terry yelled louder and louder, "Slow, slow!" which I dutifully repeated, only to have Jack almost maniacally yell, "Go, Go!" I later concluded that the exhaust vapors had gotten to him.

Around and around we went, faster and faster, as neither Terry nor I could figure out which turnoff we should take. Then Terry chose a turnoff and drove out of the roundabout, simultaneously turning off the ignition switch; a good idea it seemed, but the front wheel of the Fiat hit the curb that was buried in snow, bending the wheel mount!

We limped to the youth hostel, each of us as wobbly as our right front wheel. The next morning, after shelling out a good portion of our remaining cash to get the wheel and the accelerator cable fixed, we decided we had had enough of Geneva, so we set off for the famous beer halls of Munich.

To Munich

How could we resist! We arrived in the early evening. Here, for the first time, I got drunk—really, really drunk. Fortunately, the Germans, no strangers to overdrinking, had designed the Hofbräuhaus bathrooms with large open drains in the sinks! Then, even more glorious, I discovered that on each side of the sinks were—handlebars. Yes, handlebars whose sole purpose was to assist patrons in remaining upright when singing to the sink. I was not the first to need them, but need them, I did.

Late the next morning, nursing my first real hangover, we learned from other hostellers that the Winter Olympic Games in Innsbruck were only a two-and-a-half-hour drive away. The Olympic Games! Who could resist?

So, off we went on a harrowing, circuitous drive up and through the mountains. It was well worth the effort. We arrived late, of course, and found no room in any of the hostels. With our funds seeping away, we were getting a bit nervous, but hey, the town was like a carnival. We partied well into the night until some newfound friends invited us to sleep on comforters on their living room floor. Soon we were fast asleep. Life was good.

We were up early due to the racket of fellow sojourners preparing to join the crowds on the slopes. If we were willing to climb the hills above the finish line, we were told we could watch the end of the giant slalom competition for free, and that is what we did.

Olympic Winter Games Innsbruck 1964

This was a great time to be a young American abroad. America was respected and admired, and casual acquaintances treated us with hospitality and friendship wherever we went. So lavish the bonhomie of our newfound friends, they urged us to stay on, but we explained that time was running out, as we had to get back to Florence to drop our car off before making our way back through Yugoslavia to Greece.

As we were about to leave, one of our new friends yelled out, "Wait, wait," as he ran into the next room. He quickly returned with three large USA patches he had just purchased from a vendor on the slopes. Our friend had the patches in one hand and a bottle of glue in the other. "Here," he said excitedly as he immediately started gluing the patches onto our bags. "No matter what you hear," he went on, "Americans are loved all through Europe and especially in Eastern Europe." It turned out to be a lifesaving gift.

No doubt, in Egypt and in Europe, there was an undercurrent of anti-American sentiment building, but it seemed more manufactured by political factions. In the streets, Americans, alone or in small groups, were welcomed, respected, and liked by the common folk. Certainly, this was true for Terry, Jack, and me. Such kindness, as well as gratitude from the older generation for our role in WWII, was not just a bromide but a lifesaver.

Time Was Running Out

The path before us was daunting. We had to find our way back to Venice, then through Yugoslavia in the midst of winter, and then on to Athens. We had to do all of this before our ship left Piraeus—in six days!

As we passed from Switzerland into northern Italy, the weather took a turn for the worse. Nasty, in fact, as dark gray billowing clouds piled up against the rugged mountains. Snow fell lightly at first but intensified as we reached the summit. We later learned that the summit road was closed not long after we passed through.

The conversation was sparse, as was our cash. So, we traveled through the night, enduring rugged ups and downs and circuitous travel, now a necessity, both to return our rental car in Venice on time and to conserve our precious cash. Reaching Venice was only the first milestone. From Venice, we had to travel over 1,100 miles through the middle of Yugoslavia in the midst of winter to get back to Greece in time to board our ship in Piraeus. Plenty of time!

We arrived in Venice in the late afternoon, just in time to turn in our Fiat. Standing by the side of the road, we discussed the sad state of our finances.

I decided to hitchhike back to Greece, enduring Terry and Jack's ridicule. "Look," I said, stating the obvious, "time is not the problem. Money is the problem!"

Jack replied immediately, "No one will pick up three of us, and we know from our train ride here what Yugoslavia is like in the middle of winter—frigid, dark, and desolate." Jack said, a bit hysterically, I thought. Then, theatrically, pulling out his trusty travel guide, he said, "See the index! Do you see anything about Yugoslavia? Nothing, not a word," he said with his voice rising. "And who in their right mind would pick up three guys hitchhiking their way through Yugoslavia?" he went on, now verging on panic.

"Well then, that settles it," I said, "I guess we just have to split up!" That broke the gloomy mood, as Terry and Jack both broke into laughter.

But I was serious.

I walked over to the curb and stuck my thumb out, enduring their continuing snickering and ridicule. "Do you even know where you are going?" Terry said sarcastically.

"First Trieste," I replied, pointing to the highway sign just a few meters away, indicating, "Trieste 169 kilometers."

I was about to go on when Terry turned apoplectic: "Trieste is at the border of Yugoslavia." He pointed to the map as if I didn't know.

"Yes," I said, "and from Trieste, there is a highway to the center of Yugoslavia that joins with the main freeway that goes all the way to

Greece!" I said, pointing to the map, somewhat agitated for not being taken seriously.

Now they were laughing hard when I walked over to the Trieste sign. But they stopped laughing when I stuck my thumb out and, almost immediately, a guy in a small car pulled over and opened his door. "Trieste?" I said. He waved me in. I threw my bag into the back seat, gave Terry and Jack a short wave, and shouted out the window, "See you in Athens." Then, I was gone.

I learned later that upon my leaving, Jack and Terry were in near shock. They talked a bit, and then, of course, they followed suit.

On My Own

Little was said during the trip as I knew no Italian and my driver knew no English. About two hours later, around nine o'clock, my ride pulled over at a dark intersection where there was a sign marked "Trieste." *Great!* I thought. Thanking the driver profusely, I got out of the car and watched it drive off into the night.

Then, I looked down the longest, loneliest road I had ever seen and saw only one small light in the distance. All else was dark. So, I picked up my bag and started walking through a darkened town. As my eyes adjusted, I could see glimmers of light peeping through curtains and shutters of homes in the hills, but in the town, nothing. So, I just kept walking.

The light at the end of town was all I thought of. Any light is better than nothing was the extent of my reasoning. It seemed the entire village had retired for the night. Nothing was open. The light I saw from a distance turned out to be illuminating one lonely mailbox.

I looked around. All the shops were dark.

Then, I discerned a glimmer of light seeping faintly through the shutters of one of the shops. I walked closer. The light was from a little restaurant, clearly not open, but there were shadows of two people moving about inside.

I walked to the door and tapped softly on the glass, causing both figures to startle. The larger of the two shadows approached the door, and then the blinds spread open. I could see that one of the shadows was of a middle-aged lady of some girth. I gave her a timid wave and my most friendly smile, making sure she could see the USA logo on my bag.

She continued to peer at me and finally opened the door, saying something in Italian that I took to mean, "Our restaurant is closed." but whatever she said, she said it kindly. So, I gestured and said in broken English while pantomiming, "Sleep, sleep on floor?"

She hesitated a moment; then the clouds parted as a young lady about my age stepped forward, saying in nascent English, "Where come from you?" (or something like that). Then, "Where are you going?"

I tried to explain but quickly realized that my explanation would make no sense to any sane person, regardless of their nationality. So, I just repeated, in the friendliest manner, I could muster, "Sleep, on floor?" pointing to the USA patch on my bag accompanied by my best thespian pantomime.

She turned to the older woman, her mother, for a brief discussion, and then the grace of the One whom I did not know yet was bestowed upon me. In slow but good English, the daughter said there was a room over the kitchen with a bed and a bathroom, and I was welcome to stay the night. I told her I didn't have money for a room, but a place on the floor would be good. "No, no, you sleep upstairs. Go," she said, waving me up. Both mother and daughter followed me up, showing me the bed and bathroom and, yes, a shower. After saying good night, they turned to walk back downstairs, but the mother said something firmly in Italian, which the daughter said, somewhat shyly, "First, shower, then sleep." The mother then provided a towel, and she showed me, rather firmly, to the shower. I wondered why she thought I needed a shower?

That night, so many years ago in Trieste, I met two Good Samaritans. Their example of hospitality to a stranger stranded in the middle of the night has stayed with me all these years, both as an example and a mandate.

I awoke to a brilliant morning. The ladies served me breakfast, though I tried weakly to protest. When I asked if I could wash dishes as a way of saying thank you, they just smiled. Soon, I was on my way, but this memory remains a debt I have gladly repaid many times over by offering gracious hospitality to wayfarers.

Not as Easy as I Thought

I was lifted up and carried along by the memory of hospitality graciously extended to me the previous evening. The walk from Trieste to the Yugoslavian border was easy, but things got strange when I reached the border. Getting through the border was simple, but as I stood roadside with my hand out, waving, which was the polite way to ask for a ride, driver after driver whizzed by, waving kindly, but no one stopped. It was maddening, strange, and frustrating until finally, a young American businessman, who I learned lived in Trieste, stopped. "Where are you going?" he asked.

"I am trying to get to the central freeway that runs through Yugoslavia." I said, pointing to the highway in red on my map, "So, I can hitchhike to Greece." I said matter-of-factly.

He looked at me as if I were out of my mind. Shaking his head, he said, "Look, the drivers of the cars that are passing you by are like me. They are driving over the border to get gas as gas prices in Yugoslavia are controlled by the state, so gas is nearly seventy percent cheaper in Yugoslavia than in Italy."

"More importantly," he said, looking at me with pity, "the highway you are hoping will get you to the central freeway is closed for the winter!"

"Oh." I said after a pause, "That explains a lot."

"Yes, I guess it does," he said, looking at me with pity. He pulled over at a gas station. "Look," he said, pointing at my map. "See this crooked road going north?" he said, indicating a small curvy line going north to Belgrade. "It's your best bet," he said. "No, you're only bet is to take a bus north to Belgrade. Don't try to hitchhike as I am sure the fare is less than a dollar. Once you get to Belgrade, there is a highway that goes all the way to Athens, but God help you in finding a ride in the middle of winter all the way through Yugoslavia to Greece!" he said with emphasis.

His suggestion about heading for Belgrade seemed like a good idea. Actually, it seemed like the only idea.

I got to Belgrade late afternoon after a long, arduous journey over the mountains. Next to the bus station where I got off was a little delicatessen. I went in to see if I could get some bread and perhaps some dried meat.

A pretty Yugoslavian girl about my age was in line ahead of me. As she was walking away, apparently having heard me trying to communicate my request in pidgin English she thoughtfully said, "What is it you want?" Her English was much better than my imaginary Serbian-Croatian-Slovakian travel dictionary could muster up for me, which was *nothing*! "Some type of snack, some bread and cheese, and maybe some meat would be great," I said.

She picked out a few things for me and, thankfully, the price was next to nothing. I then asked her what direction I should go to find the highway, pointing at my map and how long it would take for me to walk there. "If you were to walk to the highway," she said, smiling a bit, "you would not get there until after dark. I am going that way. I will drive you," she said with some authority, ending the discussion. So off we went—my second Good Samaritan and me.

Well out of town as evening approached, she pulled over where a small road ran off to infinity. I watched her drive away, her taillights merging into pinpoints, and then she was gone.

I had not seen another car since my ride turned onto the thoroughfare, and there were no cars to be seen now. To the north, west, and south—snow-covered plains stretched out into infinity.

Hard snow covered the road, bordered by two-foot berms of snow on each side. My hoped-for direction of travel, the southeast, had snow-covered mountains stretching across the horizon, formidable, rugged, and forbidding. I knew it was these mountains through which I must travel to reach Greece, a journey of over six hundred miles. There were no signs of life here—no cars, no lights, neither near nor far; even the heavens were veiled. On I walked. I began to wonder, a little late, if perhaps I was crazy.

I walked with purpose for a considerable distance, thinking surely a car would soon pass by and deliver me, but each time I paused, the mountains seemed to be no nearer. Hope was now a stranger.

I had no idea how long it would take me to get to the mountains, much less what I would do if I did. Knowing that walking was better than standing still or sitting down, I walked just to generate some warmth.

"Surely, a car will pass by; surely, there must be a village where I can seek refuge." But there was nothing. I trudged on.

The gray sky gave way, deepening into gloomy evening, quickly turning into darkened night. I could see no stars, no moon, no lights—near or far. A gray shroud enveloped the dome of heaven. Fear, my only companion, is all that pushed me on.

Finally, giving in to my exhaustion, I sat down on the berm, ignoring that I was inviting a slow death. Snow fell lightly, and soon I was asleep.

I do not know why I woke up, but I did so with a jolt that lifted me to my feet. Brushing off the light snow that was doing its best to cover me, I stared at a new sight. The canopy of clouds had lifted. The stars shone brilliantly in the deep sky, and now the argent moon was showing brilliantly upon the mountain to the east. I watched, mesmerized by the brilliance of the light. A shadow was growing bigger and bigger as I stared, stupefied.

Then I heard a mighty roar from behind. I turned just in time to see a fast-moving bullet of a car speeding by, swerving to avoid me. I didn't have time to react.

Remorseful that I had been sleeping rather than on alert, I watched the taillights narrow in the distance. What should I expect taking such a fool's risk, hitchhiking through Yugoslavia during the Cold War in the middle of winter? How could I have fallen asleep? What kind of fool would fall asleep alongside a frozen track of snow? Then, suddenly, the taillights brightened. The car was slowing. Could it be, could it really be? One moment I was looking forlornly at fading taillights, but now bright backup lights were coming toward me! The car was backing up! I stood, unbelieving, motionless.

"They're backing up to me," I said, as if in a trance. The car stopped beside me, the passenger window came down, and an attractive young blond lady smiled, saying, "Want a ride?"

I was dumbfounded, speechless, really.

The driver, who turned out to be her husband, leaned over, saying jovially, "If you want a ride, you have to get in!"

Still frozen physically and mentally, I was finally able to blurt out, "Yes, yes, I would very much like a ride."

"Well, then you have to get in the car!" the wife said, smiling, motioning toward the back door. I came to my senses, virtually leaping into the car, dragging my duffel bag with me.

"It was a miracle we saw you along the side of the road, an honest to God miracle," the woman kept saying, "with the white USA posted on your bag. I kept telling my husband he is an American." I listened, stunned, having all but forgotten the labels we had been given only a few days before.

"Where are you headed?" said the driver, a snazzy young man just a few years older than me.

"Athens," I replied, and both of them started laughing.

"Your second miracle," said the husband, "That is where we are going, so lean back, my friend, get warm, and get some sleep," he said, throwing a blanket on me. "You can help drive after you get some shuteye."

We saw no other car that I am aware of until early morning when we finally reached the border. By then, I had been driving for a while, and we still had a long way to go.

Before this, I didn't believe in miracles. However, the facts cannot be disputed. After not seeing a single car for more than six hours; being exhausted to the point of not being able to walk; falling asleep on the side of the road; being covered with a light dusting of snow; and then, somehow awakening and being brought to my feet just in time to be seen; because of a label saying USA in bold white letters, posted on my duffel bag by a stranger; I was in no position to dispute the wife's conclusion—it was a miracle.

I knew not what to say, but I was thankful for being saved.

It turned out the driver and passenger were a young American couple on their honeymoon. They had picked up a brand-new black BMW in Munich and were on their way to Athens.

When we reached Athens, the couple insisted upon delivering me to the youth hostel. I thanked them profusely and waved goodbye before it dawned on me that I did not have their names or address. I had no way to thank them. Hopefully, they will read this chapter and know that their kindness resonates with one lonely sojourner to this day.

Terry and Jack arrived two days later, together. I was greatly relieved and overjoyed to hear their voices coming up from the stairwell, ecstatic really, as I had spent two nerve-racking days with no idea where they were or what I would do if they did not show up before our boat was scheduled to sail.

Being a practiced thespian, however, as they came up the stairs, I assumed an attitude of casual repose, leaning slightly over the landing. I heard them babbling about what they would do if I didn't make it to Greece in time to catch the boat. "Have a nice trip, gentlemen?" I said in my best baritone. "You had me worried."

They looked up in shock. Then, spotting me above, they raced up, pounding on me ecstatically, then even a hug or two.

I must say, it was the first time Terry expressed joy in seeing me, and I returned the affection, though I couldn't help but put a dig in. "Aren't you glad that you don't have to explain to Mom how you lost me in Yugoslavia?"

He laughed heartily, then gave me a genuine smile and said, "Yes, yes, I am!" giving me another hug.

So, all was well, except for the inconvenient fact that we were as close to being busted as three guys could be, and we still had two days before our ship sailed for Alexandria. After the two-day sail, we still had to make our way back to Cairo. All in all, we were in a sorry state.

So, we followed the most rational course that came to mind. We marshaled our few remaining Drachmas, went downstairs, where we knew we would find a number of hostellers at the sidewalk café, and purchased a bottle of cheap wine, bread, cheese, and olives; then sat down to enjoy our last meal as we considered the gloomy state of our finances.

Fortunately, our passage back to Alexandria and our train tickets to Cairo were pre-purchased. All we had to do was survive without food for the next two days after paying our fee for the hostel and survive on the two-day voyage back. So, things were not all that bad!

Then another miracle happened. A fellow hosteller told us there was a clinic that would purchase blood for about ten dollars a pint only a few blocks away. Ten dollars each would be just what we would need to get back to Cairo. It seemed that once again, we might be saved.

On the way to the clinic, Jack said flat out that he would prefer to starve if the clinic wasn't spotlessly clean. Terry and I agreed that we would head for the door if we didn't see the needle coming out of a sealed package. Fortunately, the clinic was spotless and, more importantly, staffed by a bevy of young Greek nurses who were abuzz to find three young Americans at their doorstep.

The senior nurses, however, maintained a strict discipline that prohibited fraternizing. Terry and Jack went first, behind the cotton curtain, and soon reappeared, saying, "Nothing to it." They waved the Drachmas they had earned. Still, having never given blood before, I was a bit nervous.

Lying down, I looked up at the prettiest nurse. She smiled, but almost immediately, the room was swimming. I felt clammy and cold, and then I clicked out.

How long I was out, I do not know. I could hear commotion from somewhere and Terry yelling, "I want to see my brother!" rather loudly, followed by "I want to see my brother now!"

Then Terry and Jack burst into the room and, as Jack told the story later, over and over again to our friends at the American University of Cairo: "There he was, sitting up with a ring of the prettiest Greek nurses you would ever see, one patting his forehead with a wet towel, another offering him dishes of olives, until the head nurse shooed them away, giggling of course."

I remembered little of what happened, but I never tired of hearing Jack tell the story.

So, this time, we actually managed our hard-earned funds well, and to the best of my recollection, the remainder of the trip went without mishap. The weather was balmy, considering that it was winter, and the Mediterranean behaved. Now, the only issue was how our adventure would be received at home.

Home

Home was great. We told the whole story over the dinner table and then later in the evening as well. We held nothing back. The recounting of our story marked a turning point in Terry's and my relationship with my parents. Mom was shocked, but Dad hung on every word and clearly enjoyed every moment of our adventure.

When Mom left the room for a moment, Dad directed both Terry and me to check in with the embassy doctor for a blood test. This clearly was a turning point in the parent-child relationship, and though both of us made clear there was no need, Dad laughed. "I am not worried about your morals, just your health, as there is no telling what you could have picked up when giving blood."

CHAPTER TWENTY-FOUR

Rhythm of the Streets

We entered Egypt with the best of intentions: to represent the best of our country, to listen first, and to engage with courtesy and respect. We read the books recommended by State, and I took them to heart. I did my best to learn Arabic script, an almost impossible task for me given my as yet undiscovered dyslexia and the mirror-like reversal of Arabic script.

So, I set out to learn spoken Arabic. This also was a formidable challenge made more difficult by the good intentions of my Egyptian friends at the American University of Cairo (AUC). Most of them were fluent in no less than three languages—Arabic, of course, English, and French. Consciously or unconsciously, my Arab friends would switch to English when a member of the Anglosphere was present. If a conversation became heated, rapid-fire Arabic would breakout until order was restored.

Since I was intent on learning at least colloquial Arabic, I ventured out to the streets of Cairo, where my primitive efforts were actually encouraged. In the shops, on trains, and in cabs, my pathetic efforts were not only encouraged, they were met with delight. Shopkeepers, policemen, waitresses, and taxicab drivers were all thrilled by my nascent efforts to communicate in their native tongue. I enjoyed myself immensely in these ventures.

I picked up enough street Arabic to shop, get directions, and exchange pleasantries with the people of the street: waitresses, elevator operators, police officers, and shop proprietors. In fact, every time I initiated a conversation, a small crowd would gather around to help me with my efforts. They would point out directions, laugh good-naturedly at my pronunciation, but then repeat each word slower and slower until someone would yell with joy, "Good, good—you speak Arabic!" to which I would reply with a wide grin, "I speak Arabic, yes!" Laughter would then break out as my new friends of the street would repeat, "Yes, yes, you speak Arabic!"

My budding Arabic was not as well received by my AUC friends, who said, "English, please Roger, the hour is getting late," always with a kindly smile. Occasionally, I would surprise my Egyptian AUC friends by interjecting into their "off-stage" Arabic conversations with a word or two that demonstrated I understood at least the gist of what they were saying.

Such moments deepened my friendships, but then I embarked upon a larger challenge; I tried to understand the complexities of this civilization struggling to enter the modern world.

The Gifts of Ancient Egypt

When I learned that I would be joining my parents in Cairo, I hit the books hard. However, little of what I read prepared me for the reality of Egypt.

I read that Egyptians had an unparalleled mastery over the arts of mathematics, civil engineering, and stone cutting. These three arts were required to design and construct the world's greatest stone buildings of their time, including the four-sided triangular pyramids faced with structured casing stone. Across the great river, we saw the three pyramids of Giza, bathed in yellow light, dominated by the Great Pyramid, known as the Pyramid of Khufu or the Pyramid of Cheops. Fifty stories high, the grand structure is acknowledged as one of the Seven Wonders of the Ancient World and the only one that remains intact to this day.

With my binoculars, I made out the Sphinx, glowing in the same yellow illumination. I felt I'd stopped breathing, and the world stood still. This was my introduction to Memphis, Egypt's first capital city and a UNESCO World Heritage Site. Our family spent many days exploring the remnants strewn around Memphis and the surrounding desert, where the massive statue of Ramses that adorned the great temple of Ptah was first found. Once discovered, this magnificent tribute to the greatest Pharaoh of the nineteenth dynasty of Egypt was moved to the Cairo Museum.

These are the structures I gazed upon from our Nile Hilton balcony on our first night in Cairo.

Later I learned of the monumental effort involved in barging the stone hundreds of miles south from Aswan, building the canals to transport the granite from the Nile to Giza, and moving huge stone blocks into position for shaping. However, what struck me as nearly miraculous was the precision with which the blocks were placed, such that, as measured by the North Star, the Great Pyramid of Khufu was aligned within one-tenth of a degree of true north.

When the barges arrived near Giza from Aswan, the massive blocks would be precisely cut, meticulously shaved, then pulled up spiral ramps by slave labor in corkscrew fashion for their final placement, creating the magnificent structure of the Khufu pyramid.

The resulting structures deserve the appellation of *Wonders of the Ancient World*. I can attest to the stunning moment when one views the intricately carved hieroglyphics for the first time: the resplendent palms, papyrus reeds, and other symbols of fertility etched into the walls and columns to comfort and placate the ancient gods and the living pharaohs. Incredible obelisks rose four stories high, and the Sphinx still gazes upon the eternal city from across the Nile, unmoved since my first night in Cairo.

Carvings on the temple walls and columns reflect the ancient mythology of the Nile River Valley as the "Island of Creation." Pillars, often shaped in the design of palms, papyrus, and lotus plants, also echo the creation story of Adam and Eve and the Garden of Eden.

These great temples and pyramids, born of the genius and mystical visioning of men and women, were inspired by the belief in an afterlife, but these dreams came at a terrible price. It was not dreams that moved 2,300,000 massive blocks of granite from the upper Aswan Basin 434 miles to Giza. Nor was it dreams that elevated ninety-ton blocks into place to construct the great pyramids, the temples of Memphis, and the temples of the Valley of the Kings. It may have been the dream of some, but the toil and sacrifice of hundreds of thousands of men, women, and children turned those dreams into reality. In the end, it was the mighty flow of the Nile, year after year, century after century, through blue nights and white stars that turned the dream into a kingdom. Think of this when you behold the monuments of modern life.

Giza

Our father drove the Tempest Lemans convertible to and from Maadi and out to the Cairo Airport. Still, it was on our trips out to Giza along the open desert roads that the Tempest was let out to run—and run it did, along the Nile, the canals, and desert roads leading to Giza. I understand that today there is no unused space between Cairo proper and Giza, but in 1965, there were plenty of open roads. Terry and I were allowed to take turns behind the wheel on these desert trips, and we let her rip.

Outside of the summer months, the desert weather is quite comfortable as long as the wind is not up. So, three times a year, Mom and Dad would organize an adventure to the Pyramids of Giza, a few miles south of Cairo. My parents were well known for their hospitality, so usually several families would join us on these adventures.

With the pyramids and Sphinx in the background, we explored all the surrounding area, in and around the desert roads and on the hardpan surrounding the great pyramids between shallow rolling dunes. Finally, we would find a good spot to spread out our picnic paraphernalia. We would park the Tempest anywhere we wanted. After raking a clean patch, we would lash our shade tarps together, deposit a cooler with beer and lunch meats, arrange some camp chairs, and light up a small portable hibachi that Dad brought from Japan.

Once settled, we'd explore, looking for trinkets from millennia past in the swales of the dunes. We found ancient beads of various colors made of sand quartz and sometimes greater treasures such as scarabs and Roman coins. Remnants of civilizations past were all about, left behind by those who, over the centuries, risked their lives to plunder the spoils of the tombs.

These pirates of the desert engaged in a deadly game. Pharaoh's guards, courtiers, and soldiers who were fortunate enough not to be interred with their king, guarded the treasures of the tombs. While being ruthlessly pursued and mercilessly treated, thieves spilled booty near the pyramids. As archeologists discovered new passageways to the underground, more treasures became available.

Pale stone, clay, and glass beads of various shapes and sizes were abundant. We assembled small collections while sitting in a camp chair or on an overturned bucket. We only needed patience and a practiced eye to survey the vast land. Casual glances or distracting chatter, however, rendered little.

Most of the beads were hollow tubes either drilled or formed of clay around straw before firing in a kiln. Most were just a sixteenth to an eighth of an inch long, but some were up to an inch in length. We learned that the colors, bleached by the sun, could be partially restored by applying cooking oil or olive oil.

Our trips to the desert seemed to play a role separate from casual treasure hunting. Often Dad brought some of his professional friends out with us, and usually, they would wander off to chat without being disturbed. Years later, I questioned Dad about these sub-rosa get-togethers. He replied, "The desert can keep a secret." Make of that what you will.

Herb and Dad in Giza

The Great Pyramids

Political Intrigue

When we arrived in Cairo, the cold war was at its height, and competition, disinformation, plots, and counterplots abounded, just like *MAD Magazine*'s cartoon "Spy vs. Spy." All this bubbled beneath a thin layer of civility. Egypt was the pivot point. The battle for the hearts of other African countries was a serious one.

Gamal Abdul Nasser, then the president of Egypt, was a complex man with many strengths, as historians would attest. Still, as an affirmed socialist in the vein of Marshal Tito, most of the Egyptian commercial class despised him. Undoubtedly, Nasser was intent on nationalizing Egypt's major industries. As an avowed secularist, he had virtually no support from Egypt's many religious factions.

Regardless of religious, social, or political bias, most pundits acknowledged he was a master when it came to playing the Soviet Union and Eastern Block against the West to Egypt's great benefit. He enticed the USSR to invest billions of dollars in Egypt (when such numbers really meant something) to construct the Aswan Dam. In response, the United States pushed back with aid packages of its own, such as the one that brought my father to the country.

Nasser's ruthless suppression of the Cairene mercantile class, confiscation of property, and imprisonment of resisters— whether due to their faith or their politics, seemed unbounded. His most radical campaign was to suppress the Muslim Brotherhood, which many believe cost him his life, as well as the life of his successor Anwar Sadat who died by assassination. The Muslim Brotherhood remains a powerful force in Egypt to this day.

Many of my friends at AUC were of the mercantile and banking class. Their families bore the brunt of Nasser's imposed socialism, and they suffered greatly. To them, Nasser was a thief—dangerously naive, but clever and duplicitous.

Interestingly, the prevailing power struggles did not disturb the social collegiality of AUC, which had students from Russia, Poland, Czechoslovakia, Hungary, Korea, Indonesia, Malaysia, and many other countries. We had lively conversations and many serious debates, but never once did political issues interfere with the equanimity of our social interactions.

These undercurrents, as well as the stratification and fragmentation of the Egyptian culture, rippled beneath the surface of Cairene life, touching our lives as well.

Expatriates—The Three Stages of Adjustment

We arrived in Egypt late summer of 1964, with Nasser appearing to be in complete control of the country. It is not unusual for expatriates who lived in the Middle East for any length of time to experience three stages of adjustment upon their first introduction to the country.

First comes the excitement of a culture like nothing experienced elsewhere in the world. Egypt, before Nasser, was unique for its depth of history, culture, and robust commerce. Only Lebanon was its economic rival in the area.

The novelty of this exotic country never wears off, and for me, every day was a new gift of the mystery of the Orient. Yet, the longer I stayed, the more I learned about the culture and the intrigue just below the surface.

The merchant class was under attack because of Nasser's socialism. Multi-culturists and western religions were highly suspect. Several conservative Muslim sects, including the aggressive Muslim Brotherhood, were forced underground by Nasser's regime. They are still very active today.

Mom, nearly six feet tall and the wife of a Marine who had traveled the world for decades, was not easily intimidated. Yet, she would not venture out alone unless Terry or I served as her conscripted escort.

Throughout my two-year stay, I wandered the ancient streets of "Cairo: The City Victorious," as Max Rodenbeck described it in his excellent book of the same name, absorbing everything I could. Over time, I learned my desire to see everything and befriend everyone drew attention to me. Late in my stay, I realized I was never alone.

In time I learned my safety was in part due to the fact that informants were everywhere. The more complex and fluid question was—*informants to whom?*. Every neighborhood, I learned, was controlled, much like the early gangs of New York or South Chicago. There were free agents who lived outside of established boundaries and harbored many loyalties. They played a dangerous game. Those whose loyalty was not comfortably pegged were watched carefully. They were vulnerable to any misstep.

Since I had a penchant for being on my own and readily conversed with strangers, wandering the streets at odd hours, I became well known to those doing the watching, as they became well known to me. For the most part, I wandered undisturbed, as my encounters were always innocent and free of political issues. If the conversation wandered into politics, I quickly demurred and steered it back to cultural or historical issues.

Eventually, I learned the pattern of the streets, the call of the minarets, and the social structure requiring deference to those of stature. Though the maze of the streets was complex, getting lost was virtually impossible. If I did lose my way, at no cost, a local shop owner would have a youngster guide me to where I needed to be. It was understood but not required that the guide receive a small tip or *baksheesh*. Please note that baksheesh should be understood as a thank you gift. One should never ask "How much?" for such a service.

So, like most expatriates in the Middle East, I learned enough of the street and enough Arabic to get by, and most of all, I learned the rhythm of the interchanges, the subtle patterns and nervousness of the street, and how to know when things were amiss.

In short, I learned enough to be accepted and never once felt otherwise.

CHAPTER TWENTY-FIVE

Full Throttle!

The emerald surface of the El Alamein Lagoon lay before us, clear and calm but not for long, not with our DC-3 ripping through the air, propelling us forward, my father at the controls. The bucolic serenity of the El Alamein Lagoon, with its beautiful water and sandy bottom surrounded by palms and deep reed banks, was not for us to appreciate right now. The thrust provided by two Wright R-1820 Cyclone 9 engines demanded total concentration as we skimmed the lagoon's surface. We had work to do.

The morning was scheduled for certifying the Alexandria International Airport Flight Control System, specifically its ability to spot air traffic that wandered outside of prescribed flight corridors. The in air team (Dad's team) had complete instrumentation required to ensure the accuracy of the ground-based readings, including altitude, speed, and direction of all flights within its reach. It was critical that the data provided by the ground-based systems be identical to the airborne instruments. The process was tedious, requiring flying precise circle routes at precise altitudes.

I was not looking forward to the process, as I felt like a moth circling a light bulb from every possible angle and height. When we arrived, we found a major surprise. All of the navigation instruments were in boxes, waiting for installation. Worse, there were only two "technicians," neither of whom had any training in flight control instruments. It seemed the Alexandria International Airport team was hoping the Cairo team would assemble the flight control instruments and train the as yet unidentified technicians.

To put it mildly, there was disappointment all around. We had no choice but to cancel the flight check as there was nothing to check. Ever the diplomat, Dad smoothed over the disappointment saying, "We can conduct an inventory to ensure you have all the right equipment. We will do our best to get you qualified installation contractors and instructors to manage the ground equipment. Then we can get started with training."

When I left Egypt two years later, the equipment was still in crates. In the moment, there was no room for reflection. As with much of my life, memories and reflections were sealed away. Of course, time has now become my most precious commodity, so I document these memories and reflections for future generations.

As a consolation, Dad hosted his and the Alexandria team to an early lunch at a popular Alexandria restaurant. The goodbye lunch was a lot of fun, and I got a chance to see Dad's famed charm up close.

Soon we were off banking hard, first over the Mediterranean, then west, flying along the coast, as low as we could go, of course.

Shuffling through my guidebook, I had a great view of the Citadel, the famed Alexandria harbor, and its lighthouse. My excitement remained as we flew over, and since the flight test had been canceled, I committed to making a return trip over spring break.

Dad and his number one "CO," Captain Hossain Jawad, were in the cockpit after the abandoned mission to check the flight control facilities at Alexandria International Airport. I was strapped out of the way in the jump seat behind Hossain, much like a duffel bag. We were on our way to survey the northwestern quadrant of the Qattara Depression, the deepest geological depression in the world.

We traveled on with little to draw me out of my reverie.

In June 1964, I graduated from Mira Costa High School in Manhattan Beach, California, after moving fourteen times between kindergarten and high school graduation. I attended schools in places such as Bakersfield Elementary, in Bakersfield, California (kindergarten), Corona Del Mar Elementary, in Corona Del Mar, California (Kindergarten); Sunset Beach, Oahu (first and second grade); Pearl Harbor Elementary(third grade); Bakersfield Elementary (third grade), Santa Ana Elementary (fourth grade); Far East Command, American Dependent Schools, Japan, (fifth grade); Bakersfield Elementary, (fifth grade for two months); Santa Ana Elementary (sixth grade); Francis Willard Junior High, Santa Ana, California (seventh grade); Wasatch Junior High, Salt Lake City; (eighth grade); Olympus High School, Salt Lake City (Freshman) and Skyline High School, Salt Lake City (Sophomore and Junior); and, finally, my Senior year, Mira Costa High School, Manhattan Beach, California.

Okay, it was an unsettled life. Interestingly, with only two exceptions during my childhood education, I had never been able to settle into a school for more than a year. It was not too bad when we had base schooling, as in-and-out moves were more the norm than the exception, and new students introduced new energy. However, when we were encamped into stateside schools, we were the strangers, and by the time we settled in and made a few friends, we were off again.

After high school graduation, there was no doubt I was adrift. Neither of my parents were college graduates, so they provided no assistance in considering and preparing for my future. My grades were not terrible, but not exciting. I considered applying for a theater scholarship to Cal State Long Beach since I was well known in that field, thanks to Mrs. Reed and my awards at the Long Beach Theater Scouting Competitions. Though I enjoyed theater, I knew it was highly unlikely it would be my career. My success with debate taught me that I thrived on intellectual challenges, but I had no clue how to make a career in such pursuits. In short, I had no idea what to do.

Out of the blue, once again, a miracle happened. I learned about Dad's Middle East Assignment and the American University of Cairo. I put on a full-court press to join my parents in Cairo, as did Terry, who was finishing his first year at the University of California, Santa Barbara, on a full scholarship.

We were embarking on a cultural and social revolution that I knew nothing about. For the time being, all felt good: new friends, new ideas, new music, and new morals. Music was changing, from the Beach Boys to the Beatles and soon to the Rolling Stones; warfare was changing from fixed battle lines to jungle and tunnel warfare; social norms were changing from true love to free love. I did not know at the time that we were frogs in a slowly heating pot of water, and soon the water would get hot, very hot.

John F. Kennedy was assassinated during my senior year of high school; the Fair Housing Act had passed prohibiting an owner in California from refusing to sell or rent property based upon race, leading to the only time I had ever stood up to Dad.

In this context, I joined my parents and Terry to take advantage of this once-in-a-lifetime opportunity. Now we were there.

Dad preferred that his trainees fly as low as conditions allowed, even when he was just observing (as he was then), because he wanted his trainees to be "all in, all the time." And, did I mention, whenever possible, Dad's first choice was for full throttle? In truth, Dad knew when to pull back, but he pressed the limits of perfection when instructing or observing. His view was to never waste a moment in the air, even when touring. He believed the best lessons were learned when students were pressed to the limits of their ability.

That is why he was the best damn pilot in the US Marine Corps. It is also why he excelled at the Federal Aviation Administration and then at the Agency for International Development, where he was currently working.

I know there are thousands of best damn pilots and friends of the best damn pilot, ready to contest any such claim. I heard it so many times growing up, not from Dad, but from his friends, those who couldn't stand him, and those who served with him flying Corsairs during WWII, and those who flew with him into hot landings in Korea and throughout the South Pacific during the Formosa stare down, and those who flew with him throughout Africa and then Northern Thailand during the Vietnam War, flying into places that God knows he should not have been and that he couldn't talk about.

Even into his eighties, friends meeting Dad for dinner would, much to his embarrassment, have him paged as the world's greatest aviator. This joke proved embarrassing when Bob Prescott, founder of Flying Tiger Cargo, responded to the page even though it was meant for Dad. Prescott was more than gracious and said the only way to settle the issue was to merge the parties together for a drink, which they did, even though by then, Dad had been off of alcohol for over a decade. So, he shared a ginger ale with one of the world's two greatest aviators.

Enough diversion, it was Dad's view that pressing limits provided the best opportunities for training, and it was relentless training that kept one's mind focused, clear, and sharp. Dad was never one for wasting time. Even when he was just wasting time, he observed, challenged, and absorbed. That is, unless he was drinking, then all bets were off—except that he never drank within forty-eight hours of flying.

The Qattara Depression

We hugged the coast at low altitude, continuing westward toward Marsa Matruh. Today it's an interesting beach resort due west from the bustle of Alexandria, but in 1965, it was a bit of nothing halfway between Alexandria and the Libyan border. From Marsa Matruh, we veered a neat southeast course toward what I was keen to see, the Qattara Depression, the largest land depression in the world. It was more than 7570 square miles and 84 miles at its widest and at 436 feet below sea level, the third deepest.

The desert rippled with endless waves of sand as lavender shadows undulated, all shifting toward the western horizon where Libya lay. It seemed incongruous that the more we gained in altitude, the more forlorn I felt, as I was drawn into a mindless journey with my fellow sojourners, the dunes of Libya, my only companions, who knew nothing of me. I seemed drawn into eternity.

My introspections were interrupted when Dad notified the Cairo tower that we were diverting south to the Qattara Depression to test below sea level navigation. Our aircraft was furnished with the newest civil aviation technology for ground to air navigation systems flight checking. This technology would be of little use once we entered the depression since we would be out of range of any flight control system.

Dad gave Hossain his new vectors, which split the northern shoulder of the depression neatly from its NW corner to the SE rim, the sun behind us. We were to make several passes at altitude, getting a feel for the depression, and then, when comfortable, we'd descend, each time from the west so the sun would be at our backs.

He gave a quick verbal reminder to Hossain to pay no attention to the instruments since "we are not flying a submarine, so our instruments cannot be relied upon below sea level." Hossain granted Dad a slight smile, responding that he would maintain an altitude of no less than 500 feet below the rim of the depression but would go lower at Dad's direction for the level passes. By all reports, the northwestern approach would start with an immediate dramatic drop, a steep descent of terrain over wind-eroded bedrock with sharp spires and upheavals rising several hundred feet above the sloped surface. Dad would plot visual markers of interest on what was an essentially barren map. When we passed midway, the surface level of the depression would reportedly level out; we would see the floor of the depression, barren salty lakes and at least one freshwater lake dotted with greenery, numerous sand pillars, and a few actual outposts. We would continue on a straight course until we reached the opposite rim and then return for several other passes.

I was excited beyond words. I could sense Hossain's anticipation, but he was too controlled to reflect any nervousness or even excitement he may have been feeling. Dad's expression, calm voice, and actions were strictly business, so down we went.

I had seen the depression only on my map of Egypt. Its outline was gnarled into a shape that reminded me of the comedy and drama masks I had become familiar with in my high school theater class—with the northeastern face looking to Cairo and the inverted southern face to the southwest. The components apparently joined back-to-back along a west to east axis, rotated slightly on a northeast to southwest axis. The effect was as if two court jesters were doing an inverted jig when something went terribly wrong.

I could see the cookie-cutter outline from miles away. When we approached the canyon rim, we were flying low, of course, with no more than a hundred feet clearance. Since the terrain around the depression was flat in every direction, there was no concern, except on my part, when the northern ridge seemed to drop suddenly away. The feeling was like stepping off of the Empire State Building. Sharp towers, fittingly minaret-like, rose hundreds of feet from the descending slope of the depression as if calling the devout to worship from islands in the sky.

I reminded myself repeatedly that we were maintaining a constant elevation, even though my depth perception informed otherwise. The steep drop, broken only by the 918-foot-high escarpments, marked the northwestern edge of the adjacent El Diffa Plateau. As the western slope disappeared below us, Hossain started his descent and quickly leveled as my vertigo relaxed slightly.

As we descended, it seemed we were entering a lost civilization. Pillars rose up from the floor of the depression, created by the interplay of salt, weathering, and wind. The layers of sediment that passed my window fascinated me. They were a journey back in time. I did not know how many years back, but certainly many hundreds of thousands of years were now laid open before me.

A few shallow briny lakes appeared, dotting the valley's surface in resolute isolation. Then, we spotted the green foliage of the single freshwater oasis, a few palm trees, and a few mud-brick homes that bespoke of life, reinforced by Jeep tracks leading off to who knows where. I wanted more than anything to be on the floor of the depression, walking the shores of the lagoons, following tracks to distant horizons.

Throughout history, the great Libyan desert and the Qattara Depression have guarded Cairo against every attempt at a western desert invasion. I looked at that desert from my jump seat window and wondered how anyone could envision such a campaign. Of course, the Qattara Depression had nothing to say about a strike on Cairo from the air. That was altogether a different matter.

We completed the planned passes when Dad announced his last vectors, taking us along the northern curve of the depression, which was shaped like a teardrop, with its shallow point facing northeast directly toward the Nile Delta and Cairo. I found, however, that the shape and depth of the northern curve were more like that of a medieval lance, a thin curved blade atop a long pole. Interestingly, the Northern Curve tapers out at elevation just before the Nile Delta, with the tip of its lance pointed directly at Cairo. It was then Dad said, "Hossain, it's time to trim some trees." I do believe I saw Hossain smile just a bit as he took the controls.

CHAPTER TWENTY-SIX

Alexandria

Between the generous month-long winter break and the freedom of the summer vacation, AUC provided only a week off for Spring break. The springtime weather in Egypt was glorious. Terry would be returning to UC Santa Barbara when the school year was over, so this was our last opportunity to explore the area together.

As we bemoaned the brevity of our time off and scoured the travel magazines for vacation ideas, our good friend, Eliot Giuili, graciously invited Terry, our friend Richard, and me to enjoy his family's beach house in Alexandria. For years, Eliot good-naturedly teased that we just showed up, but we all knew he had given us the address and a photo to guide us to his bungalow.

For me, this was an opportunity to explore the great city of Alexandria, romanticized in the blockbuster movie *Cleopatra* that had opened in Los Angeles the previous year. Having played Mark Anthony once and Caesar Augustus twice in high school productions, I knew the story well. I was captivated by the city where Cleopatra ignited her famous tryst with Julius Caesar, having her servants smuggle her into Caesar's palace in a rolled-up carpet. Though I was fully aware of how this famous tryst turned out, I couldn't wait to get a head start on the week.

Finding the ticket window for Alexandria seemed nearly impossible in the chaos and near derangement of the huge Ramses Train Station.

Our efforts quickly turned into a Kafka-like dream with false starts, dead ends, and a crushing stream of passengers. Fortunately, a well-dressed young Cairene man stepped forward. "You look lost," he said with a smile, and we quickly corroborated his assessment. After learning we were going to Alexandria, the polite young man offered to assist in negotiating the best accommodation for our trip. We followed him to the ticket booth, and after a bit of haggling, he turned with a smile, assuring us he had negotiated an excellent cabin for a little baksheesh, a small monetary gift. Then, he graciously led us through the maze of people directly to our cabin. We demonstrated our gratitude with a generous tip.

As a practical matter for most Anglicized passengers, First Class travel was required, not an elective. Fortunately, our cabin was quite comfortable. So, we settled in as Richard ordered three Stella Beers from our attendant, expecting we would arrive in Alexandria in a little less than three hours, in time to catch a cab that would take us to Eliot's beach house well before evening. We leaned back, enjoying our departure from the station.

Life Was Good

We relaxed, chatting casually as our train made its way out of the station and then out of Cairo. We were entranced with all that was going on outside our window, and all was seemingly going well until one of our fellow passengers asked, "Where on the Red Sea will you be visiting?"

"Huh?" one of us responded, confused by the comment. "We are going to Alexandria."

"Oh," the passenger said; then, after a brief pause, he leaned forward, inquiring, "Do you know this train is going east to Port Suez on the Red Sea?"

"Alexandria," another passenger said helpfully, "is the other way."

"What?" one of us said. "We are going to Alexandria."

"No. You are going to the Red Sea."

We looked at each other as a vigorous discussion was taking place among our cabin mates regarding the best course for dealing with our predicament. A small crowd gathered outside our compartment door. Seemingly, each member of our audience was anxious to share their opinion, but the consensus was unanimous. We were going the wrong way.

The three of us sat in stunned silence until Richard voiced the now obvious. "We are heading to the Suez canal?"

"Yes, Port Said on the Red Sea," said our fellow passenger, relieved that all was right, now that we knew where we were going.

"We will arrive in several hours," another passenger added, also looking relieved.

We looked at each other until one of us said soberly, "We are going the wrong way."

Morose silence ensued until one of our new friends said obligingly, "It is a fascinating town. Lots of history." He overlooked the fact that we would be arriving in the middle of the night.

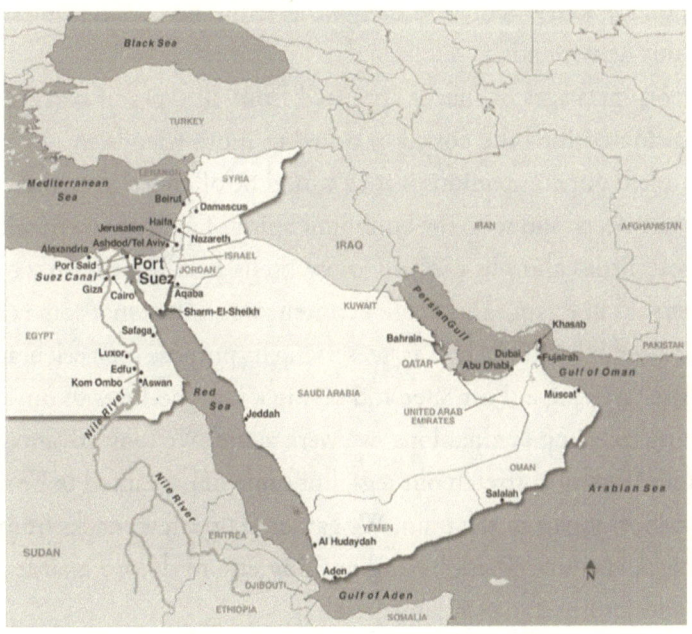

Map showing Cairo between Port Suez and Port Said

Now a crowd was forming outside of our cabin as our conductor quickly restored order. "You have no choice but to stay on the train until we arrive at Port Said," he said with authority. "Once we reach Port Said, you have two options. After a brief layover, you can take the train coming back from Port Said to Alexandria, arriving at midnight. Alternatively, after an hour's stop at Port Suez on the Red Sea, you can get out and stretch, have some food and get back on the same train as it travels north along the Suez Canal. Once it reaches the Mediterranean, the train heads east to Alexandria." I was following closely on my map, and indeed, Port Said was the easternmost point of the Nile Delta. "If you take the second option, you will arrive in Alexandria at six o'clock tomorrow morning. That is best for you as you can sleep most of the way."

We were thankful for all the advice we received from our cabin mates. Still, we were more than a little morose about our detour until Richard chimed in, flashing his infectious smile and stretching out his arms, "What is there to complain about? The couch is comfortable. The food is good, and the company wonderful," he said, earning smiles from our new friends.

Soon, packages of snacks appeared from all types of parcels. The aroma floated into the corridor, drawing more friends to our door. Terry asked our companions if they would be offended if we ordered a few Stella Beers, and soon the bonhomie spirit of unexpected friendship filled our little cabin. Just so you know, Stella Beer was the only brand of beer sold in Egypt. The alcohol content was so low that some called it near-beer, but it had a beer taste, serving its purpose for a celebration.

After arriving at Port Suez and saying a few goodbyes to our well-meaning traveling companions, we were alone. We took advantage of the hour layover to stretch our legs, but none of us wanted to be more than a short jog from the train. We gathered up a few snacks from the late-night vendors. Then, having nothing else to do, we boarded the train and returned to our compartment.

Our conductor came by several times, making sure he knew where we were. The good news was that we were on schedule to arrive at

Alexandria in the early morning, refreshed and ready to go.

We were comfortable in our compartment, swaying with the rhythm of the tracks, enjoying the cool air from the delta. I looked into the darkness, wondering at the mystery of where this would end. Soon I was asleep.

I awoke in the near light or, as Dad would say, "Oh-dark-hundred," but what I came to call the time of silence. We were somewhere in the Nile Delta. I do not remember stars, conversation, impatience, or discomfort, but I do remember I was not unsettled by our setbacks, as such things were not new to me. We would miss a night in Alexandria with our friends, but I was accustomed to taking things as they came, just as I had many times before and just as I would in times to come. Trains in the night bearing me on was all that mattered.

We stopped a few times for no apparent reason. I saw papyrus reeds thick in the ponds, having yet to bend to a breeze, and an early grayish mist spread over the delta. Dim was the morning light; I nodded off again.

Soon, Alexandria

I awoke to an early morn, the eastern sky sporting a rosy haze. Not knowing how far we had traveled or how far we had to go, I settled into a repose that served me well on many journeys past, as it would on journeys yet to come. We were traveling, and I was content.

We made several stops at small villages, the names of which I cannot recall. I had no way of knowing whether we had passed over any of these villages on flights with my father. My repose began to give way to subtle anticipation as the great city of Alexandria drew near.

Seaside bungalows and small hotels appeared along a misty shoreline, though I could detect no signs of life. The coast curved hard to the south, jostling Terry and Richard awake. We were traveling through the rolling dunes of the western verge of the delta. Dotted by grayish-green succulents, the coastline was coming alive with signs of civilization sprouting in clusters.

We reached the outskirts of Alexandria. *Falukas*, their triangular sails partially hoisted, were ready to catch the morning wind, waiting to be rewarded for their efforts. I felt languorous watching barges and yachts that remained strapped together. Smoke from small charcoal fires settled in as if to whisper, "Not yet, not yet." Then we passed through the quiet fringes of the city.

For nearly an hour, we maintained this leisurely pace. It seemed forever. I dozed, but soon the pace quickened, a walking pace for sure but then—a trot. Our conductor wandered through, stirring those who still slept, giving a friendly wave. He stopped to exchange pleasantries as we provided him with more than the expected baksheesh before we arrived.

Alexandria

A few early morning passengers disembarked with us, and they disappeared quickly through the lofty baroque station, leaving us suddenly alone in the rosy glow of the high walls of the station, wondering, "What's next?"

Misr Railroad Station, Alexandria, Egypt.
Image via Victorianweb.com.

There were no attendants, no passengers, no vendors. We were alone in the stunningly beautiful arcade of the station with its stained-glass windows, seemingly disappearing upward into the rosy vault of heaven. The ticket booths were empty; the connecting vestibules were empty; the adjoining halls and the grand portico all were empty. We walked slowly out of the portico into the roundabout, hearing only the echoes of our progress as we made our way to the plaza.

There were no policemen, and the restaurants and hotels were shuttered tight. None of the many shops were open. So, we settled on a bench in the middle of the plaza to consider our options. Eliot's instructions were straightforward: "Just hail a cab and give the driver our name. He will find us. It is a short ride, and unlike Cairo, cab drivers in Alexandria are all honest, as everyone knows everyone. They will take you right to our retreat." I had kept the black and white photograph he had given me, so what could go wrong?

First of all, there wasn't a taxi, car, bus, police officer, or even a phone to be found. And, of course, we didn't think to get Eliot's phone number. Besides, we wouldn't have awakened him this early in the morning unless we were in dire straits, which was far from our current circumstance. So, in lieu of waiting until a taxi showed up, we strolled west along the promenade until we found an open restaurant or snack shop.

Fortunately, my guidebook had a simplified map of the harbor. It was a beautiful walk. The crescent-shaped harbor, exquisite with its expansive romantic esplanade, curved gently to the west along a row of pensions, hotels, and apartments.

All was aglow in the misty pink light of morning. The small café at the point of the esplanade was not open, nor were the hotels or the shops, but it did not matter as we were living in a fantasy world.

After a while, we decided to give up our search for open establishments. Finally, Richard suggested, "We know Eliot's place is on the beach to the west, and we have the photo, so let's just keep walking." We did, and fortunately, we had packed light.

Rounding the promenade, we saw a seemingly endless beach gently curving into the western horizon. "Hurray, we are on the right track," I said, letting my sarcasm hang.

"A trek to the end of the world," Richard acknowledged.

We decided to settle in on one of the sidewalk benches. It was a lovely day, so I said, "All we need is a beer," which earned me a few chuckles. But then, almost magically, rounding the corner was a Stella Beer delivery truck. We sat somewhat dumbfounded as the truck navigated the narrow drive and stopped just a few storefronts away. Opening the panel door, a burly stockman loaded his dolly with cases of Stella Beer, then wheeled it before us to the café door, which he opened with a key.

"The delivery guy must know the Giuili Beach house," I said, pulling out the picture, showing him expectantly. Richard chuckled, as did Terry, who laughed outright, but then the driver, looking closely at the picture, said, "Yes, yes, I will take you there." We had been around long enough to know that "Yes, yes!" means—"I will find a way." Which means, "Allah will provide." For the trade class, "I do not know" is not a polite answer.

He was friendly and persistent, beckoning us to squeeze into the truck's cab, which was cozy but manageable. Our duffel bags were stuffed safely behind us.

"Allah provides," I said, causing our driver to smile broadly.

"Yes, yes, Allah provides!"

So Off We Went

We rounded the corner of the road, which seemed to run to eternity. Soon we were shouting out, "There it is, Eliot's home!" and showing off the photograph.

"Allah provides," said our driver. We all echoed him. We offered a generous tip and bought several cases of Stella beer, which I am sure was at a premium. Even though only a few folks were awake that early, we made a big hit driving up to Eliot's beach house in a Stella Beer truck.

Over time, the story took on epic proportions, "Like John Wayne riding to the rescue," one of Eliot's friends said.

The veranda of the beach house faced the sea, of course. There was a roasting pit where kabobs of various meats seemed perpetually available, along with a remarkable variety of traditional Egyptian dishes, all incredibly delicious. Mom was a great cook, and she was a bit incredulous when I raved about the vegetable dishes we enjoyed since I rarely touched vegetables. To this day, I remain a great fan of Egyptian cuisine.

The following days were great fun. Paddle tennis games were a constant, along with lots of swimming, napping, drinking, and simply lounging around. The evening parties went late into the night as we gathered around small fire pits on the beach. More fun, more stories, and then, late into the evening, we retired to the veranda, where soft cushions, pillows, and light blankets provided for a comfortable sleep.

Too soon, it was time to head home from our perfect trip, but I was suffering substantial guilt for not visiting even one of the magnificent museums of the ancient world. I guess I was becoming a true denizen of Egypt.

We left Alexandria midday, the third day of our stay, tired and more than a wee bit spent. I was looking forward to sleeping most of the trip back to Cairo in our first-class cabin, and thank goodness, there was a bit of air-conditioning, so my hope for a nap did not seem unreasonable.

The Return Trip

On any given working day, the Nile River was alive with energy. *Falukas*, their white sails spread wide, plied the great river. Their decks stacked high with bales of cotton, crates of produce, sacks of fruit and nuts, and livestock tethered or strapped together again stirred my wanderlust. Majestic white and black herons swooped by, culling the shallow waters for small fish, trekking through the mud to snare snails or clams along the shore.

Our accommodations were comfortable as long as the train was moving, but counterintuitively, the air conditioner quit whenever the train slowed down. At about the halfway point of our journey, we came to a major depot crowded with freight, much of which was to be loaded onto our train.

The temperature and humidity in our cabin rose quickly, causing Richard to take what seemed to be a reasoned response to our circumstances. He stood and started pulling down the window of our compartment to allow some air in. "Stop!" screamed one passenger; "No, no!" shouted another, but the window was now partially open.

Richard turned from the window, saying a puzzled, "What?"

"Close the window, close the window!" our fellow passengers shouted, all nearly hysterical. Not knowing why Richard turned to do as he was told, but it was too late. Immediately a large sack, thrown by someone on the platform, hit him in the stomach knocking him nearly over.

"Close the window, close the window!" the passengers shouted but, again, it was too late. As Richard finally turned to close the window, he was hit in the chest with a suitcase, and then the crowd hoisted a very large woman in full black peasant garb into the window. She immediately settled her formidable girth onto Richard's lap, still pulling bags and bundles into the cabin.

Richard's eyes were as large as saucers, but there was nothing that he or any of us could do as streams of boxes, bags, and children were pressed through the window while passengers mobilized, attempting to throw boxes and bags back out the window.

It was mayhem. Arguments broke out as our small compartment was about to burst. Through all of this, the heavy *fellah*, or peasant, remained on Richard's lap, nearly obscuring him from view, except for his bulging, astonished eyes. To his credit, he maintained an Alfred E. Newman grin. Finally, the conductor stormed into our cabin, yelling at the top of his voice, gesturing for the interlopers to climb back out the window as he attempted to throw baggage and boxes back onto the station platform. But his efforts were too little and too late.

The tumult grew as train personnel blocked the entrance to the corridor. More and more travelers without tickets prevented baggage and passengers from being shoved back out the window. Finally, after a tremendous amount of pushing and gesticulating, the conductor and the earliest interlopers worked out some type of compromise, and the earliest new passengers were allowed to stay. It was an event to remember.

Soon, we arrived back in Cairo. Our remarkable, circuitous, improbable journey and Eliot's hospitality will never be forgotten!

Postlude

Through two remarkable coincidences, I reconnected with Eliot and his beautiful wife, Mariola, whom I had met for the first time at the beach house. Our reconnection was simply miraculous, the result of a chance run-in at a coffee shop in Union Square, San Francisco, just a few weeks after I graduated from law school. However, my chance encounter was not with Eliot but with Kosey, another AUC classmate from Egypt.

As I was standing in line at the coffee shop, my attention was drawn to a group of young men speaking a mixture of Arabic and French. One of them seemed vaguely familiar. He kept glancing at me as I glanced at him with that look of *do-I know-that-guy*? Then both of us exploded at the same moment with identical enthusiasm. Soon we were laughing and hugging as everyone in the coffee shop stood somewhat agape at our joyous reunion.

I quickly learned that Kosey was with Bank of America, San Francisco. He later became a vice president for the international side of the bank. As we caught up, I asked Kosey if he knew what had become of Eliot. I was terribly worried about him because of the forced diaspora of Cairene Jews after the six-day war. I had lost track of Eliot. I only knew that he and most Jews from prominent families were given two days to leave the country, taking only one suitcase for an entire family. I spent years not knowing what had happened to Eliot and Mariola.

Kosey looked stunned. "You don't know?"

"No," I said with some alarm.

"Eliot and Mariola are married and living in Alameda."

"No!" I erupted again, and by now, all the customers were joining in with the celebration. "No, no!" all of us were yelling.

"Yes, yes!" Kosey was saying joyfully, pounding on me until our frenzy finally settled down. We spent several hours catching up, and many of the customers hung around to hear the rest of our story.

We immediately planned a reunion, which was a great occasion. Eliot became the chief economist for the San Francisco branch of the Federal Reserve, and his lovely wife Mariola became a professor of economics. Remarkably, for years, until his death from cancer, Eliot and Mariola lived only fifteen minutes from our home.

CHAPTER TWENTY-SEVEN

The Valley of the Kings

Terry would soon be returning to UC Santa Barbara, and I had to face the fact that I would likely follow him back to California the following year. We didn't have bucket lists back then, but at nineteen years of age, the sense of diminishing time hung heavily over me.

Mesmerized by the National Geographic my grandmother had given me as a gift, I devoured every article on the Nile River and Egypt. I longed to explore some of the ancient temples in the Valley of the Kings before they were literally swallowed up by the Aswan Dam, which was scheduled to be operational in five short years. The global community was outraged at the indifference of the Egyptians and Russians to the loss of these magnificent monuments carved into the face of the cliff three thousand years before.

Though it was impossible to predict at the time, experts from all over the world mobilized to save these magnificent historical edifices and monuments. This massive undertaking required precise stone cutting, heroic relocation efforts, and substantial funding from global partners to extricate the Abu Simbel Temples and move them to higher ground. This effort began in 1964 and was completed in 1968. The temples themselves were actually carved into the face of a cliff, much like our very own Mount Rushmore here in the United States. Instead of four faces of past presidents, the Abu Simbel temple shows four colossal seated figures of Ramses himself, all about sixty-seven feet in height.

Having learned of the terrible fate facing many of the temples in the Valley of the Kings, and not knowing that they would eventually be saved, I was nearly desperate to see as many of these famed and astounding monuments as possible. At my request, Dad arranged for me to join a scheduled flight check of Aswan's air navigation equipment from Aswan to the Egyptian border with Sudan. The result was a flight up the Nile in one of the DC3s maintained by USAID, but it was more than that. It was a flight back in time with a deep sense of urgency as, day after day, the dam came closer to completion.

The night before our flight to Aswan, I spread out my National Geographic map, intending to learn as much as I could about the great river. I was aware that the precise origin of the Nile was unknown and that which was known was often disputed. Both National Geographic and the Smithsonian agreed that the river's two main sources, the Blue and White Nile, merged high in the Great Plains of middle Africa, initiating a journey of over nine thousand miles to the Mediterranean.

I settled into the jump seat of our DC-3 as we departed Cairo to track the Nile to the south, in reverse of its flow. The river was placid as we left Cairo, but not for long. As we approached the Sudan border, the topography changed dramatically, and the flow of the river accelerated, generating impressive rapids above the Valley of the Kings. Below me, riverbanks melted into bogs as channels stretched out, east and west for miles, then conjoined again.

The sky was filled with birds, Egyptian geese, and ospreys, majestic with their six-foot wingspan, seemingly darkening the day. Fish were in abundance, as were their predators.

Through raging rapids with rocks looming up from the deep, the muddy river raced. Layers of sediment revealing its history, I saw the water plunge deep into unknown pools, only to burst upward again. It rumbled through jagged rocks, exploding the river's surface, funneling, then slowing, only to race again. Finally, I saw the great river slow as it entered into what T.S. Eliot might have had in mind when he penned,

"The still point of the turning world." Here the current of the White Nile joined with the Blue in the dry throat of the northern desert. I noticed especially here how time passes yet into eternity. My ruminations of that time some fifty years ago, inspired me to write this poem:

Night Visions

I drift south
for how long, I do not know
Finally, the river opens into broad places
two miles wide or more
In the darkness of my dream or my vision, I know not which
the canopy of the night sky opens above me
revealing again the deep blue silhouette of the first of the great pyramids
One by one, I pass them by, toneless and mute, hundreds of miles apart,
each great in stature, seeming as sentinels
warning those who dare venture further
of the might and power of the kingdom they are about to enter

CHAPTER TWENTY-EIGHT

On My Own

"Summer turnover" was part of life for expatriates whose tour was coming to an end. As for others, most found ways to be elsewhere during the scorching summer months, whether on a vacation or home leave, anywhere but Cairo. Cairenes of means would escape to their summer homes on the Mediterranean or elsewhere in Europe. No one with means would choose to stay an entire summer in Cairo, where the daytime temperatures spike at 120 degrees, seldom breaking below 95 degrees. That is, no one but Dad, who for some reason felt the need to see how his aircraft and pilots functioned in the unmerciful Cairene summer.

The city was like a specter during the heat of the day. Temperatures above 120 degrees Fahrenheit were not uncommon. When combined with frequent summer sandstorms, the city's inhabitants stayed indoors, emerging only when the evening breeze from the Nile provided some relief.

I experienced a few of these sandstorms that required that we shutter up and then fill every opening, slot, split or crack and cover our nose and mouth with a fine wet cloth. I was determined not to spend the summer in Cairo.

The Sell

So, I informed my parents that I wanted to tour Europe during the upcoming summer.

"Who will you be traveling with?" Mom asked, cutting to the chase. This was the delicate question I had been expecting, for which I had no good answer. All my expatriate friends were headed home, and my Egyptian friends were scattering to various locations in Europe and the Mediterranean.

"That is still unclear," I said, but I quickly rattled off a list of friends I planned to visit in Europe, each of whom had expressed excitement about the possibility. I exaggerated a bit. The great thing about my strategy was that it was all based in fact, and as a good friend of mine said, "If the truth works, why not use it?" to which I responded, "I think you are on to something."

Uncharacteristically, Mom bored in. "Fine, but who will you be traveling *with*?"

I replied, "Well, all the details have not yet been worked out."

Dad seemed to be enjoying the jousting, but Mom was not amused, and she pressed on. "Well then, how about sharing those details that you *do* know?" Dad loved watching Mom at work.

Knowing this would happen, I was ready with my list of "friends." I started with Eliot because my parents approved of him.

"Eliot is going with you?" she asked, knowing that Eliot was a sophisticated cosmopolitan.

"No . . . but when Eliot found out about my adventure, he wrote to one of his best friends, Jean-Paul, whose family has a flat in Florence, giving him the approximate days I would be there. Jean-Paul wrote back right away, saying he would definitely have room on his couch for as long as needed."

Mom's blue eyes were turning a cold gray. "How long have you been considering this junket?" she said, drilling down on me. I pulled the letter out and showed her the postmark. This technique of presenting the strongest evidence first served me well in later years as a trial lawyer.

The second friend I talked about was Nadia. Telling Mom about Nadia was also somewhat of a trump card as Nadia was a compelling friend. The daughter of a well-known Egyptian industrialist and a former Miss Sweden, Nadia was beautiful and charming. Oh, and did I mention that I almost accidentally killed her cat when we were studying in the second-floor library of her home in Maadi? But that is another story.

"Nadia?" Mom said, somewhat taken aback.

"Yes," I said though the invitation was little more than a "You must stop by if you visit Sweden."

"Nadia assured me that her family had assured her that they would welcome a visit from me," I explained. I immediately knew there were too many "assureds," so I quickly moved on. Dad listened in silence as Mom continued the inquisition.

Now things were getting a bit dicey as the third friend was a friend of my friend Jane. Jane was a student at AUC who was living with her aunt, a lady with significant responsibilities with the embassy. My parents knew her aunt. Jane's parents were with the US Diplomatic Corp stationed in Switzerland. Tragically, they had died in a car accident two years earlier when the family was posted in Switzerland, resulting in Jane living in Cairo with her aunt and closest relative.

Jane and I had dated a few times, and our relationship was more down than up. Anyway, a few months before, Jane had informed me that, for reasons I cannot recall, her friend from school in Switzerland was coming for a visit and Jane was hoping I could arrange a double date. I thought that my friend Jack, from our winter vacation adventures, would be a great candidate, a suggestion Jane quickly endorsed, a little too enthusiastically, I thought. And, once again, my instincts were right.

Knowing that Jane's aunt and my parents were attending an embassy affair, I suggested Jack and I prepare the dinner so that Jane could enjoy the time with her friend, and since we would be taking care of dinner, she could send her servant home early. Yes, I was a kind and thoughtful person without a duplicitous bone in my body, just trying to give the hardworking servant a night off. Jane readily agreed, a little too quickly. *Hmm*, I thought.

Jack and I arrived that evening, loaded with boxes and bags full of wonderful ingredients. As gentlemen would, we urged the ladies to "Relax, enjoy the wine and leave the cooking to us." Then, Jack and I ensconced ourselves in the kitchen along with a nice bottle of white French wine. Gallantly, we occasionally stepped out to the living room to freshen the ladies' glasses while protecting the kitchen door from entry.

Having retreated to the kitchen, we clanged and banged on pots and pans, muttering occasional mock insults under our breath. When some of our clanging and curses became a bit too loud, the ladies made efforts to invade our territory, but we repelled the invasion saying, "Not now, please ladies, patience pleeeaaase!"

So, after more clanging of metal spoons, rattling of dishes, and occasional cursing, Jack and I sat in the kitchen, sipping more and more wine, occasionally coming out to the living room with smudges and splatters on our aprons to engage in small talk. Then after a few sips of wine, we would return to the kitchen and our great work.

Soon the delicious smells of chicken cacciatore wafted from the kitchen into the living room. The meal, of course, was actually prepared by our very talented family cook, Mohammed, and sealed in Mom's large food containers that we used when having parties around the pyramids. We brought the food into the apartment cold, so no smells would give us away, and we had stuffed fresh vegetables on top of the boxes to provide a touch of authenticity.

Finally, exhausted, we announced the salad course was ready and said we would assemble it at the table.

It took Jack and I several trips to bring the salad components to the dining table, which included: the thoroughly washed and shredded romaine leaves (just as Mohammed had taught us); shredded parmesan cheese (grated by Mohammed); horseradish and chopped anchovies, both precisely measured out into small bowls (by Mohammed); and small cubes of bread pre-cooked in olive oil with garlic infusion (by

Mohammed)—which we warmed and stirred in the frying pan just before serving in the dining room. Jack and I actually cooked and crumbled bacon slices, as Mohammed insisted they must be cooked fresh and served warm. It was a challenge, but the bacon came out perfectly cooked, crumbled, and, yes, hot.

We were very proud of our preparations.

We brought forth the wooden salad bowl at the table, which we seasoned with several cloves of garlic gleaned from their skin earlier by Mohammed. We then crushed the garlic against the interior of our wooden salad bowl while daintily covering our fingers with a paper napkin to prevent a lingering unpleasant smell. I then squeezed the juice of one lemon and added one tablespoon of Worcestershire sauce and three quarters of a cup of olive oil, all of which were in small sealed bowls previously prepared by Mohammed. I then smartly swirled the ingredients around the bowl with a whisk, as Mohammed had taught us.

Roger and Mohammed

The mélange of scents wafted through the room. We added the shredded and torn lettuce leaves and mixed and tossed them with all the ingredients in the salad bowl. Finally, Jack spooned the Parmesan over the salad.

The ladies were stunned. "Salad is served," Jack said, his tall, lanky frame standing, poised and confident, with all the pomp and circumstance such an occasion deserved. At each serving, I filled the wine glasses from the lovely bottle of French wine that Jane's aunt had so kindly provided. The ladies had been looking at each of us quizzically, with an edge of skepticism during the assembly, which lingered through the serving, but soon, the aroma emanating from the Caesar salad quelled any skepticism. Following the salad course, the chicken cacciatore confirmed our culinary expertise.

From that moment on, the dinner went very well. We had a lot of fun, but it was soon apparent that Jane was more interested in Jack than in me, and that would have put a chill on the evening except for Jane's friend, who was clearly interested in me. Before the evening was over, we succumbed to the obvious. I learned later that Jane's friend asked if she could communicate with me regarding my summer trip. Jane had no problem acquiescing to her friend's request, as Jack was her primary objective.

And that is how I ended up in Geneva the following summer. I truncated the story quite a bit for my parents, "You remember Jane's friend from Switzerland?" I said with confidence.

The fourth and last "friend" was an adorable redheaded girl I had noticed walking through the Commons in late spring 1965. She was looking around a bit befuddled, which I later learned was her normal state of being.

Chivalry was ingrained in me, particularly if a pretty girl was at stake. "You seem as if you might be lost. Can I help you?" I said in a gentlemanly way, as drilled into me by my parents.

She was an art student on a three-week spring break from the American University of Vienna. Being a gracious host, I offered to familiarize her with Tahrir Square. With an attractive Texas drawl, she smiled and said, "Thanks so much, but all of the classes will be held at the museum; we have been touring the area around the square for the last few days."

"Great. I will know where to find you and when you are finished with your classes, perhaps you will allow me to show you some of the sites not on the tourist maps."

She smiled graciously, giving me the address of her school and dormitory. She didn't tell me how restrictive the school was about male visitors, nor did she tell me of her restricted curfew hours, but I viewed such matters only as tactical issues.

So, that was four, and I thought four wasn't bad as they were strategically spread out across the continent.

Now the hard part: how should I tell my parents I want to tour Europe during the rapidly approaching summer—on my own?

Trying to finesse either of my parents would result in a quick and perfunctory rejection. So, I set upon a straightforward approach. I knew Dad would want details, and Mom would want some form of security so that the perils of last winter's journey would not be repeated. I had prepared my presentation meticulously. I stated where and how I would travel, where I planned to stay, and who I would travel with. "Terry and Richard are headed back to the States by way of Asia. Many of my friends are headed back to the States for summer leave; my Egyptian friends are headed for summer homes in various places in Europe, and I have several invitations to visit them this summer."

"And who would you be traveling with?" Mom said casually but directly, immediately getting to her most significant concern.

"I want to travel alone. It'll be a good experience for me to be on my own." Gulp! There it was.

Mom remained calm, but her big blue eyes opened wider than usual, and her back straightened as she took a deep breath.

"I have it all worked out," I said, opening my travel journal.

Dad looked on, not giving away anything.

"Why alone?" Mom said in an even voice, but I knew she was marshaling her attack against my plan.

So, I launched, "I think it is time I was on my own. Dad joined the Marine Corps and went off to fight a war when he was my age (a bit of an exaggeration), and I just think it is time for me to be on my own."

Dad said only, "What are your plans?" and I knew that the decision was made as long as I didn't do anything stupid.

"First, I will procure a Euro-pass. It's one of God's gifts to young travelers, pre-paid rail travel and some ferry services to virtually anywhere one could want to go in Europe; first-class cabins (shared, of course) for three hundred and fifty dollars for unlimited travel for ninety days." Dad was not passive, and he tested the depth of my plans. I responded succinctly and rapidly to each question: "I will stay at youth hostels; they charge only three dollars a night, including breakfast." I added, waving the secular traveler's Good Book, *Europe on Ten Dollars a Day*.

I had not yet mentioned the length of my trip, but now was the time. "I developed a budget for ninety days, three dollars for each night's stay, including breakfast. Then for other meals and incidentals, seven dollars a day." Europe was a deal then.

Sensing I was on a roll, I headed for the barn, "Ninety days would be nine hundred dollars." Mom wasn't concerned a lick about my budget, but she was very concerned about me traveling alone. After all, I was her baby. Now was the time to replay the friends card, so I reminded them about my four friends who encouraged me to visit. "So," I concluded, "I will always have a place of refuge."

Dad weighed in. "Am I correct that three of the four are ladies?"

"Why I hadn't thought about that, but you are right." And I knew then that the deal was sealed with Dad as he looked at Mom, saying, "Remember, when I was his age, I was fighting a war." Again, a bit of an exaggeration, but the point was made.

I was home free. I could sense it when Mom said, "What if he is in an accident?"

Dad closed the discussion. "Remember, he'll be carrying the black passport." Each of us had received a black passport, exclusively given to diplomats and their families, when we arrived in Cairo. Case closed.

I am certain Dad was not familiar with the term *coming of age*, but he innately knew this would be a pivotal experience for me, even more than my experience the previous winter, as this time I would be on my own and out of Terry's shadow. He was right. The summer of 1965 was the year I changed from a boy to a young man, but nothing came easily.

Once I got the go-ahead, everything fell into place, and soon, I was off on what seemed to be the same Greek freighter I had taken the winter before. This time the weather was clear and balmy. I stood on the deck, considering Dad's last words as he saw me off. "You can't plan for everything." He said, looking me in the eye. "So, if you get in a pinch, act on what your gut tells you is right. But whatever you do, act." *Always the Marine*, I thought, wondering what the hell that meant. "Trust your gut," he added, and almost immediately, I learned.

Trust Your Gut—and Act!

On this trip, there was no storm, so the sky remained blue from Alexandria to Greece. I made friends with a few crew members. A cook took me under his wing, providing me a few plates of food from the galley from time to time and a bit of wine. They were interested in America, and I was interested in their lives on the sea.

Just before disembarking at Piraeus, my friend the cook took me over to the rail, asking me if I could do him a great favor. "I am supposed to meet my brother to go to my father's eightieth birthday," he said, pointing and waving enthusiastically to his brother on the dock below, who was waving just as enthusiastically back. "Now they tell me I have galley duty and can't leave the ship until midnight," he said sorrowfully. "My father's birthday is tonight! Would you take the birthday present down to my brother?"

"Sure," I said without much thought, thinking he had been kind to me, and it was the least I could do.

So, he gave his brother another wave, nodding his head up and down and patting my back. "Thank you, thank you so much!" he gushed. "Come with me, and I will give you the present to give to my brother," he said, pulling me into a dark passageway. Passengers were starting to disembark, and I was getting a bit nervous. I had my duffel bag slung over my shoulder, ready to go. He quickly took a brand-new Rolex watch out of his pocket and started slipping it onto my wrist.

"No, no, just put it in my bag," I said.

"Just wear it off," he said, shaking loose of me, and before I knew it, he was gone, and the watch was on my wrist.

I was stunned. People were disembarking. "Don't worry," rung in my ears as I looked out at his brother waving at me, "My brother will meet you as soon as you get off the gangplank. There will be no problem, really no problem," echoed in my ears.

Yes, there were all sorts of red flags, and yes, I knew something was wrong, but I wasn't thinking; I just let myself be pulled along by events. I walked down the plank with my heart racing. The cook's "brother" grabbed me roughly by the arm as soon as I stepped off the gangplank and steered me around the corner, where he summarily stripped the watch off my arm before I knew what he was doing. Then he was gone. I hadn't even felt it coming off, I thought as he disappeared into the crowd without even a thank you.

I was more than a little stunned. I was scared, but then I was furious, not at the con artist but at myself. Bad enough for having been used, but worse for not stopping immediately when I sensed something was wrong.

I learned several lasting lessons from this event, which I have since shared with the junior high and senior high Sunday school classes I teach: First, when confronted with important issues, never succumb to pressure from others; rather, listen critically to advice, but in the end, take responsibility for your decisions. Second, be prepared to alter course as events change or your thinking matures. Third, keep thinking, evaluating, and looking for ways to improve circumstances for yourself and others. Finally, and most importantly, when the moment requires action—don't talk, act!"

As a retired trial attorney, Sunday school teacher, and father, lecturing is what I do best.

The Saronic Gulf in the Aegean Sea

Even with Eliot's emphatic assurances of Jean-Paul's warm, welcoming response, I admit to harboring more than a bit of trepidation. "Knowing your travel plans and very tight budget," Eliot had informed me, "Jean-Paul will take care of you. As soon as you get off the ship, find your way to the ferries headed to Venice. However," he advised, "I urge you to take the ferry that travels through the Corinth Canal. This route is a bit longer, but it is the trip of a lifetime."

Reviewing my travel book, I learned that the Corinth Canal is a very narrow passage connecting the Gulf of Corinth with the Saronic Gulf to the west, ultimately opening into the Aegean Sea on the eastern side of the Isthmus of Corinth. What was memorable to me was the canal itself.

The sheer limestone walls of the narrow canal reflected the light of day, from misty grays in the morning light to brilliant orange, red, and mauve in the late afternoon. The canal was so narrow, only pleasure crafts and small ferries could pass through. Thus, the decision to travel through the canal required tradeoffs. Those wanting faster travel or greater comfort should select a larger ship. I have never regretted choosing such less traveled courses as prescribed by Robert Frost in *The Road Not Taken*, which seemed to guide most of my travel decisions.

We reached the canal in less than three hours, traveling first counterclockwise south of the island of Salamis and then nearly due west to the eastern entry of the canal.

The Corinth Canal.

As we entered, people waved from the bridge rails on high as they did with each succeeding bridge. I waved back but felt like a speck looking up from dark obscurity to the sharp-edged shadows slicing the canyon walls diagonally—dark gray below, exploding light on high, a horizontal rainbow playing on the canyon walls. With each successive bridge, witnesses lining the rails cheered us on our way. Our craft's mighty trumpets boomed in reply, sending echoes out to eternity.

We Soon Entered Open Sea, Then Slept

We passed into the open waters of the Gulf of Corinth, a wide-open stretch of sea, as the sun was near setting, but I had long been asleep. Most of our journey would be in the dark, so I would arrive in Venice refreshed the next morning when I would make my way to the train station, which I understood to be close to the port.

"There are many restaurants near the Venice train terminal that serve cheap breakfast croissants," Jean-Paul informed me in his earlier letter. You will be in Florence before noon, depending upon how early you get going. Call me when you arrive at the train station," he told me.

I did just as Jean-Paul advised, and all went well.

Arrival Florence

The payphone was in my hand, but I hesitated, considering what type of reception I, a total stranger, might receive. I still wasn't sure what I was getting into, though I had Eliot's firm assurances, and Jean-Paul had been solicitous and welcoming from the moment he learned of my plans to visit. To my relief, he answered the phone before the third ring. Jean-Paul somehow knew it was me as he gave me a gracious "Hello Roger" before I had a chance to identify myself. Jean-Paul gave clear instructions about the bus I should take and the plaza stop where I was to get off. "Just a short ten-minute ride. When you exit the bus, look straight across the plaza; and you will see a pink stone apartment building. Look up to a second-floor balcony; my friend and I will be waving at you," he said.

And so, things went, as he was at the balcony rail waving at me, along with his friend, just as he had said.

I do not recall the plaza's name, but it was just a few blocks from the Ponte Vecchio, the famous arched bridge, which was one of the top five sites I had aspired to see while in Florence. All went well. I got off the bus, looked across the small plaza, and saw two people waving at me.

I waved back, but there was one potential problem. The "friend" was a pretty strawberry blonde with long hair. She was very pretty (or did I tell you that already?) who happened to be, well, topless. Completely topless!

Walking across the small plaza, I sheepishly kept my head down until Jean-Paul yelled, "I will buzz you in!"

"What do I do?" I asked myself as I walked into the stone-paved foyer that opened to an impressive winding stone stairwell. I looked up to see Jean-Paul and his friend smiling down and waving from the first-floor landing. I am confident that all young travelers know the relief of a harbor safely reached. Such were my feelings as I walked up the stairs, and it helped immensely that Jean Paul's companion had now donned a blouse, diaphanous as it was. I soon relaxed.

I beamed with joy at my arrival and the warmth of my greeting. Quickly I was escorted into their lovely flat, a spacious one bedroom, one bath apartment with an open living room and a kitchen that had a brick oven and sleek pendant lights with rose oblong shades. Jean-Paul waved me toward a comfortable-looking couch, telling me that it was where I would be sleeping and that we would share the bathroom. All seemed very comfortable, and I effusively expressed my delight. The living room opened to the large balcony I had seen from below. As I surveyed the plaza, he reminded me I was welcome to stay as long as I liked.

"Well then, Jean-Paul, we shall grow old together!" I said, which garnered a good laugh.

La Dolce Vita

The gracious welcome I received extended throughout the entire three days of my stay. I relaxed and exhaled long and deep, succumbing to the immense joy of being in Florence. Soon after I settled in, Jean-Paul suggested taking a short stroll to the famed Ponte Vecchio medieval bridge over the Arno River. "There is a café we can visit near the entrance and, if you like, you can take a walk through the shops." I learned later that Italians don't enjoy walking like the British and Americans. Italians will scale mountains and ski rough terrain, but just walking seems like a waste of time.

So, we set off with my guidebook in one hand and my camera at the ready. Gracious to the end, neither cringed when I dug out my camera, but they gave me a grateful smile when I laid it down. Later, when I went out alone with my camera, I found that Italians did not seem to mind an American by himself, taking the time to treat the photo to be taken as art rather than just a rushed memory. I had been taking photos for many years, changing perspectives and enjoying the moment, but I seemed to gain some respect on these ventures from those passing by, some of whom would stop for a moment to share a comment, ask a question, or offer a suggestion.

I learned that gracious hospitality is the norm rather than the exception when traveling, yet none could be more hospitable than Jean-Paul and his friend. So, I fell in love with Florence, and I treated each moment as a romance that perhaps one day I would share with one who loves *the moment of being* as much as I do. My friendship with Jean-Paul remains strong in my mind all these years later.

Three days went woefully fast, but I was committed to my travel plan. As I prepared to leave, I learned that there was no straight-line rail service from Florence to Vienna, my next destination. I would have to disembark just north of the Italian border in some little town whose name I cannot remember. Then, I would have to wait for over an hour for the train coming from Germany, which would take me to Vienna. It was a good plan. What could go wrong?

The Stranger on the Train

All went well on the first leg of my journey. I disembarked shortly after midnight just north of the Italian and Austrian border to a well-lit but deserted platform, which was probably Klagenfurt. I was the only passenger to disembark, and I remained the only one on the platform of the deserted station. So, I waited for the connecting train that would deliver me to Vienna at around 9:00 a.m.

I was cold but equipped with my burly travel coat, and I waited out the time without any company whatsoever. When my connection arrived, I boarded quickly. All the cabins were dark, except for one lighted cabin where I heard a lot of soprano voices joking and laughing. *Ah, companionship*, I thought, so I knocked and opened the sliding glass door to find four young ladies about my age. They startled, but I doffed my cap, saying with my best smile, "I came in from Florence, and I am on my way to Vienna. All the cabins are dark, and I didn't want to disturb anyone, so I was wondering, could I join you, ladies?"

After a moment of stunned silence, one of the women said something like, "Ladies, we can't leave this poor fellow out in the cold. I vote for letting him in." The others agreed with mixed levels of enthusiasm. The ladies wanted to know where I was from and why I was going to Vienna. I didn't like saying I was going to visit a girl there since I really didn't know if she wanted to see me anyway, so I said simply, "I am meeting someone there, but it won't be a long visit."

That got a few quizzical looks, but the same young lady who invited me in pressed on. "Well then, if you are not going to tell us why you are headed to Vienna in the middle of the night, how about telling us where you are coming from?"

I diverted again, saying she had a sweet midwestern accent, somewhat like my mom, who was from Ohio. She laughed again and asked, "Just how many accents does your dear mother have? As a matter of fact, I am from Ohio." We both laughed.

But she pressed on. "Where are you from?" she asked.

"Cairo," I said. She looked at me a bit skeptically. "Would that be Cairo, Illinois?"

"No, Cairo, Egypt." I replied, laughing, "but I admire your wit." I thought this would be a good time for a cigarette break, as I needed some air. I went through the corridor to the exit door and pulled down a glass window. The wind felt great as I stuck my head out. I let go of the handle, only to have it spring up with a substantial force. The window hit me hard on my right cheekbone, leaving a two-inch slash, causing me to jerk my head up hard and bang it into the top of the window frame. Pulling the window down, I lurched back, my knees wobbly, my head reeling. Stumbling, I made my way back into the compartment, not thinking about the blood flowing from just below my eye down my cheek and onto my t-shirt. When I was greeted with a chorus of gasps, shrieks, and ululating squeals, I realized what a frightening sight I must have been.

Of course, the ladies wanted to know what had happened to me, but I wasn't about to admit the truth since that would make me out as closer to one of The Three Stooges than to James Bond. Instead, I authoritatively said, "Never mind! but if anyone inquires, please say I have been asleep." Now, I wasn't asking anyone to lie because no one would be inquiring about an event that didn't occur, but it was a deception, a habit I had to cure myself of in the years to come.

So, I curled up with my duffle bag, and the next thing I knew, one of the ladies was shaking me awake. We were in Vienna, and all of us were in a hurry to disembark. I got the hotel's name where the Ohio traveler would be staying, so I was looking forward to my visit.

I enjoyed Vienna. The city was magnificent and dazzling, and both ladies were intelligent, cute, and a lot of fun. The red-haired art student I had met at AUC was in class all day and was only available in the evening. So, my Midwestern friend and I walked the city during the day. Honestly, I wasn't prepared for the city, just as I wasn't prepared for any other part of my trip other than a superficial route plan and my four contacts. A sad commentary on my vagabond schooling experience was that I knew little to nothing about the great cities I was visiting.

Fortunately for me, my new friends were well prepared to make up the slack in my education. During the day, my Ohio friend and I toured museums, picnicked in the parks, and told stories about our friends and families. Then in the evening, my artist friend and I would go through the same light flirtation rituals but never took it further. My fondest memory of these days was hiking through the mountainous parks that looked down on the city.

My artist friend and I enjoyed the small amount of time she could manage. As for my friend from Ohio, we had a lot of fun touring the city and the nearby parks by day, and we spent a few nights strolling through the town when she was not engaged with her traveling companions. I can honestly say we were just good friends.

Geneva

Coming into Geneva was much different from six months before when Terry, Jack, and I struggled over the summit. This time I was traveling first class. The sun was shining; the mountain passes were a lush green sprinkled with small white dots, as lazy cows rested in the sun. I felt fat and lazy myself as I watched the scenery slip by. All was well with the world. I had written to my friend regarding my expected arrival date.

I received a welcoming reply with the apology that while her parents were looking forward to my visit, they could not accommodate a guest, so they had made arrangements for me at a nearby guest house. I was a man at ease, and my repose was well warranted as things worked out.

Her parents were very welcoming. We spent the afternoon getting acquainted, and then they drove me around Geneva, pointing out the sights, including the famous jet d'eau fountain in the middle of Lake Geneva, which spurts water nearly 500 feet in the air. I didn't know it at the time, but I wondered why my friend and her parents graciously took my camera, directing me to pose on the walkway over the lake so they could take my picture. They retired quickly, taking cover, leaving me to get drenched from the unexpected shower. They laughed at their prank, which was a common initiation for newcomers to Geneva.

Lake Geneva's Jet d'eau.
Image via Wikimedia Commons.

We had a great time. Her parents arranged and paid for a beautiful dinner at a nearby restaurant for the two of us. It was very, very romantic.

My time in Geneva remains one of my warmest memories.

La Ville des Lumieres

I had no idea one could have a romance with a city, and as it is with any affair of the heart, memories only sweeten with time. So it was with the "City of Lights" and me. I had the good fortune to know Paris as a youth, singing for wine on the banks of the Seine, then, while visiting with my children, and as a mature professional when I visited after being accorded the great privilege of speaking before The Hague on conflict resolution.

I enjoyed each and every one of these visits, and Paris has never lost its charm. It is my time as a young man, however, that I keep coming back to when in search of my soul.

Again, I arrived midmorning. I set out to find the closest youth hostel, map in hand, but the energy of the moment swept away my plans, leading me to the Avenue des Champs-Elysees. I meandered along the sidewalks, wide-eyed, as I neared the Arc de Triomphe. Cars buzzed around, horns blared, and folks defied death, crossing through traffic while elegant *gendarmes* directed the world from their pedestals, acting as if someone was actually paying attention to their policing.

I spotted a burly Scotsman on the sidewalk. It was not hard to pick him out as he had a great red beard, was wearing his billowy white blouse over his kilt with his *sporran* or pouch hanging low in front, and his gilt hose and ghillie brogue shoes.

What a man he was, and I figured he would know as much about the city as anyone, and I was right. "Can you tell me where the nearest youth hostel is?" I asked, brandishing my map.

"Aye, laddie, am happy to tell ye, but it do ye no good; they're all booked through the summer, lad." I am sure my face showed everything I was thinking. "But nay ye worrie, laddie, we have all the space at our bit (flat), if ye don't mind sleeping on the floor. Help me sell the rest of these papers, and I introduce ye to our tribe." I didn't mind at all.

It turns out that several vagabonds shared the fourth-floor flat where he was staying. It was much less orderly than a youth hostel but had no toll. It was a vagabond commune before I knew the meaning of the word vagabond. Folks slept where they could; informal groups formed to muster up means and play music. There was lots of alcohol but no drugs. Given my circumstances, I was grateful to stay there.

Thus began my two-week love affair with Paris.

The patron of our commune was in his midtwenties. He had the only two flats on the top floor of a four-story apartment building on the left bank, only a few blocks from the Seine. Rumors were that he, or his parents, owned the entire building. The bottom three floors were rented out, apparently at a premium, but he enjoyed the company of the bohemian set. It all worked out, even though I didn't really know what a bohemian was at the time.

I quickly fell into the tug of my Scottish friend's magnetism. The *Tribune* didn't care how my friend sold his papers or who sold them as long as he turned over the street price of the papers sold, minus a small commission for the day's work. We had no territory restrictions, so we could tour as we sold, and as soon as we met our quota, usually by midafternoon, we were off on our own. My friend would be "off the book" if the purse did not balance, so we were scrupulous about our accounting.

When we were done with our papers, we would square up the purse and head back to the tribe. Then we might take a well-earned nap or have a late lunch, depending on the doings of the night before. One afternoon I took off early to shop for a birthday present for Mom. Her favorite perfume was Jean Patou's Joy, and in my wanderings, I discovered the biggest perfumery I had ever seen. In fact, it was the only perfumery I had ever seen.

I entered the store with great trepidation because it was so fancy. Light refracted from every surface, so I could not be sure if what I was seeing was real or a reflection. The store representatives were dazzling in their sleek fashions, seemingly refracting light themselves from their jewelry and haute couture. I walked through the store somewhat stunned and too intimidated to chance an inquiry.

After being ignored for some time as I stood by the counter, one of the salespeople, a very pretty lady, apparently was told to assist me. She approached, exuding an ambiance of *must I?*

"I would like to purchase a bottle of Joy perfume," I said. She looked at me somewhat quizzically as obviously Joy was a premier brand and more than somewhat expensive.

"Very nice," she said, appraising me. "You have good taste for a young man. Is this for a lady friend?"

"No." I said somewhat uncomfortably, "It is for my mother, for her birthday." Her practiced sophistication faded away. It was as if I were her little brother, her precious little brother, standing before her.

"She started speaking rapidly to the other ladies, and soon I was surrounded by beautiful ladies asking me in fluent French, of course, "Your mother, how tall is she?" and they were stunned when I told them. "How old is she? She is pretty; she must be pretty? Is she married?" And on and on it went. I was stunned, flattered a bit, and more than somewhat embarrassed, but I enjoyed the moment so much that I didn't realize that each lady was having me sniff a fragrance that she sprayed or dabbed on my arm, my neck, or my cheek.

Finally, carried away by the moment, I purchased a 1.6-ounce bottle of Joy Eau De Parfum at a cost substantially more than my limited budget, which was unbelievable, as the bottle seemed so small.

I headed back to our apartment, not noticing the funny glances coming my way until my Scottish friend took a large whiff and said, "Goodness man, ye smell like a French whorehouse, laddie. I let ye be alone one day and see the trouble ye bring home." I was stunned and slightly offended, but his good-natured chuckles soothed the moment. And, of course, all the other fellows wanted to know just where this perfumery was; but I wasn't about to tell them, and, besides, it was time for my nap.

Early Evenings

For our small band of vagabonds, the sweetness of the evening sky as dusk settled in warmed our hearts, spurring the kindness of newfound friends who responded generously by contributing to the hat.

This was not the time for working the tourists overtly; rather, it was a time for fun, ballads, and sweetness. Peter Paul and Mary, the Kingston Trio, and the Limelighters were the main fare, and soon enough, a few folks would join in our fun as we sang about poor Charlie not being able to get off the MTA or out of the Tijuana Jail. We sang "Puff the Magic Dragon" and "If I Had a Hammer", songs by Glen Yarborough, and on and on. These songs were the rage, and soon our small group would expand, some newcomers joining in by clapping or singing while others listened, as folk music was popular throughout Europe at that time.

I would pull out a hat, which I always held onto, partly for security but mostly because I learned in my short time as a thespian that eye-to-eye contact meant everything, particularly with small groups. So, in the spirit of good humor, amiability, and, this being Paris, *bonhomie*, I gave each audience member a personal opportunity to extend some small thank you for our efforts. People would come and go but rarely failed to contribute to the hat that I passed around.

As the evening settled in, when the purse was adequate, one of our band would purchase some cheap red wine, a few loaves of bread, sausage, cheese, and savory mustard. We would scout a new perch somewhere along the right bank promenade with a view of two of Paris's many bridges and cathedrals. We turned to quiet talks about travels past and travel to come. Occasionally, if the purse had been particularly good, we would head over to the left bank cabarets, and perhaps we would head home with the morning sun.

Early on, I questioned my Scottish friend regarding why we didn't set up on the more collegial left bank. "Ahh, Laddie, it's very simple. The left bank is for tips while the right is for the intellectuals."

Adieu to Paris

After nearly three weeks in Paris, it was time for me to go despite the sorrow of leaving friends. I have had the good fortune to revisit the City of Lights on several occasions, and, with each visit, my memories walk along with me. Memories sweeten with time, and so it has been with Paris and me.

Trouble

It seems unfair for rough times to follow the sun, especially after Paris. Barcelona was warm, brilliant, and vibrant, but I was not prepared for the mess of the summer crowds. Of course, the youth hostels were full, but it seemed not to matter as the frantic revelry was nonstop, deep into the night, a night of intertwining currents. I thought then of the whirling dervishes as their dance approached near fever pitch. Still, here, in Barcelona, there was no concurrency, just faces, arms, and legs flashing as indistinguishable streaks of light, intertwining within a stream and moving on to places unknown.

The only hotel room I could find the first night was in a seedy part of town, with a narrow cot-like bed up multiple flights of stairs. I awoke either early morning or late day; I am not sure which, but I quickly found that I did not sleep alone. I had heard of bedbugs but never before had I experienced them.

After scrubbing myself as clean as the tepid water dribbling from the lavatory faucet would allow, I packed and headed outside. I quickly found a locker for my gear near the train station. Then, to pay my respect to Mr. Hemingway, I headed to the arena, not because I thought it might be exciting but because I was told it was the one experience that captured the machismo spirit of Spain.

So, I went but came away horrified. The bull in a ring has no more charge over its fate than the convict strapped in the chair. I would not return.

Slow Route Home

For a number of reasons, I was anxious to head for Stockholm. I wanted to dissolve the bad taste of Barcelona, but more importantly, I hoped to see Nadia and Sweden, so I resolved to make my way to Stockholm as quickly as possible.

But once again, my friend Robert nudged me toward the road not taken. Instead of heading directly to Stockholm, I decided to go west, along the southern Pyrenees to the heart of the Basque community and the Bay of Biscay.

Having been born in Bakersfield, California, I was familiar with the Basque community that had left their homeland in the western Pyrenees, straddling the border between France and Spain on the coast of the Bay of Biscay and settled along the southwestern slope of the San Joaquin Valley, but I knew little about their history. Instead, I was drawn by the rugged Pyrenees Mountains, the Bay of Biscay, the valleys and grand mountains, and the deep coastal waters of the Atlantic. I wanted to see as much of the Pyrenees as I could manage, traveling through the heart of the autonomous Basque country. Most of all, I wanted to see the Bay of Biscay piercing into the Iberian Peninsula from the Atlantic at the border of Spain and France. All in all, I was pleased with the circuitous, western route rather than the direct route to Paris, then Stockholm.

Using my Euro-pass, I boarded the Spanish line to the Pyrenees at the Barcelona train station. As was my custom, based on advice from *Europe on $10 a Day* to avoid additional hotel fees, I boarded the night train and slept through the night until we reached Villefranche de Conflent, the transfer point for the Little Yellow Train of the Pyrenees.

I awoke to the splendor of the Pyrenees playing peek-a-boo with the early morning mist. Apparently, for some time I had been traveling through Basque territory without knowing it.

The tracks of the Spanish line deadended at a dirt path in the foothills about forty yards from the Little Yellow Train station. Passengers were required to disembark from the Spanish line and hand-carry their luggage up the hill to the Pyrenees train station with the aid of pushcarts. I had no idea what to make of this transfer, but I was game for whatever was to come.

The cute little yellow train that awaited us would have been more at home in Disneyland than in the Pyrenees Mountains. In fact, I heard that these Little Yellow Trains may have inspired Disneyland's trains.

Some carriages were covered, some opened to the sky. Of course, I chose the latter. I followed my fellow passengers onto the train, and thankfully, my passport and Euro-pass were accepted for boarding. Only then was I able to take in the magnificent panorama below. The reward for our labor was a breathtaking view of the Bay of Biscay, where I hoped to spend a few days.

We were at a considerable elevation, and I could see a few small towns scattered below. I relaxed. Finally!

Francetraveltips.com
Photo by J. Chung

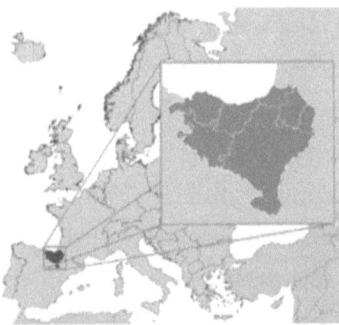

The Pyrenees straddle the border between Spain and France.

Although I knew nothing of the Little Yellow Trains of the Pyrenees, I soon learned of the practical reason for these restrictions. First, the rugged topography of the Pyrenees did not allow for an axel width greater than thirty-seven inches for rail traffic, significantly limiting freight and passenger service through the Pyrenees. The second and most significant reason for the restricted axel width was the narrow tracks that protected against conquering armies from the north and south. In fact, these restrictions proved to be a powerful prophylactic.

The Pyrenees

The route through the Pyrenees mountain range is narrow, steep, and rugged. Consequently, the train's pace was erratic, slowing, then accelerating with a sense of purpose, only to slow again. I did not complain, mostly because I was used to such travels.

We were traveling the mountains where the French, British, Portuguese, Spanish, and Germans had engaged in countless battles spilling the blood of their enemies. It is estimated that the repetitive Napoleonic Wars resulted in somewhere between two-and-a-half and three-and-a-half million military deaths.

I found in my travels a paradox. The sense of solitude strikes me the hardest in the midst of crowds, while isolation graces me with a sense of contemplation, repose, and, sometimes, remorse, though I know not why.

I could not help but see in these bucolic valleys and beautiful mountains the bodies of the fallen. Here in these mountains were the sites of so many battles. How many? I remembered my senior high role in *The Skin of Our Teeth*, a Pulitzer Prize-winning drama by Thornton Wilder about war, and my English class, where each of the students was required to memorize and present a short poem. I chose the antiwar poem *The Grass* by Carl Sandberg, who penned, "different were the wars, but the cost was the same. Pile them high at Gettysburg / And pile them high at Ypres and Verdun. Shovel them under and let me work; I am the grass; I cover all."

Is it possible to have a sense of being without experiencing both exuberance and loss? I was beginning to think not. Certainly, the Pyrenees' great mountains and verdant valleys, the picturesque villages clothed in the morning mist, and the rugged, majestic mountains above enthralled me. But reflecting on all of the battles that took place in the Pyrenees, I wondered how the blood of the fallen could have been washed away; a monument, a plaque, is that all? "I am the grass; I cover all."

I did not know that my generation would soon fill the streets in protest of the Vietnam War or that thousands of my contemporaries would be coming home in coffins. It was early, but the reaper was sharpening his steel.

I eagerly disembarked at one of the quaint villages, the name of which I cannot recall. The morning mist veiled the surrounding peaks of the Pyrenees. It had been slow going through the night with several long stops, and now I was anxious to explore.

I confirmed that with my Euro-pass, I could check my bag, hike through some of the lower meadows of the Pyrenees, then board the evening train that would reach Paris just past midnight. So, I headed out with my canteen and a light meal to carry me through the day. I was careful not to undertake anything challenging as I wanted to arrive in Paris and then in Stockholm without incident.

The trail was easily managed at lower elevations. All worked out as I was easily back in time to purchase another light meal to take on the train. I was quite tired, just as planned.

We crossed several summits and traversed many valleys, each spectacular. The scenery changed with each turn. Soon the sun disappeared behind the rugged ridges to the southwest. We lurched and swung about, only to pick up speed again, but I was accustomed to unsettled rides, and I slept.

Paris

Near midnight we entered the great perimeter of Paris; it would still be some time before we reached the station. I was apprehensive about changing trains in such a cavernous and intimidating structure. Fortunately, a director (I don't know what else to call him) gave me a fold-up brochure and then pointed to the incredible pictogram hanging from the Gare de Lyon Station ceiling. The director was clearly proud of the multi-sided information board hanging from the rotunda high above the hurrying passengers. It was lit with various colors, coordinated by route and destination. Colored electronic routes pointed off to different branches of the station, and the colors of my intended route remained constant as I followed the arrows up or down stairways.

Sweden and Nadia

So, there I was, getting ready for my next adventure—Sweden and Nadia. I knew that my Euro-pass would get me to Stockholm, but I wasn't sure of the particulars. Working through my map, it seemed we were taking a very circuitous route, but it turned out to be efficient and interesting.

Our train started out traveling east into Germany, then north to the sea and the German city of Puttgarden. Here we disembarked and were quickly guided onto the largest ferry I had ever seen. According to my map, we were at the dividing point between the North Sea to the west and the Baltic Sea to the east. Sweden split the two seas, almost connecting with the northern shore of Germany.

Once onboard the ferry, I found my cabin and went back to sleep though I had slept most of my journey since leaving Paris. The good news was that I would arrive in Stockholm midmorning.

Although I found the Stockholm map nearly indecipherable, I was determined to find Nadia's apartment. After many false starts, to my great relief, I found myself at the front door of her building.

A Major Disappointment

The previous spring, when I had told Nadia of my plans for the summer, she quickly suggested that I visit her in Stockholm. Wonderful! Even better, Nadia assured me that her parents had several guestrooms so I could stay with them. I thanked her profusely but, silly me, did not set a date or anything close to a date. I must have thought Nadia would just be waiting for me to show up.

When I rang the buzzer, a girl opened the little peephole in the door, and Nadia's sisters greeted me somewhat apprehensively. It soon became apparent that they did not speak English. After many hand gestures and much gesticulation, I discovered Nadia was not home. She was in Spain. What?

Getting nowhere talking with Nadia's sisters, it was clear that they would not let me in. Nadia and her offer of free lodging were gone.

I spent the remainder of the day mulling over options, but my travel log tells the story best.

"My dwindling funds are an issue, but to make things worse, Sweden does not accept Euro-passes. Double-worse, I could not get a straight answer from the desk clerk or Nadia's sisters about when she would return."

Sometimes I wonder about myself. When I reconnected with her after the summer break, I discovered that she was only in Spain for a long weekend.

I was disappointed but had no intention of remaining in Sweden to wait for Nadia. Soon I was back on a ferry headed to West Germany and, from there—Berlin. My diary summed it up, "Long train ride to Germany—ominous it seemed to me, but I slept through the night."

East Germany

The East German Bundepolizei treated me somewhat harshly. Worse, they tried to keep my passport. This was my first experience with Cold War tensions, and I was taken aback. My father had made it clear, "They can stamp or rub your passport all they want, but don't let your passport out of your physical possession." As a result, I got into a bit of a dispute with the East Berlin Port authority when they demanded I turn over my passport. Though shaken by their demand, I did not give in and held on to my passport with a vise-like grip. After that unfortunate incident, things began to look up.

According to my travel log:

"Met a girl on the train to Berlin; cute. I tried to act a bit older, but she knew better. As she was also going to Berlin, we palled up for a while. Met an older couple who took us under their wings as surrogate grandparents and tour guides. They were very kind and spent half a day showing us the sights."

It was the summer of 1965, just four years after the Berlin crisis when the wall was constructed. West Berlin was an island of freedom amid communist oppression and ground zero in the conflict between the Soviet Union and the United States. As a result, West Berliners adopted an attitude of fatalism, determined to wring every bit of life out of each moment, and it showed.

On My Own, Again

My time in Berlin seemed like the movie *Cabaret* that I saw many years later, and certainly, the town lived up to its reputation for indulgence.

Most interesting were the telephones next to each patron in the taverns. Each patron stood at a café table with a telephone post in the middle and five telephones for each table. Patrons could survey the room. When they found someone of interest, they would call the phone next to the person they wanted to speak with. And the rest was up to them.

If the night turned raucous, who knows how many patrons would crowd the posts, or perhaps a liaison might blossom.

To me, these posts were emblematic of Berlin's postwar fast-paced, high-energy clubs, open twenty-four hours. The people there lived life in the moment. Ah, Berlin, how I look forward to seeing you again!

Arrival Florence

I was looking forward to seeing Jean-Paul again, but it was not to be. As it turned out, Jean-Paul had let out his apartment for the remainder of the summer while he went off to vacation in Spain, and his tenants had no interest in my sad story.

My purse continued to dwindle. My ticket back to Alexandria was not interchangeable, so I had to survive for three and a half weeks before I could board the Greek freighter that would take me back to Egypt. However, my problem was more immediate as I only had funds to support me for another three days.

"Well, that shouldn't be a problem," I said sarcastically to myself. "As long as I can go three and a half weeks with little to no food while waiting for a ferry to take me from Florence to Piraeus, then to Alexandria, everything should be fine!"

The Power of One Thing at a Time

Find the closest hostel, then find out if they need help—any help, and then . . . well . . . pray for a miracle! In my travel book, the nearest hostel was a good walk into the hills above the Fountain of Ponte Vecchio at the entrance to the bridge over the Arno River.

Thirty minutes later, I reached my destination.

A delightful lady at the desk responded to my question about work, but her answer cut to the heart. "I am so sorry, all of our positions are filled," she said sadly.

I didn't know what to do, but I thanked her as politely as I could, then started back down the hill, but for no discernable reason, I thought she just didn't really understand. So, I turned around and walked up the hill, returning to the hostel to plead my case once again. But this time, before I could say a word—she gushed.

"Oh, I am so happy you came back! I will make a position for you somehow, but for room and board only."

Great! No, wonderful! Thus, my love affair with Florence continued.

Meet Thomas Angel

If you have the joy of travel, sooner or later, you will encounter forces of nature, those who lift the spirits of everyone they come to know. So it was with Thomas Angel.

Thomas was almost impossible to characterize—a dishwasher, bigger than life, a living oxymoron charging through Florence on his motorcycle, wise and learned. He had first come to Florence looking for his father's grave, an American soldier who died in battle during WWII, then stayed to learn the language and culture of his father's final resting place. During our breaks, Thomas and I cruised the streets of Florence on his bike. Once, in a somber moment, we cruised to the hills above to the place where his father was buried.

In the evening, after we finished cleaning up, we would relax on the patio overlooking Florence in all of its glory. We were allowed only one glass of wine from the house barrel. Still grateful for the privilege of being in Florence, singing along with Thomas' guitar and talking late into the night was enough for us.

Because I worked and lived in the hostel, patrons almost always expected me to be Italian, and I was often embarrassed by the Americans who treated the staff so poorly. I heard such things as "The dumb wop wants us to clear the table," and I admit sometimes my response was not polite.

However, I did surprise a patron or two when they thought I was Italian. One memorable morning when Thomas and I were in the kitchen, a young American lady came up to the service counter saying very slowly in English, "Senore, do you have a spoon?"

I looked wide-eyed at her, giving her a fork.

"No, no," she said, this time, very slowly. "Do . . . you . . . have . . . a . . . spoon?" as she pantomimed someone using a spoon. This back and forth continued several times as I gave her some other kitchen item—a knife, a glass, a napkin, all delivered with great sincerity as I watched Thomas' shoulders shake with stifled laughter.

I could see she was getting more than a little perturbed, so I said, "Tom, can you help me out? I can't understand what this lady is saying."

My little joke quickly went over with the boys, but strangely not with the girls. Everywhere, I heard guys saying, "Do you have a spoon?" while the girls remained unamused.

By the next morning, there were three small bouquets on each table with a note saying, "To the ladies, please excuse our little tease." By dinner, there were new flowers and a new note: "To the gentlemen, all is forgiven but don't forget to bus your dishes."

Beautiful Days

I will never forget those wonderful days. Soon I would be back in Egypt, miles away from Europe. There are many ways to say goodbye to a friend, but leaving a city is a different story. Thomas knew of my sorrow, and he did his best to lessen my pain, as did the staff. All I can say is thank you.

CHAPTER TWENTY-NINE

The Deep Desert

Progress was slow, very slow, if measured by modern travel, perhaps a bit faster than the ancient caravans whose well-worn trails we were now tracking. Our small caravan of two desert Jeeps shepherded the world's largest desert tanker truck, which I christened "the Leviathan," and which swayed and rolled as we journeyed into the deep desert southwest of Cairo.

It was early fall 1965. We were ferrying the most precious commodity known to man through this driest of drylands—fresh drinking water, along with other incidentals required to sustain the wildcatters of Pan American Oil's Deep Desert team.

I had just returned to Cairo after my first summer trip to Europe to find a new friend, Sandy (George) Triefenbach. Sandy remains one of the most remarkable men I have ever known. Somewhat on the short side for a University of Missouri freshman linebacker, he was rugged with broad shoulders and a face befitting of a man of action. All was a bit askew, with eyebrows exploding here and there above a pugnacious nose, which would have been a bit unsettling but for his magnificent, somewhat crooked, and infectious smile, which seemed to make all things right—except when he was upset or angry. I saw him that way only twice, and then it was a face that could make a man's blood run cold.

It was immediately apparent he was a man to be reckoned with, and we were inseparable over the following year. When I asked him how a guy on scholarship at the University of Missouri ended up in Cairo, he said simply, "Raja, let's just say it was best that I no longer be around."

So, Sandy and I quickly became fast friends. He was living with his uncle in Maadi, a short walk from our family home, and of course, was enrolled in AUC. Sandy's uncle was the representative of Pan American Oil's Sahara territory, from the Red Sea to the Libyan border and as far south as it was practical to explore. Those familiar with Middle East oil production in the 1960s know that Sandy's uncle appeared to have drawn the short straw when it came to territorial oil licenses. While vast quantities of oil were found throughout the Middle East, including many locations on the Sinai Peninsula, Egypt's southwestern desert was overlooked by providence. Well, after well came up dry (three wells would be discovered decades later).

In 1965, however, it was the hope for oil that enabled Sandy and me to head into the deep desert southwest of Cairo on a Huckleberry quest for adventure. To put the great truck into perspective, I had Sandy take a photograph of me standing on my tiptoes peering out from under the wheel well of this beast.

We started out as passengers on the tanker, which rolled and keeled. At the first opportunity, we opted for the Jeeps, one driven by a young roustabout from a country unknown, the other by a young engineer who had just returned to the desert after a month touring Europe. The captain of our leviathan was an infectious young Aussie who never adequately explained how he came to be there. He seemed to be on a journey to nowhere.

Recall that I described our water truck as the largest in the world, not the fastest. We loped along, the sun still low in the eastern sky, our caravan casting long, morning shadows toward the western desert. We made better time than walking, but not much—no matter. It was a journey out of time, and I remained alert and keen on every bit of the adventure. By midmorning, the terrain changed a bit, from hardpan strewn with rocks to larger and larger swales of sand, requiring judicious decision-making by our steward. Each dune posed a choice between circumnavigating the sand-filled swales or summiting a rocky hardpan hill. In either event, our progress slowed.

Our driver's instincts and manifest skills instilled confidence that we were in good hands. We traveled on as the endless rocking motion beckoned complacency. Off to the western horizon, ridges burst through the sand, bulging high above the desert floor, extending west like the tails of dinosaurs with spiked rocky platelets.

We left Cairo at dawn, ceaselessly lurching and tilting, the landscape indistinguishable and hypnotic, our progress measured only by the sun. At long last, the caravan stopped for a break. I walked about stretching my legs, thinking this must be what it would be like to land on the moon. After a short respite, the captain sensed our restlessness and invited each of us to take the wheel of one of the Jeeps, with the roustabout and engineer as our passengers. Hot damn!

Within minutes we took off for a few divergent explorations, just as I imagined the scout of a wagon train might have done. We enjoyed the freedom of frolicking around the dunes but were careful not to lose sight of the massive, lumbering water truck, which kept us on course. We were strapped in tight with sturdy roll bars protecting us.

It was great fun, indeed, and our captain enjoyed giving us a bit of freedom, urging us to dodge and weave and race—we even went airborne at times, though we were well short of reckless.

The captain, comfortable with our judgment, directed us toward some rugged terrain to survey the area we had been tracking. It was a rugged climb, and I admit to some trepidation, but we quickly summited. Resting against the roll bars, all the world was before us: to the west Libya, to the south the deep Sahara, and to the east, far beyond our horizon, the Nile and the Red Sea. The mystery of this moment, the seamless sand and patterns of broken rock, stunned us into silence. It was as if chaos had momentarily bowed to the design of a god unknown.

Soon we rejoined our caravan. In the midst of a long sandy swale was a single small shade tree. It was the only tree we would see in our entire journey. We spread a cloth under this bit of filtered shade, enjoying a short respite and lunch, wondering how this singular tree could thrive alone in this desolate place, but the desert did not answer.

It was a moment of mystery. I recall no conversation, just looking out at the flat horizon that spread in all directions, except for the gray rocky ridges in the west. Once again, I felt the desert calling.

We Drive On

After lunch, the roustabout and engineer took over the driving, and we resumed our steady pace. It seemed only a moment until our driver nudged me awake. We had summitted the northern ridgeline of the deep east-west rift, affording us a view of the trailers and oil rig below, nestled into the sandy basin where the camp was located, now covering an ancient fault line. Years later, I saw Stanley Kubrick's *2001: A Space Odyssey*, and when the camera panned to the crater below to reveal the Monolith, I was immediately reminded of my first view of this base camp in the middle of nowhere, in Egypt's western desert.

We descended into camp with the last of the desert sun giving way to the horizon and the western desert turning to lavender before our eyes. As the desert light was extinguished, magnificent stars appeared, first one by one it seemed, followed by a sprinkling, and then as rain from the heavens.

Over dinner, our guide offered us a foretaste of the sites we would be exploring the next day. "Tomorrow, you will have the rare opportunity to go where very few people have gone. These places are not shown in a travel guide, and most people have never heard of them. You will encounter a petrified forest, with as many as thirty large trees, forty to fifty feet long and up to five feet in diameter, with thousands of smaller fragments strewn over miles, right here in the deep desert. Then within twenty-five miles of our camp, you will find irrefutable evidence of a fierce tank battle from World War II."

We were intrigued and gripped by his recounting of the World War II battles waged in the deep desert as the German General Rommel coveted Egypt's great ports and cities and the Allies fought intensely to defend them.

"Ghost battles!" I said. Sandy, who fancied himself a WWII expert, was skeptical as he was sure that tank battles did not reach this far south, but our guide said only, "Well, wait and see, then you can tell me what they are."

Later that night after dinner, I walked the valley floor as the silver moon ascended. I sat alone on a sandy dune outside of camp, wondering—as I had in the middle of the Pacific and as I had in the desolation of the Utah mountains—how can all this be?

Adventures in the Western Desert—Day Two

We awoke before dawn, the camp already alive with activity. I had fallen asleep thinking of the similarity between our just-completed journey and my ride years earlier into the red rock canyons of Utah. As with Utah, the second day of our journey did not disappoint.

Now, leaning up against his Jeep, our guide directed us. "See how the ridges of our valley fan out," he asked, pointing to the horizon beyond the open desert. We were far enough to the west that we could see a series of similar-looking ridges lined up north to south mile after mile. "Fascinating territory, like you have never seen, yes?" Indeed it was, and we nodded accordingly.

"Now, look again at the two ridges of *our* valley," he emphasized. "See each ridge, north, and south, surrounding our camp. Each ridge that marks the boundaries of our camp curves out north and south, while the other ridges are parallel, straight, and east to west. Then see how they stretch out farther to the west than any of the other ridges. Just stay within sight of these two ridges," he said, making sure we were looking up and down the ridgeline as he was pointing, "and you will be fine. Got it?"

But he wasn't done. Smiling, he pointed straight to the west. "Not far, straight out and then to the south," he said, "you will find the amazing sites I told you about last night. You will see the tracks in the sand that were compacted by the tanks decades ago. All trace was buried by the sand and the wind, only to be uncovered again."

Still, there was more. "In addition to the tank tracks, you will find the petrified trees I told you about last night, scattered about for miles. Thousands of pieces litter the desert floor, preserved by the sand and heat for how long, no one knows." To me, these things were unimaginable.

We couldn't wait. As we drove toward the vast western horizon, I experienced the same feeling I had when flying near the Libyan desert with Dad on our way to the Qattara Depression, wanting nothing more than to roam the distant dunes.

I am pleased to report that we followed all of the instructions and admonitions we were given. As a result, the day was splendid. Neither of us wanted to press the limits here in the middle of nowhere. But more importantly, we wanted to show respect and appreciation for Sandy's uncle and the reminder he'd given before sending us off—"Remember, you are representing me. And you, Roger, you are representing your father."

I knew Dad occasionally spent time with Sandy's uncle, a retired Marine colonel. I learned this from Sandy, not from my father. When I asked Dad how he came to know Sandy's uncle, he replied saying simply, "Well, he is a retired Marine, just like I am." To me, his remark rang just a bit strange.

On Our Own

We were jazzed. We played a bit, racing about in the sand, catching some air under our wheels, but soon we settled down. Then we came upon the tank tracks! Unimaginable, yet real. They went for miles and miles and not just straight tracks. They whirled all about, charging, lurching, and spinning, the ephemeral remains of a long-ago saga, then they just disappeared.

We exited our Jeep, walking in silence. The ghosts of valiant warriors all about, remnants of a battle waged long ago, a testament to death and valor, all now lost in time. I am reminded as I write of Ecclesiastes 1:14 "I have seen all the things that are done under the sun; all of them are meaningless, a chasing after the wind."

I broke from my reverie when I saw Sandy's deep perpetual lip curl had assumed a contemplative repose. We were each lost in our own thoughts.

We drove deeper into the western desert at a more reasonable pace, constantly checking that our valley remained in view. We explored this strange and intoxicating land, and as promised, we came upon fields of petrified trees, bits and pieces mixed with intact sections as much as five feet in diameter, all strewn about as if by a mighty Arthurian Galapas gone mad; all ravaged by time. We were stunned and silent as we walked among these fallen giants, wondering how long ago they had reached for the sky and how vibrant and verdant this barren land must have been.

We never lost sight of our valley, but as the hour was late, we could see that we had traveled far. So, we headed back to camp, relaxed and immensely grateful for the opportunity we had been given. We kept a steady pace until, with the sun low but still above the horizon, we entered our valley. We were tired and more than a bit sore from all the jostling, so a hot shower was in order.

I couldn't wait for dinner as this was when we would present our gift to our hosts; a fifth of Jack Daniel whiskey recommended (and paid for) by Sandy's uncle. As you might have suspected, the bottle was uncorked well before the end of the evening.

I did not make it to the pouring of the last drop as I was exhausted from the day's adventures. Before turning in, I made my last visit to the desert stars. The white mountains were aglow as I had seen the night before. Always at such times, I reflected upon magnificent nights past, drifting to the darkest nights in the midst of the vast Pacific Ocean, sailing to Japan and the high mountains of the Sierra and high plains of Utah. Still, tonight all seemed different as this ancient land gripped me. Seldom had I experienced ages past as I did in the last two days, and I did not want to lose this moment. So, I turned and turned and turned again, looking up, taking it all in. Perhaps somewhere in the night, the whirling dervishes joined in my dance.

Our Return

I did not want to wake up. I heard the bustle of the roustabouts and cooks, but the thought of moving my head was too much. I ached everywhere. *Thanks, Jack*, I thought, not for the first or last time. But I rousted myself. I gave myself and every aching muscle a pep talk, and then I just "Marined up."

My pep talk may have been good enough to roust me, but from the laughs I received upon entering the mess hall, I was fooling no one. My only solace was that when Sandy emerged, he got a bigger laugh, by far, than I had received.

The jokes soon died down, as the men were anxious to get to work, and each wanted to say their goodbye, all promising to look us up when on leave in Cairo.

I expected the journey back to be long and arduous. There were five of us all together, three in the cab of the water truck and two in the accompanying Jeep. I did all right for the first few hours, but by lunch, I was lurching and jerking in response to the terrain, falling against one shoulder and then the other. When we stopped for lunch, I revived a bit but soon started nodding off again.

Our driver stopped our leviathan and got out a well-padded mat from behind the back seat, which he then threw onto the enormous hood of our behemoth, saying to me, "Lay down for a nap."

When it sunk in what he was saying, I was aghast, "No, no, no, thank you very much, but no."

But our driver assured me, "No, no, it is common. No one falls off. We loop cloth around your feet and hands," he gestured emphatically, "You will be fine!"

"What if the truck rolls over?" I asked, more than a little concerned.

"Never happened before, never!" was the emphatic answer, and by this time, everyone was laughing and encouraging me. Sandy snickered, his crooked smile at full bloom, "If you don't take him up on it, Raja, I will." That was all it took. I climbed up on the hood.

It was like being on the bow of a ship. I had a good-sized pillow so I could enjoy the scenery, and the straps had plenty of slack, tight enough to keep me from falling off the hood but sufficient for me to sit up cross-legged if I was so inclined. I did so for quite a while, feeling like a Sultan loping along through the desert on his majestic camel. After a bit, I laid back, enjoying the rocking motion, and soon I was asleep, dreaming, I am sure, of sailing the waters of the world.

It was unforgettable. After a few hours, Sandy and I traded places and gazing out upon the desert, mesmerized and more than a bit tired, I considered the mystery of our journey. The midday sun waned into the afternoon as the outskirts of Cairo began to emerge from what had been for hours a melted, monochromatic horizon. Now, it was a dance of variegated colors, coalescing into distinguishable forms, first orchards, and palms, then structures. I was home.

CHAPTER THIRTY

The Six-Day War 1967

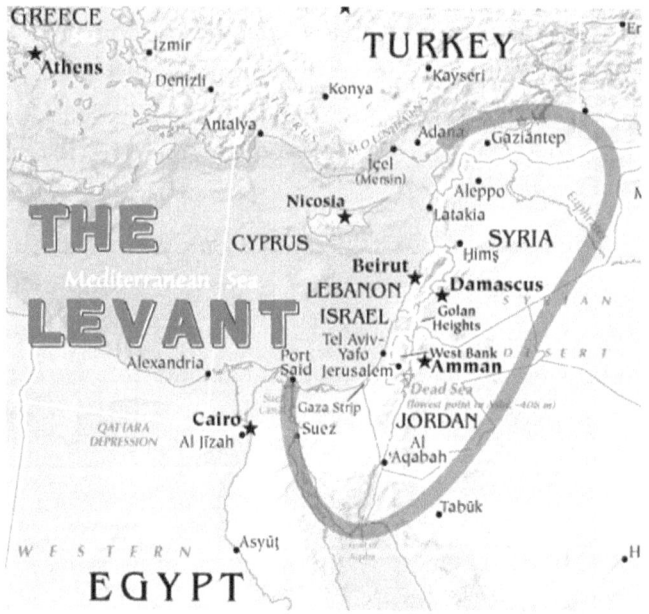

The Levant—a historical geographical reference to the Eastern Mediterranean Region of Western Asia

"In the Middle East, secrets are easy to come by, Roger. The challenge is distinguishing the truth from what appears to be true," Herb confided. "Just remember, some secrets might actually be true. In any case, the truth must be vetted with a healthy dose of skepticism."

Secrets were a dime a dozen in the Middle East. The objective was to make sense of the secrets, as a few may be accurate but useless, while others may be false but very useful indeed. In 1960s Cairo, there were few secrets that one could really rely upon. The secret igniting the Six-Day War was one of them. History depends upon who controls a particular narrative at any given time. Such is the fortune of war.

The *Britannica* rightfully points to an Israeli airstrike on Jordan, an air battle between Syria and Israel, and Soviet disinformation that resulted in a significant escalation of tensions between Israel and the coalition of Jordan, Syria, and Egypt.

In our neighborhood, provocations were not unusual. But the level of vitriol was reaching the breaking point even by Middle Eastern standards in the second semester of my sophomore year at the American University of Cairo.

The Rumors Were Right, Partially

Rather than a normal Middle Eastern folderol, it appeared that this time Egypt, Syria, and Jordan were preparing for all-out war against Israel. Virtually every one of my friends and acquaintances from The American University of Cairo was either packing up or was already out of harm's way.

My girlfriend Dewi, whom I had been in love with for the past year, had been whisked back to Indonesia by her parents without even the opportunity for a farewell. Given Dad's position with the United States Agency for International Development, our leaving Cairo was just a matter of a phone call, which was soon to come.

At my parents' insistence, I returned to the States as soon as school was out in June 1966, while my parents remained in Cairo until just two weeks before the Six-Day War began in May 1967. At that point, they left Cairo for Italy before returning to the States later in the summer of 1967.

The moment was emblematic of my itinerant existence with one exception; this time, I was returning to a new life on my own. The worst I can say about my nomadic existence was it was interesting.

One day, I Was in Egypt, and the Next Day I Was Gone

My mother's brother and his family took me into their home in Cincinnati, Ohio, for the summer when I found myself having to leave Cairo suddenly. There was no one else to help me. I give full credit to my Uncle Chuck and Aunt Eileen for taking me in, without warning, in unusual circumstances, even though they didn't know they were taking me for the whole summer. Well, life was good!

We had a lot of fun, and they treated me very well. Having two young grade-school-aged daughters, they were not ready for a worldly young man used to independence. After hearing my aunt admonish us, "I had better not see a single footprint on the living room carpet," I admit to teaching my cousins how to lift each other's legs like a wheelbarrow while leaving only handprints on the living room carpet.

Thankfully, my aunt forgave me, and to this day, we talk every couple of weeks.

The Rest of the Story, I Could Only Read About

Through news accounts, which I obsessively scoured, I learned that the streets of Cairo were electric with rumors of war. Tensions peaked in May of 1967 when Egypt insisted that the United Nations peacekeeping force withdraw from the Sinai Peninsula. The peacekeepers had been stationed there since 1956 to monitor the situation at the Suez Canal.

Nasser immediately sent Egyptian troops to patrol the area and closed the Gulf of Aqaba, virtually blocking Israel's port city of Elat. A week later, a mutual defense pact was signed between Jordan and Egypt, which ceded command of the joint armed forces to Egyptian control.

The Arab Coalition confidently announced its intentions and ability to force Israel into the sea. Nothing could have been further from the truth as Israel responded quickly and decisively. In June of 2017, Bret Stephens wrote in the *New York Times* for the fiftieth anniversary of the Six-Day War, "Arab leaders declared their intention to annihilate the Jewish state, and the Jews decided they wouldn't sit still for it. For the crime of self-preservation, Israel remains a nation unforgiven."

On June 5, 1967, Israel launched a surprise attack in response to the mobilization of and threats from the Arab coalition. The first attack destroyed 90 percent of the Egyptian air force on the ground, and a second crippled the Syrian air force. Without Arab air support, Israel captured the Sinai Peninsula to the Suez Canal and the Gaza strip within three days. Jordanian forces joined the fight but were no match for the Israelis and were driven out of Jerusalem and most of the West Bank.

The UN Security Council called for a ceasefire on the third day of the conflict. Jordan, Egypt, and Israel quickly accepted it. Syria, however, continued fighting until Israel decisively captured the Golan Heights after intense, crippling hostilities. Syria, the last combatant, accepted the cease-fire on June 10.

Unanswered Questions

In reconciling the news reports of the Six-Day War with my own experiences, I was left with many questions that have never been fully answered.

First and foremost, how could the Israeli Air Force destroy the Egyptian Air Force on the ground without being detected by radar? How did they know it was possible to attack the Egyptian Air Force under the radar?

Could it have something to do with Dad's work circumnavigating the Qattara Depression? After all, before Dad's flight checks, there was no useful map of the coordinates of the area. And if they flew below sea level, they would be virtually undetectable!

Or were they undetectable because the Egyptians had not unpacked and installed the ground-to-air navigation systems that the US had sent them, like those in Alexandria? If those systems had been installed, wouldn't the Alexandria Tower have detected the Israeli planes in time to sound an alert?

Why did my parents insist that I leave Cairo a year before the Six-

Day War? And more importantly, why did they stay until two weeks before the war began? What were they doing in Italy during the war and right after?

What was Dad talking about with his colleagues during our frequent trips to the desert in Giza? Did he take other people there when we weren't with him? What did they talk about? Why did they go there? What did Herb mean when he told me that the desert doesn't tell any secrets? How did Dad know Sandy's uncle?

Why was our house the only one threatened by a mob the night the Marine House was burned to the ground? Why were the protestors in a well-organized formation rather than a mob? Why did their actions seem so choreographed and coordinated?

Why did we live in such a secluded area surrounded by water and privacy hedges of thorny bushes? Why did we have a guard stationed outside our house every night?

Why did the Marines salute Dad when we first got to the base in Cairo? How did they know who he was when he was in civilian dress? He hadn't been a Marine for more than five years.

Why did we have such a formal, in-depth orientation when we arrived in Cairo? Why were we advised that we were constantly being watched and listened to? Was every American treated that way? Were all ex-pats surveilled or just our family? And why?

If we didn't have cars and weren't allowed to drive the Lemans, why did Dad want Terry and me to get driver's licenses? Did he suspect that we might need to get away suddenly?

I may never know.

Black Hawk Down

The movie *Black Hawk Down* was released in 2001 to rave reviews, and I was almost certain my father would be interested in seeing the film with me.

The film takes place in 1993 when the US sent special forces into Somalia to destabilize the government and bring food to the starving population. The special forces flew Black Hawk helicopters into the capital city of Mogadishu to lower the soldiers onto the ground. But Somali forces launched an unexpected attack that immediately brought down two of the helicopters. The movie continues as the US soldiers struggle to regain their balance while enduring heavy gunfire.

Since my dad had been a Marine and spent three years in Northern Africa in the 1960s, I wondered if he may actually have been in Somalia. So, I asked my dad if he would like to join me.

"Yes, I would," he said, sounding somewhat guarded.

So we went, just the two of us, to the theater.

As we drove home after watching the movie, I asked my dad if he had ever flown into Somalia.

"Yes," he replied somewhat abruptly.

Ignoring his reticence, I pressed further. "Well, what were you doing there?"

"What the hell do you think I was doing?" he said dismissively.

His non-answer spoke volumes.

Mementos

Shortly before my father's death, it became clear it was no longer safe for him to be in his home, where he had lived alone since losing my mother several years earlier. So we took on the grim task of moving him into a residential facility. As we packed his belongings, we came across many extraordinary keepsakes.

First, was a burgundy-colored official passport along with a red pamphlet entitled "Permit to Possess and Carry Arms." None of us had ever seen either of these documents, so we examined them carefully. Inside, we found a list of weapons that my dad was apparently permitted to possess and carry as he traveled. The list was long and sobering, including weapons such as grenades, machetes, guns, and swords—and more interestingly, the list was in Arabic. In addition to the approved weapons list, my dad's passport had stamps from infamous countries like Somalia, Israel, and Libya.

Next was my dad's cane that he had bought in Burma. It had a silver plate between the black handle and the wooden cane with an ornate embossed design. Though we had seen him use it for years, until we examined it carefully, we hadn't noticed that it was actually two pieces. Grabbing the handle, we pulled it apart, exposing a two-foot-long sword hidden inside.

Perhaps the most cherished memento was my parents' photo album, which displayed many pictures with my mother's handwritten captions, sometimes humorous and sometimes poignant. Somehow, with their brief captions, these photographs tell the story of my parents' relationship, their deep friendships, their passion for life, and their extraordinary adventures. The centerpiece of the photo album was a picture of a military helicopter parked on my parents' back lawn in Thailand. Their lawn butted up to a retaining wall on the edge of the beach of the Bay of Siam. The picture showed a dozen surly, tough-looking soldiers from an Army special forces company, which I understand to be the predecessor of the Green Berets, posing in front of the helicopter. My mother's caption made me laugh out loud. It read simply: *The boys stopped by for lunch.*

Every time I look at the painting of the view from my parents' back lawn looking over the Bay of Siam, I can still see the image of the helicopter parked on their lawn and the soldiers posing in front of it.

Painting of the view from Harry and Irene's backyard on the Bay of Siam (and their picture in the lower left corner).

A treasured souvenir of Mom's was a plaque inscribed:
To: Irene Hughes (One of the guys)
From: Detachment A-10, 46th Special Forces Company (Airborne)

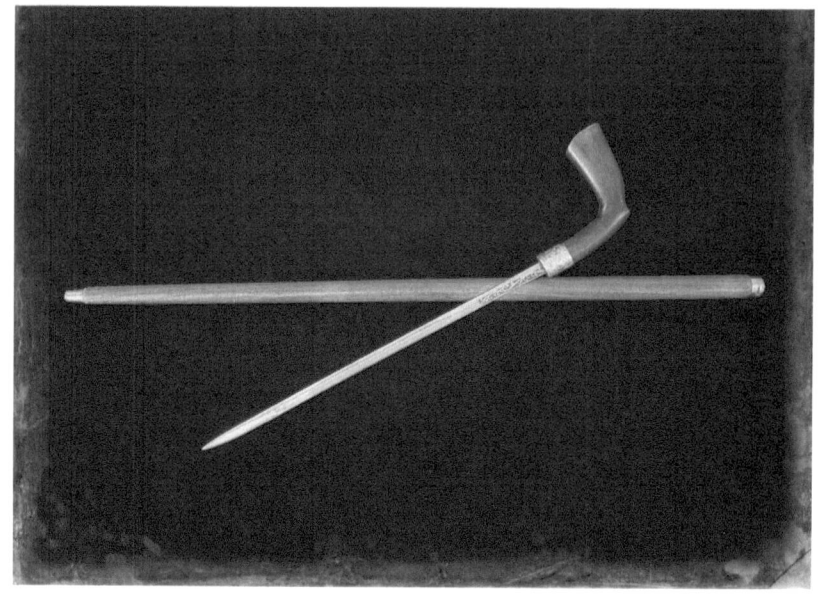

Harry's incredible hidden sword from Burma

Harry's international weapons carry permit.

Part Five

CHAPTER THIRTY-ONE

Return to Bakersfield

We knew from friends in Bakersfield that my grandmother was failing. Though I didn't realize it at the time, I, too, was struggling. Within a few days of my arrival, it was clear to me that my grandmother's decline was worse than our friends had realized. Since my parents were in Cairo and Terry was in college in Santa Barbara, the daunting responsibility of helping my grandmother fell on my nineteen-year-old shoulders.

When I left for Egypt, the Beatles were lamenting their "Hard Day's Night," and the Beach Boys boasted their ability to "Get Around," but upon my return from Cairo, increasing numbers of young men were coming home from Vietnam in body bags. So many, it was easy for Barry McGuire to convince us we were on the "Eve of Destruction." All of this was the result of a war taking place in a country that few Americans could identify on a map.

It was a difficult time, and I was alone.

When I returned to Bakersfield, I discovered that my grandparents' old house where Dad was born had been torn down, and the surrounding orchards had been cleared for a small housing development. My grandmother never sold any of the property that she and my grandfather had accumulated, but she continued to rent out ground leases for the development along Brundage Lane. Her income from those properties was modest but provided some financial security for the rest of her life.

I was given the heartbreaking burden of preparing my grandparents' house for sale and my grandmother for the transition from her home of more than twenty years. When my parents eventually returned from Cairo, it would be only for a short leave, and then, almost certainly, my grandmother would be going into assisted living.

Dad's good friend Johnny Barber helped me make a plan. "The old clothing will go to the Salvation Army," Johnny proclaimed. "Whatever furnishings your grandmother wants to keep, you should keep until your parents return from Cairo. The rest can be sold, given away, or taken to the dump as you see fit. Just tag them according to where they are going."

Sounds simple. However, my grandparents' property consisted of my grandmother's house and the three outbuildings on her property, which were literally stuffed to the rafters with all sorts of "trophies." My grandfather accumulated those trophies from unlucky gamblers at his establishment and kept them over the years as bounty. Terry and I devoted endless hours admiring those treasures and creating imaginary adventures with them throughout our childhood. Those trophies had long been abandoned, collecting dust—until now, when they became my burden.

Living With Ghosts

I worked hard every day into early evening for months cleaning up the carpets and furniture and tagging what was to be sent to the Salvation Army, what was to be tossed, what would be stored, and what should be put in the safe.

It was a chore, but hard work never bothered me. In fact, I enjoyed it. In the evenings, I would walk through the house, measuring my progress and taking my time revisiting old memories.

The kitchen overlooked the breezeway where my grandfather had passed away many years before. Beyond the kitchen to the left was a small dining area that had hosted all of our family dinners celebrating birthdays, holidays, welcome homes, and send-offs over the years. The dining area opened into the living room, where family and friends congregated while Fujisan had roamed freely.

Beyond the living room was the hallway leading to the guest room on the left, where my parents stayed during periodic overnight visits. Further down on the right was my grandmother's master bedroom, with the bathroom between the two bedrooms. On the other side of the breezeway, attached to the garage, was a second guest room with a bath where Terry and I stayed during periodic overnight visits and where I now lived with my grandmother.

Keepsakes from my grandfather's gambling saloon were scattered throughout the house: most notably, a four-foot-tall mahogany and brass pedestal and a two-foot-long bull horn that had adorned the wall behind the bar at Pickett's. The dining room hutch contained a collection of beautiful crystal goblets and vases, which I spent a lot of time admiring as a child, though we were admonished not to touch them. Fuji-san's cage was in the living room on the right side of the door leading to the hallway so that Fuji would always be included in the festivities. Dad's picture from fighter pilot school when he was nineteen year's old with his aviator's leather helmet and goggles was hanging in the hallway next to the master bedroom.

It was a small house brimming with memories.

The evenings troubled me. Every room held memories of returning to my grandmother's house, the closest thing I had to a home base before we were whisked off to the next faraway place like Japan, Hawaii, Salt Lake City, and Cairo. And memories of people whom I missed, like my grandfather and my childhood friends.

My grandmother understood what was happening and showed resignation and sorrow about her transition, but we didn't talk about it. We shared an early dinner together every night; then, after cleaning the kitchen, I would take long solitary walks along the canals, returning to the house after dark.

Aunt Montana

The first time I met my great-aunt, Montana McCoy, was in late August 1966. She and my grandmother had been estranged since 1917, when my great-aunt had refused to acknowledge my grandmother's marriage to my grandfather due to my grandfather's previous marriage and divorce. Sixteen years after my grandfather's death, just after my return from Cairo, my great-aunt Montana made her first and only trip to California.

The occasion was to reconcile with my grandmother and witness Montana's son assume the position of head chef for the new governor of California, Pat Brown. As I was living with my grandmother at the time, I was able to meet Aunt Montana. The sisters' reconciliation was a long time coming and clearly a success.

My Visit with the Machados

The Machado family had lived next door to my grandparents since the home on the corner of Hughes Lane and Terrace Lane was built. Andy Machado was truly one of the nicest men in the world. As I have mentioned before, he was like a surrogate father to Dad when he was growing up, and now, he was to me as well. Andy represented normalcy and kindness and had a wonderful smile and a caring heart. Just what I needed at this difficult time.

While I was visiting the Machado's one afternoon, soon after returning from Cairo, their daughter June, who was a few years younger than Dad, stopped by for a visit. Soon, the conversation turned to Dad and my grandfather when June said how sorry she had always felt for Dad. Her comment took me aback as I thought of Dad as an intimidating, larger-than-life war hero. When I pressed her on the issue, she looked surprised and gave me an appraising look before saying, "Roger, didn't anyone ever tell you that your grandfather was known as 'the meanest man in Bakersfield?'"

"What? No, I didn't know that. He was always nice to me. And in fact, I don't remember him ever being mad at me, unkind, or even harsh with me. You have to be kidding!" I said as I looked to Andy for help.

He gave me a sad shrug. "Roger, your grandpa was always respectful to me. He helped me out with many things. But there were a lot of men who would walk across the street rather than cross paths with your grandfather. Especially if they owed him money or if he had been drinking—which was most of the time. Don't get me wrong, he was honest and hardworking, but he would take even a sharp look as a dare. In fact, if he had been drinking hard, he would challenge even a look away as an affront that could easily lead to a physical confrontation. And there was no doubt in anyone's mind that he was always armed. Men and women would just move to the other side of the street if they saw him coming."

Years later, when Dad came back from Thailand, I told him about my conversation with Andy. He only nodded and said, "Your grandfather had a lot of demons and more than a few enemies, some real and some imagined, but he was always ready for whatever happened." Dad went on. "He was hard on me, though we worked things out eventually. But he always treated your mom and your grandmother with respect, and he treasured you boys."

My grandmother passed away in 1969 while Dad was stationed in Northern Thailand with the USAID. He came back for her funeral but seldom returned to Bakersfield after that.

As for me, I continue to consider Bakersfield home.

CHAPTER THIRTY-TWO

Fuji-san—A Tribute to a Great Bird

Our parakeet Fuji-san was a noble and mischievous bird who was loved and revered by our entire family. We have many happy and some hilarious memories, which I have shared already.

I feel compelled to write a tribute to Fuji-san and to share some of his adventures after moving from Salt Lake City to Bakersfield to live with my grandmother. You may remember that Fuji and our new English Pointer, Penny, did not get along. It was no surprise that a bird dog and a parakeet could not live peacefully under the same roof. Fuji tormented and insulted Penny unmercifully at the risk of his own life: "Bad Dog, Bad Dog!" Fuji would cackle with glee.

Sadly, the decision was made that Fuji and Penny could not survive under the same roof, but the solution was a good one. My grandmother was living alone in Bakersfield, and she was happy to welcome Fuji-san into her home to keep her company and to enable us to visit him whenever we were in town. They got along very well as my grandmother, a devout Christian woman who was virtually deaf, never understood that Fuji was repeating the profanity he had learned in the Marine barracks. Good thing!

The Denouement

The match worked wonderfully for several years as the pair got along famously. Then, near tragedy struck, a prelude to Fuji's ultimate demise.

We were visiting Bakersfield from Utah for Easter. My grandmother apparently left the refrigerator door open for just a moment while dinner preparations were underway. Seizing the opportunity for an early tasting from the "salad bar," Fuji-san flew unbeknownst to us into the refrigerator and made a beeline for the salad bowl.

Shortly after, we were all called to dinner. My grandmother, whose eyesight was as deficient as her hearing, did not see Fuji-san, lying still in the middle of the salad bowl, "wheels up," as Dad would say when she brought the salad bowl to the table.

You can imagine the uproar when suddenly, perhaps in honor of Easter, Fuji-san arose from the bowl with a flurry of flapping and squawking. "He's alive!" we all shouted. After being treated to a warm towel wrap, he fully recovered to provide my grandmother with many more years of enjoyment, as she would confirm with us during our weekly phone calls.

Fuji-san and my grandmother's relationship continued for many happy years after the Salad Bowl Incident, as it was referred to in the family, until he passed away.

At the end of the day, there was no replacing Fuji-san, who was one of a kind.

CHAPTER THIRTY-THREE
UOP and Leo

Now What?

Once again, I was on my own in trying to determine my future. I didn't know what schools I should go to, what field I should study, or whether I should even continue my studies at all. My parents were still not available to help, and Terry was back at UC Santa Barbara on scholarship pursuing his degree. Terry had returned home from Cairo and resumed the life he had left and I didn't see him much. He lived a complicated life, but married, had children, and eventually published a novel toward the end of his life called *Paradise Burning*.

At the time I returned from Cairo, I was still adrift, not knowing what I should do with my life.

My good friend Steve Ladd helped me set the course for my future.

I first met Steve in my senior year of high school, just before heading to Egypt. He had joined my childhood friend Don Barber on a surfing visit to Manhattan beach. Though none of us could surf, we were great at talking up the girls and formed an instant bond that remains to this day.

After I finished preparing my grandmother's house for sale, Johnny Barber offered me a job at Barber Pontiac. As I renewed my friendship with Johnny's nephew Don Barber, who was on summer break from UC Davis, I also spent time with Steve. He had returned to Bakersfield after attending the University of the Pacific (UOP).

Steve and I became inseparable. He is a man of great heart and great intellect. At that time, Steve was also somewhat of a rebel. He had a very fast car and wasn't afraid to put it through its paces. On the other hand, I was looking for a no-frills, reliable car. Through my job at Barber Pontiac, I was able to buy a used (and I mean *used*) Studebaker Lark. Very few people know the car at all, and those who do are probably laughing at me. But for two years, the car was a loyal soldier. In fact, as long as I owned it, I rarely put oil in the car, and it returned the favor by getting me where I needed to go with no breakdowns or maintenance.

As I had only my elderly, infirm grandmother in Bakersfield, and my parents and brother were nowhere near, the Ladd family took me under their wing. Steve's father was the head of engineering for Kern County, the largest landowner in the San Joaquin Valley. I was fortunate enough to benefit from the kindness and support of the Ladd family, and I enjoyed living vicariously through all of Steve's adventures.

Why College, of Course

As we cruised around, enjoying the summer of our youth, I learned that Steve would spend the fall semester at Bakersfield Junior College before returning to UOP. As his wingman, and with no input or advice from any family to the contrary, I decided to register at Bakersfield Junior College as well, a decision my parents fully supported.

Steve's magnetism and charisma were a powerful influence on me, and my relationship with his family filled the void of being on my own without my brother or parents. After the semester at Bakersfield Junior College, still having no other input, I followed Steve to UOP.

There were other advantages to registering at the University of the Pacific. It was just a four-hour drive north on Highway 99 from Bakersfield, so I could check in on my grandmother regularly. Additionally, UOP was one of the few western schools that offered a degree in International Relations, my chosen major.

My time at the University of Cairo went a long way toward my acceptance at the University of the Pacific, so off we went to J&J Apartments in Stockton, California, home of the main campus of UOP.

Pledge Party and the Morning After

Infamous stories are still told among our fraternity brothers about the off-campus apartment Steve and I rented in the spring of 1967 while attending UOP. Steve was in his last semester, and I was in my first. We offered our apartment for an off-campus rush party to entice possible pledges, including me, to join Steve's fraternity. At first, the party went well, but the apartment's condition deteriorated as the evening wore on. More and more fraternity brothers arrived, and more and more alcohol was consumed until—well, really, I don't remember too much about the "until" part.

I woke up late the next morning to find our last keg had been left with the tap running onto the living room carpet. The rest of the apartment was in the same rough condition. I remember going to the refrigerator for milk to put on my cereal only to find the milk had been replaced with vodka, which I discovered after pouring it onto the last of the cereal.

Believe it or not, things got worse from there. Steve joined me in the living room as we reviewed the carnage and discussed the possibility of cleaning up. Just looking at the mess left us feeling exhausted and even more hungover. If that wasn't bad enough, we found the stray dog we had picked up the day before had attacked the carpet, leaving a foot-long section of bare carpet backing next to a pile of unraveled yarn by the front door.

Hearing a knock on the door, I foolishly opened it, only to find Leo Barber standing there. He was one of Dad's longtime friends and a surrogate father to me during my parents' long absences. We learned that Leo was on his way to Davis to see his son Don, one of our best friends, who was in his last year at UC Davis.

Leo was initially shocked, dumbfounded, and speechless as he looked into the apartment, but he quickly recovered despite a long string of expletives bursting from his mouth.

Steve came to the door to see what the ruckus was about. Leo's eyes darted from Steve and me to the pile of carpet yarn by the front door, the soggy living room carpet, and the sea of dead Budweiser soldiers in the kitchen. All three of us stood there staring at each other, stunned.

Steve and I looked wide-eyed at Leo as he continued his rant. Suddenly, the stray dog, disapproving of our housekeeping habits, bolted from the hallway and ran past Leo out the front door, never to be seen again. The ungrateful mutt.

Leo gathered his senses, saying, "Roger, your dad wrote asking me to check in on you. They (meaning Mom and Dad, I inferred) haven't heard from you for six months, and your mom is worried sick."

"Oh," I said, culpably, because I was feeling guilty about not being able to bring myself to write them. Not knowing what to say, I foolishly but politely said, "Would you like to come in, Leo?" before realizing I must have lost my mind.

"Do I look crazy?" he said and then quickly repeated a little more emphatically, "Do I look @&%$ crazy?" as if he were concerned that I didn't hear him the first time.

The thought crossed my mind that, yes, he did look a bit crazy at the moment, but I thought it best to say nothing as he continued to stare incredulously about the apartment. "I am going to Davis to see Donny, and I am not going to say a word to your dad about today, but I will be back in a couple of weeks," he warned, looking a bit like General Patton, "and this place better look one hell of a lot cleaner."

"No problem, Leo," we both assured him, nodding our heads as we told him unconvincingly that we looked forward to his next visit.

When we closed the door, Steve and I sat down. We looked at each other and burst out laughing. Neither of us is proud of the incident now, but it was pretty funny then. Leo didn't return as promised, and I don't know if he ever reported our shenanigans to my father. I saw

Leo and his family many times afterward, but neither he nor I ever spoke of the incident again.

An Explanation, Not an Excuse

In hindsight, though not an excuse, I understand how I came to be such a poor housekeeper. As I have mentioned before, good was never good enough for Dad. After every long absence, the first order of business was an inspection. I don't recall ever passing inspection on the first review. One flaw would result in an instruction to not stop until we were sure we were "inspection ready," as Dad insisted.

Despite our best efforts, this protocol resulted in multiple inspections until we finally passed. I believe this practice led to my long-distance rebellion against my father after leaving home.

I became infamous within my fraternity for having the sloppiest, messiest, potentially disease-infected room in our fraternity house, and that is saying a lot. I reached the height of infamy when my brothers determined that the worst penalty that could be handed down to recalcitrant pledges was to clean my room—daily.

Steve claims that he came under my spell when we lived together at the University of Pacific, but that is not the case, as he held the honor of having the worst room in the fraternity house before me.

In any event, we both survived our college days and lived to tell about it—at least some of it.

CHAPTER THIRTY-FOUR

The Quickening of My Soul

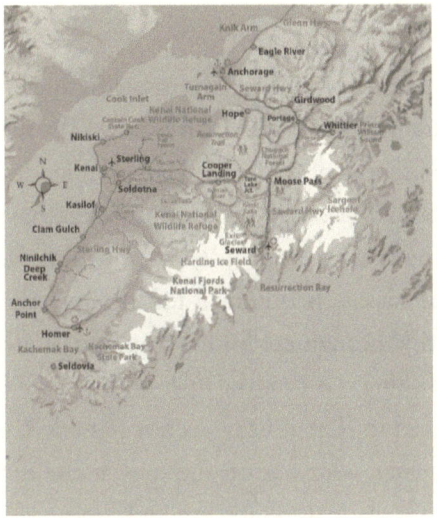

Kenai Peninsula, Alaska

My friend Steve enlisted in the Air Force in the spring of 1967 and left school immediately. My grandmother had continued to decline while I was at UOP and had been moved into assisted living. I wasn't excited about working another summer at Barber Pontiac but had no one to advise me. As a college student, I wasn't worried about the Vietnam draft yet. Once again, I was alone and adrift.

Since my parents and brother were not around, at Dad's urging, I called his good friend Herb. I knew Herb from our Cairo days, and he had recently transferred to Alaska, taking a position as the FAA's chief of air traffic control for the Pacific region. He told me he loved the state and suggested I could make a lot of money from a summer job on the Kenai Peninsula. So, in the absence of any other advice, I went off to Alaska.

I flew into Anchorage from Bakersfield and stayed with Herb for a couple of days. "I can tell you this," Herb promised. "During the summer, Kenai is boiling with enterprise. If you can't get a job there, you won't get a job anywhere." That was all I needed to hear. The next day, he dropped me at the bus station, and I bought a ticket to Kenai.

Kenai

I spent the summer of 1967 on the eastern shore of the Cook Inlet, where the primary industry was salmon fishing. The town of Kenai and the surrounding fisheries of the Kenai Peninsula fed the local economy and provided most of the jobs in the community at that time. The Kenai River flows on the northwestern side of the peninsula, located on the southern coast of Alaska. It is known for its large salmon population, harvested primarily through net fishing from beach sites. The principal location for net fishing was near the inlet of the Kenai River.

When I arrived in Kenai, I saw a crew remodeling a small house. I called to the owner, who was on the roof at the time, and asked if he needed help. He gladly took me on, and I joined his crew painting the house and repairing the roof. I asked if he would let me sleep on the porch. "I have a better idea," he said. "Take my son with you, and you can stay in my cabin for the summer. It's no beauty, but it is a roof over your head. I have five kids in this small house. He's the oldest, and he's driving me crazy."

I couldn't accept the offer fast enough. Of course, I soon discovered that the cabin was a forty-five-minute walk from the highway on a muddy road. It had no electricity or running water, but at least it had a pump, and the price was right. Best of all, my new roommate, Doug, had his own pickup truck.

The house was finished in a couple of days, and Doug and I were looking for work. We answered a help-wanted ad and were hired to disassemble an airfield matting system on an old landing field. The work involved using a five-foot crowbar to separate the mats. Each five-by-two-foot mat was bound to the next by a metal clip, which had been pounded into submission to form a two hundred-by-twenty-foot runway. The work was backbreaking and exhausting, but within a week, we were finished.

Roger's first roofing job in Kenai

Salamatof Beach

On the daily trips from our cabin to the main road, we passed a salmon netting operation at a nearby beach site. When we found ourselves looking for work again, Doug suggested that we apply for a salmon picker position. Having been born and raised in Kenai, Doug knew that the highest paying jobs were at the fisheries, and better yet, he knew some girls whose parents owned a fishing site on Salamatof Beach. They operated the commercial fishery Azarel, named after a Bible reference meaning "God has helped."

A large thick hedge from the main road obscured the view of the family enclave. The primary residence was a cabin perched less than twenty feet from the edge of a formidable 100-foot cliff overlooking the beach site. The property had several outbuildings housing the netting operation's vehicles, equipment, and a dormitory. We drove up to the cabin, and Doug introduced me to the two Honea sons working at the time. The sons were less than hospitable and more than a little suspicious of this stranger from California. Fortunately, their father, Wendell Honea, the owner of Azarel Fisheries, appeared. Though he was inquisitive, he immediately put me at ease with his warm and friendly demeanor.

He said we were welcome to work on his beach site, but he wanted us to understand the work we were signing up for. "Be there on time and work until we say the day is done and all the equipment is stored for the night. Be here tomorrow at six o'clock." We thanked him for the opportunity.

The Honea family consisted of the parents (Wendell and Joyce), four daughters, and two sons. The Honeas lived most of the year on Whidbey Island, just north of Seattle. But during salmon season, their beach site just north of Kenai was where the action was.

The Alaska Department of Fish and Game established the number of days a site could be worked and the fishing limit per day based upon the mass of the salmon runs. The higher the number of salmon that made it upstream, past the nets and anglers, the higher the fishing limit and the more days fishermen could work the site.

The Honeas often hired summer labor to help them with the herculean work of picking salmon out of stationary beach set nets. When the tide was in, all anyone could see were lines of orange buoys stretching toward the gray summer horizon. As the tide receded, more and more of the nets were exposed, flashing in the sunlight, alive with silver-blue coho salmon flashing their white underbellies as they struggled to get free.

Fish weighing less than ten pounds usually slipped through the nets as designed. The larger fish, ten to forty pounds with occasional fifty-pound monsters, thrashed against the nets as the waters that had nurtured them all their lives suddenly receded. Up and down the magnificent inlet at low tide, more and more of the thrashing nets were exposed.

Roger with three of the four Honea Daughters

Honea Family home on the cliff over Salamatof Beach site

The pickers worked frenetically as every minute was a race to pick the salmon from the net before the tide came back in. Moreover, each picker was paid according to the pounds of salmon they picked off the net. We worked individually, each with a large heavy-duty plastic garbage can fitted with a padded steel shoulder hook connected to the top of the container. The hook opened out from the side of the container so the weight could be quickly slung off the shoulder and then hoisted for dumping onto the scale hanging from the tractor. As soon as the salmon were unloaded and the weight was confirmed, we hustled off for the next load.

We rarely fit more than two large salmon into our harness buckets, sometimes three, but for one large fish, that was it. We hauled, we raced, and we sweated. We swore when the fish would not come loose; we cursed if one slipped out of the net, thrashing into the sea; we bumped and pushed, and, when I stopped for a breath, it seemed to me that I could barely discern the frantic pickers hunched over the nets from the thrashing salmon.

"Take a break when you want, but you're paid by the pound, not the hour. Take a minute for water replenishment, a quick cigarette, and then go back at it," we were told. Otherwise, we worked nonstop while the tide receded. The work was demanding and exhausting but rewarding.

The tire sling was the singular mode of transport between the rocky beach and the cliff high above. The constantly moving pulley system was secured by large spikes driven into the cliff above and through the sand below into bedrock. An old tire with an anchor tied to the top to provide weight was attached to the pulley cable, which propelled it down to the pickers waiting in the sound 100 feet below.

Its primary purpose was to retrieve the salmon plucked from the nets as the tide receded and deliver them to the cannery trucks at the top of the rocky cliff high above. However, at the end of a hard day plucking salmon from nets that stretched far out into the Kenai Inlet, the tire sling also transported the weary pickers and their equipment back to the top of the rocky cliff. The pickers, one by one, would lift themselves into the tire, give a wave, and be hoisted to the perch high above.

The salmon were wrestled from the nets and placed in plastic garbage cans, then on the tractor's scale and in pulley baskets. The pulley baskets, which were clamped to the lower cable, hauled the salmon to the top of the cliff, 100-feet above the rocky shore. The baskets were swung into the waiting haul trucks and were delivered to the cannery. As for us, the plucking of the fish from the net did not finish our day. When the last fish were loaded and on their way to the cannery, the tools, small equipment, and all the remaining stuff necessary for such an operation were loaded into the pulley baskets and hoisted up the cliff. Of course, all of this had to be done before the pickers could finally catch a ride up the 100-foot cliff.

Plucker taking salmon from the net.

The thrill of the ride always made up for the accumulation of the daily offenses to our bodies, minds, and spirits. All the effort, the pain, the accumulation of many small and large cuts and bruises, and the grit, grime, and slime that smeared us during our fourteen-hour days were ignored. Cut fingers and bruised thighs, barely felt ugly scrapes, rips here and there in cloth and flesh would soon disappear in the hot shower and clean clothes waiting above.

Roger and a fellow team member at the cannery.

We stood exhausted on the beach, waiting our turn for the lift up, showered by rain pellets here and there, empty gray mist settling in, a darkened blue sea stretching to the horizon.

Eyes shifted from the cliff, always returning to the majesty of the bay, which rippled with dark troughs topped with truculent white curls. The sky, nowhere near done, asserted its magnificence above all else; pink domed cumulus clouds erupted upward while purple mist swirled below. Above all, white clouds tinted with magenta billowed high, crowning the last of the day. What was left of the sun blessed heaven and earth with one final majestic sweep of its rays, giving a rosy kiss goodbye.

Kissed by the Anchor

The sea was the dark gray of a black goose; gray mullet trenches rippled the wet sand; intermittent idiosyncratic wonders, brackish and slick or briny darkened greens, swirling and stretching like dancers, were mysteries I could not comprehend. I wondered at the light along the horizon smeared laterally, a thin razor delineating the day's light from the darkened sea.

But it was wrong! All was inverted.

The view displaced every rational thought. At the beginning of the first day, looking down at the rocks below, I had decided that the tire sling was not for me. I would walk back up the trail, thank you. But, by the time the sun was near setting, I realized I couldn't make it back before dark. Besides, I was more tired than I had ever been, and every muscle was exclaiming—"take the ride, take the ride."

It was beautiful, beyond belief, and all went well until I was about twenty feet away from a safe landing. Then the cable stopped. Worse, it started to bounce, and I realized that a few pickers who were already safely on the cliff were bouncing the cable. Apparently, this was not an uncommon initiation for newbie pickers. I was not happy, but I played along, hanging tightly onto the tire.

The jostling caused the tire anchor to swing out. The bill of the anchor (the blunted tip of the anchor arm) smacked me hard at the corner of my left eye. I was dazed. I didn't lose consciousness, but I was disoriented and confused, dangling from my knees, looking upside-down out to sea, blood flowing. I remember being mesmerized by the beauty of the beach above and the sky below and wondering where I was. Panicked voices were coming from above. My predicament resulted from a joke gone wrong, combined with my novice mistake and a failure of instruction as to the subtleties of the tire ride.

But all was lost on me in this, my Damascus moment, the beginning of a much longer journey. For many years I flashed back to that moment, hanging upside down high above the rocky beach. These flashbacks haunted me as I sensed that I was missing something and struggled to grasp a deeper understanding of my life.

I was a hard-headed character and came quickly to my senses as I was hauled to the safety of the perch. To this day, I still bear the brand of the cross, barely discernable now, at the corner of my left eye, all because I had not known that I was to hold onto the anchor as well as the tire at all times when on the tire sling.

The Honea Family

My roommate and I were well aware of the Honea's four daughters. The Honeas were remarkable people who managed their rough and tumble existence on the border of the sky, balancing hard work with charity of spirit, keeping a close watch on their daughters and assuming the best in all of us. They were latecomers to Christ. Consequently, they had a heart for the unsaved and maintained an unobstructed view of the secular world.

Upon my arrival in Alaska, I fancied myself an atheist. I drank alcohol frequently and smoked heavily. I admit to being somewhat aggressive, even obnoxious in my views, and often condescended to or ridiculed believers.

Although the Honeas were believers and I was not, I was drawn to them—probably because I deeply needed parental figures. They consistently treated me with kindness and understanding that I did not expect and, frankly, did not deserve. They had both come to Christ as adults, so they did not attempt to evangelize with a traditional approach. Instead, they asked questions based on their heartfelt experiences. They inquired about my life and beliefs, and they invited discussion on my answers, which always led to more questions.

Though I had thought I had answers to everything, I began to feel the darkness of my views and, worse, to see that my views ultimately led to unhappiness. That didn't mean I was wrong. In fact, as I argued, "Given the history of our world, that probably means my conclusions are accurate."

"Hmm," Wendell Honea would say, "and perhaps it means just the opposite."

Eventually, I had to admit my sense of unhappiness, which made me wonder if I should at least consider other opinions.

While I was confident and forceful on the outside, I had all the insecurities and questions that come with an undisciplined, unanchored life. On reflection over the years, it became clear that the Honeas were the perfect sounding board for someone like me at that time in my life.

Who would have thought I would find the ideal repose in the wind-swept bluffs of the Cook Inlet? While the Honeas did not convert me at that moment, they caused me to temper my negativity and ego, allowing me to consider the possibility of a spiritual life.

Reunion With my Parents

One evening in late July, I returned to the cabin from work to find an official notice from the Coast Guard on my door. As the only branch of the military with a presence in the remote peninsula, my father had reached out to them from Cairo for help. The notice stated that my parents would arrive for a visit in a week and that I was expected to be there to meet them when they arrived.

How did they find me? I wondered. I didn't even have an address! And the cabin had no running water or electricity and was a forty-five-minute walk down a dirt road from the main highway. I was flummoxed, and a bit unnerved.

I had told Herb I was headed for Kenai. To my knowledge, he had no way of knowing where I was living or what company I worked for. Hell, I didn't even know how to give directions to where I now lived. The best I could do was to describe the dirt road and the trees nearby and tell friends they would know the cabin when they saw it.

After pondering the mystery and finding no plausible explanation, I went back to my daily routine until two days later when an officer from the Coast Guard with a lot of bars on his shoulder stood at my door when I got home from work.

"Did you get the notice I left about your parents' visit?" he asked.

"Yes, sir, I did," I replied with the deference of a Marine's son used to interrogations.

"They have not heard from you in several months, and your mother is worried sick about you." I felt like I was ten years old again. "So, I suggest that you be here at this time next Thursday when they arrive. This is not a request. Got it? Don't make me come looking for you."

"No, sir," I replied, resigned to the fate of facing my parents in a few days, wondering what they would think of my rustic lifestyle.

But my angst was soon assuaged when my parents arrived. They didn't seem shocked by my living conditions. They were just happy to see me—and I found that I was just as happy to see them.

We spent a couple of days catching up. I showed them around my new town and worksite. My father was intrigued by my new home and its surroundings as we explored the Cook Inlet and the communities on the Kenai Peninsula. Though he had traveled all over the world, he had never been to Alaska, and I was proud to play the role of host.

Though only a few days in length, this visit was pivotal in my relationship with my parents. I had grown tremendously since returning from Cairo, both emotionally and physically. The responsibility of cleaning and sorting my grandparents' property and preparing my grandmother for moving gave me a perspective on life that few twenty-year-olds have. My trip to Alaska, where I moved without a job or a place to stay, knowing no one, was a true challenge. That accomplishment and the extra twenty pounds of muscle I earned from the backbreaking physical labor that paid so well gave me confidence in my ability to make my own way in the world.

Of course, my parents only knew the young man I was when I had left Cairo fourteen months before. They planned the visit to reunite with their son, whom they felt responsible for. By the time they left, they had come to know their grown son with his own independent life. Our relationship was never the same. Rather than hierarchical in nature, it grew into a connection between adults who enjoyed each other's company and appreciated sharing their lives with each other—every parent's dream of a deep relationship with their grown kids.

CHAPTER THIRTY-FIVE
The Fool

Unexpectedly, I spent many of the summer evenings in discussions with Mr. and Mrs. Honea. They were deeply spiritual Nazarenes who were late converts to Christianity. They told me they had met in a bar and had an instant connection. "Before we knew it, we were married and had four children." Their story continued, "Several years later, our lives were changed forever when we became Christians and committed ourselves to God."

Having only been inside a church twice in my life, their story was foreign to me, strange, and more than a bit unsettling. But I listened. Could this be the deeper meaning I had considered as I had hung upside down 100 feet above the rocky beach? Perhaps, but, unlike the Honeas, it took many years before these initial conversations would change my life.

At the end of the summer, the Honeas asked me if I would like to stop off at their home on Whidbey Island on my way back to California, and I gratefully accepted the invitation. We arrived on a Friday, and, being Nazarenes, the Honeas informed me that they would be attending church the next day and invited me to go with them; an invitation they had extended several times in Alaska, which I had consistently declined. This time I said yes because I felt it would be ungracious of me to decline an invitation while I was a guest in their home.

To this point in my life, I can only remember being in a church service a couple of times when I was in grade school. I had no idea what to expect. It was a relatively small church, but it was packed. It was not a "holy roller" type of church, which is what I feared. Instead, it was filled with what appeared to be regular people, friends, and neighbors, glad to see each other and very outgoing. They were especially happy to see the end-of-summer return of their dear friends, the Honeas.

I settled in, not knowing what to expect. The minister, a slight man, delivered a straightforward sermon titled "The Life of the Fool." He defined a fool as someone who denied the existence of a sovereign God. The sermon was powerful to the point that I was experiencing the remarkable sensation of being pinned to the pew as the preacher's words penetrated my heart.

The message was of love, not fear; of hope, not loss; and, most of all, of belonging to the family of God. Here it was, the *family* thing again, what I most deeply longed for. Yes, I was predisposed, but again I resisted, squirming as each word seemed to pin me. Then, at that very moment, the pastor gave an altar call.

He stated simply, "If anyone here wishes to come forward to give their life to Christ, please come now."

I was gripping the pew with both hands to keep from going forward. My grip tightened as he repeated the call. I honestly did not understand what was happening as I set my jaw, buried my knuckles into the pew, and managed to make it through the call without going forward.

As soon as the service was over, I felt compelled to tell the pastor that his efforts didn't go unnoticed. I told him that I would think about and reflect on his sermon.

He looked me straight in the eye and said, "Well, I wondered who that sermon was for because it is not the sermon I prepared."

I was stunned. He went on. "I always pray before each service that my sermon will be consecrated to God's purpose and His spirit will direct my words. Thank you for the powerful confirmation you have given me today. Those were God's words, not mine."

He then asked me if I would like to give my life to Christ. I declined, saying I would have to think about it, but the truth be told, I was really trying to figure out how to get out of the church as quickly as possible.

I decided to tell the Honeas of my experience and the conversation with the pastor. They, too, were stunned. To their knowledge, the pastor had never before given an altar call.

As for me, I determined that it was time to get back to California. My mind and heart were in turmoil. I really didn't know what to think, but the pastor had given me a lot to consider.

I stayed in touch with the Honea family for more than fifty years until Joyce's death in 2019. During those years, I shared the many joys I have experienced as a Christian and my gratitude to them for helping the "fool" finally come to Christ.

ACKNOWLEDGMENTS

Writing this book has been primarily a solitary endeavor, though I never lost sight of the fact that I was writing this memoir to share my story with others. Though I spent years working nearly full-time to find the perfect word or anecdote to tell the legacy of four generations of my family, I couldn't have completed the manuscript without a great deal of help from a select group of people.

I would like to thank my lifelong friend Steve Ladd, who donated his time to edit the roughest first drafts of the book. He found errors in dates, times, and places and pointed out redundancies that I had not previously caught in my early drafts. Steve also provided a great deal of advice on the clarity, efficacy, and value of the many anecdotes I foisted on him. Thank you, Brother, for your patience and understanding during the many iterations and for supporting me as a first-time author.

Beverly Anderson, the closest person I have to a sister, donated her exceptional photo editing and outstanding proofreading talents and helped develop the ideas I used for branding the book and selecting concepts for our cover art. Though I have been blessed with many incredible family photos throughout the generations, Beverly brought them to life in a way I could never have imagined. Thank you, Beverly, from the bottom of my heart.

Thank you, B. Lynn Goodwin of www.writeradvice.com for taking on the project of editing my first book and committing to the aggressive schedule we set for ourselves. You provided the final editing, which elevated my manuscript to the quality required to attract and appeal to publishers. You taught me so much about the craft of writing and the industry standards it requires while allowing me to retain my voice as the author and narrator. Thanks for all that you have taught me.

I also greatly appreciate John Koehler and the Koehler Books team's confidence in my debut book. Their guidance, support, and editorial and artistic expertise were indispensable. I am incredibly grateful for John Koehler and Joe Coccaro's dedication to helping first-time authors like me navigate the challenges of publishing and marketing a book. Their willingness to share their experience and guide me through the process has been invaluable.

Lastly, I would like to thank my incredible wife, Natalie. She helped me sort through dozens of versions of each chapter I had amassed to build the final manuscript, which does justice to my family legacy. We devoted countless hours captivated by stories of the adventures, the challenges, the hilarity, the perils, and the triumphs of four generations of lives well-lived. Everyone involved in the process and all of my friends and family know I couldn't have done it without you. Thanks for helping me bring this family treasure to fruition.

www.ingramcontent.com/pod-product-compliance
Lightning Source LLC
LaVergne TN
LVHW091541070526
838199LV00002B/155